What the critics said

'This is a gritty Australian [...]
of our recent history – the [...]
'80s told in a no-frills sty[le ...]'
SUNDAY TELEGRAPH

'Vigorous, explosive... He is anti-romantic to the soles
of his greasy felt shearing boots... With heartbreaking
detail the narrative lifts from the exceptional to the unique,
offering proof that truthful accounts of hard times and
seemingly inexplicable behaviours can carry the seeds
of redemption within the very act of writing itself.'
Roger McDonald, THE AUSTRALIAN

'This is the real working man's Australia.'
MEN'S STYLE

'An evocative insight into men of the rural working class. He goes
further than Lawson, Paterson and other writers, dismissing any
romantic notions... Shearers may measure out their days in sheep and
nights with grog, but it is their spirit that McIntosh understands.'
Christopher Bantick, THE AGE

'An unblinking self-portrait and a vivid and emotionally
wrought tale of people, politics and animals... His prose has
a wonderful, unvarnished quality. There's also something
vulnerable and quite beautiful about the way he chooses to tell
his life story, in the process exposing his frailties and humanity.'
Patrick Arlington, ADELAIDE ADVERTISER

'Dennis McIntosh lights up the twin landscapes of the western
sheep run and the shearer's soul in a sharp, spare narrative.
Like the best of Henry Lawson, his tale allows no false romance.'
Richard Begbie, CANBERRA TIMES

PENGUIN BOOKS

BEATEN BY A BLOW

Dennis McIntosh was born in Townsville in 1958 and grew up in Newcastle and Melbourne's outer west.

The names of some people in the text have been changed to protect their privacy

DENNIS McINTOSH

BEATEN BY A BLOW

A SHEARER'S STORY

PENGUIN BOOKS

PENGUIN BOOKS

Published by the Penguin Group
Penguin Group (Australia)
250 Camberwell Road, Camberwell, Victoria 3124, Australia
(a division of Pearson Australia Group Pty Ltd)
Penguin Group (USA) Inc.
375 Hudson Street, New York, New York 10014, USA
Penguin Group (Canada)
90 Eglinton Avenue East, Suite 700, Toronto, Canada ON M4P 2Y3
(a division of Pearson Penguin Canada Inc.)
Penguin Books Ltd
80 Strand, London WC2R 0RL, England
Penguin Ireland
25 St Stephen's Green, Dublin 2, Ireland
(a division of Penguin Books Ltd)
Penguin Books India Pvt Ltd
11 Community Centre, Panchsheel Park, New Delhi – 110 017, India
Penguin Group (NZ)
67 Apollo Drive, Rosedale, North Shore 0632, New Zealand
(a division of Pearson New Zealand Ltd)
Penguin Books (South Africa) (Pty) Ltd
24 Sturdee Avenue, Rosebank, Johannesburg 2196, South Africa

Penguin Books Ltd, Registered Offices: 80 Strand, London WC2R 0RL, England

First published by Penguin Group (Australia), 2008
This edition published by Penguin Group (Australia), 2009

10 9 8 7 6 5 4 3 2 1

Text copyright © Dennis McIntosh, 2008

The moral right of the author has been asserted

All rights reserved. Without limiting the rights under copyright reserved above,
no part of this publication may be reproduced, stored in or introduced into a retrieval
system, or transmitted, in any form or by any means (electronic, mechanical,
photocopying, recording or otherwise), without the prior written permission
of both the copyright owner and the above publisher of this book.

Design by John Canty © Penguin Group (Australia)
Jackie Howe singlet featured on front cover was kindly supplied by Shear Outback,
The Australian Shearers Hall of Fame, Hay NSW (shearoutback.com.au)
Cover photograph by Tim De Neefe
Typeset in Adobe Garamond by Post Pre-press Group, Brisbane, Queensland
Printed and bound in Australia by McPherson's Printing Group, Maryborough, Victoria

National Library of Australia
Cataloguing-in-Publication data:

McIntosh, Dennis.
Beaten by a blow: a shearer's story/Dennis McIntosh
Sheep shearers (Persons) – Australia – Biography.
Sheep-shearing – Australia
9780143010685 (pbk.)

636.0833092

penguin.com.au

CONTENTS

Prologue *1*
Onion Picking *4*
A Good Worker *16*
A Working Life *24*
Warrigal Creek Station *28*
Lal Lal Station *47*
Ulonga Station *56*
Gunbar Station *69*
Windouran Station *80*
Boonoke Station *85*
Tubbo Station *89*
Greystones Station *96*
Mungadal Station *108*
Booligal Station *123*
Shearing School *132*
Barunah Plains Station *134*
Back to Lal Lal *143*
The Church *152*
The Brick Factory *153*

The Barcoo Pub 157
Blackall Station 162
Barcaldine 165
Augathella 169
Longreach 174
The Meatworks 176
Skin Sheds 181
Wool Scouring 183
Jerilderie 186
Ivanhoe 189
Bolac Plains Station 191
Barunah Plains Again 196
Titanga Station 198
The Strike 204
Devon Park Station 207
Bourke 213
Waratah Station 216
The Back Station 222
Brewarrina 225
Charlton Station 229
Butterbone Park Stud 236
Wonga Station 241
Smokey 243
The Beer Can Factory 246
Greystones Again 250
The Water Board 253
The Depot Shed 255
Billybingbone Station 262
The Road-making Gang 265
The Wide-comb Decision 268
Roof Service 273
Tumbarumba 276

PROLOGUE

I PROMISED I wouldn't but I had a drink. I woke up in my car on the side of a dirt track in outback country. Hit a cattle grid and snapped the steering wheel off. Beer bottles, some full and some empty, were strewn through the car. On either side of the track was slack barbwire, splintered posts and claypans. A few gums were scattered across the horizon.

My hair was matted with dried blood. As the sun warmed the car I started to stink. I was shaking. I didn't know what day it was. Looked like a Sunday. In the rear-vision mirror I recognised the eyes, the nose and the ears, even the skin, but I didn't know who I was. I went back to sleep.

When the sun had fully risen my stench woke me. In the distance dust rose from the track. I got out and started walking in the direction of the dust, hoping for a lift. They slowed, looked, kept on driving.

Bastards.

I remembered something of last night. I'd gone to the wrong shearing shed, unpacked my gear and waited for the other men. Dusk set in and there was no cook. I realised I was in the wrong place and left.

My head was throbbing. I didn't know whether it was from my hangover or the cut in my head. I must have been in a fight, my whole head felt sore.

Another car came along the track and stopped. He asked where I was heading. I didn't answer, I didn't know.

He said he was going to his father's sheep station and would take me there as a first step. We went inside and I sat at the end of a large dining table in an old kitchen as big as two rooms. A woman asked would I like a cup of tea. I nodded. I asked where I was and they said about fifty kilometres out of Hay, in New South Wales.

I said, 'I've worked before up this way, for Grazcos.' The women were cooking for the shearers. One of the children danced over towards me and her mother moved her back and apologised.

The tea was in bone-china cups and saucers, thin, translucent, with a red rose print. I didn't want to touch the petite handle. When I tried to pick it up the rattle of the cup on the saucer was like a road train going through the kitchen. The family turned and looked. All I could think of was my bloodstained hair, unshaven face, dirty clothes, alcoholic breath and rotting body. I stared at the rose print, smelt the aroma of the tea and kept my head down, avoiding eye contact like a mongrel dog.

The young mothers were fresh-faced, wore summery cotton dresses and had their hair tied up. The children were also beautifully dressed. One of the little girls had a blue corduroy dress with a white frilly front. I recognised it. I'd seen it somewhere before. It was the same as my daughter's dress. I had a daughter; I had children, a wife, a family.

'I've got a daughter,' I said, 'and she's got a blue dress like that one.'

They smiled, nodded and went back to talking to each other.

Lonnie's program. I was supposed to be home for Lonnie's

exercises. Fuck, what happened? My memory was jigsawed. I couldn't remember when I was last home. I think it was Thursday, or I was supposed to be home Thursday and now it was Tuesday or Wednesday. I was penniless, I had a broken-down car and a few bottles of beer. I needed to get out of here and back to my family.

The station owner's son rang the Grazcos man in Hay to see what he knew, and eventually he picked me up. We stopped off at my car, collected my tools and some clothes, and he took me over to the shed I was booked for. I dried out, went and got the car; I had to steer it back with a shifter. I had some parts sent out from the Hay wreckers. The squatter helped repair the car even though he'd heard I was going to quit. On the Friday night I subbed as much money as I was allowed and shot through.

ONION PICKING

IN 1971, JUST before I turned thirteen, we moved to Werribee South, opposite the mouth of the river. In the afternoons the school bus drove past an unkempt bay pony next to a disused dairy on an old soldier-settlement block. The noise of the bus's diesel engine and the tyres screeching along the bitumen would stop the pony from eating. She would take off down the paddock with her tail up and her nostrils flared to the wind. She had such great spirit. She was everything I'd dreamed of, sitting in a paddock on her own.

I didn't understand why she was alone. I knew one day I'd somehow set her free. I dreamed of riding her along the beach and into the waves, riding through the bush, camping under the stars and living off my wits, travelling from town to town – that was the life for me. Every night I went to bed dreaming about the adventures of Ginger and me.

Dad had said flatly, 'No horses.' They were too expensive to keep. Six kids and one income, we'd learned not to harp when it came to money. 'We can't afford it' covered everything from 'We're too busy' to 'We're not wasting money on that.' I already knew one thing about my life. If I wanted something, I'd have to get it myself.

I wondered whether, if nobody wanted her, I could have her. Or at least look after her and take her for rides. I thought that would be sort of the same as owning a horse.

One afternoon when I was visiting the pony the cocky called me over. He was in his early sixties, slightly hunched; his face was worn with heavy sagging lines and he smelt of alcohol and tobacco.

'Wanta horse, hey? I'm sellin her. She's hard in the mouth and she's foundering a bit.' Her hooves were splayed, with the fleshy parts hitting the ground. She'd go lame quickly on the road.

'She needs a bit of lookin after – not in perfect condition, but nothing that couldn't be fixed. You can have her if you buy the extras as well, right. Saddle, bridle, halters, the lot. I won't split em, understand me? Well boy, do you want her or not?'

'Yes sir, I want her but I haven't got any money yet. But I could ride her for you, and look after her and that, until I get the money. I'd brush her and take good care of her. Get her out of that soggy paddock.'

'No, no, no. I'm not wastin me time with a kid hanging around the farm, too many things can go wrong. I'm gunna sell. That's it.'

'How much do you want?'

'A hundred for the pony and a hundred for the gear, rightio.'

'I can work it off for you, if you'll let me. I'll clean the dairy and sweep the sheds and that, whatever you want. I can work after school and on weekends.'

He paused. 'Well, the onion season's about to start. The first lot'll be ready for pickin mid-December. Holiday job. Make a man of ya. Mr Pipi down the road'll be starting soon, go and tell him I recommended you.'

I went over to Mr Pipi's. He had olive skin with thick black hair but he spoke without an accent.

'How old are you?' he asked when I told him why I was there.

'I'm thirteen, nearly.'

'Not even thirteen, you're too young. This is man's work.'

'I can do it, but. I help me dad out in the factory all the time. And he reckons I'm a good worker. What are you paying?'

'No rates, it's piecework, ten cents a box. You stack your boxes at the end of each day, I want them stacked in lots of fifty. And I don't want to be paying for half-boxes. Is that clear?'

'Yes Mr Pipi, when do I start?'

'By the look of the onions, I reckon you can start in about two weeks. When do you finish school?'

'We're not doing anything at school now, so I can start when you want.'

'Call by in a week or so and we'll talk then.'

My parents agreed to let me work. When it came to money, I knew Mum would never say no. There was a tribe of us. Mum loved babies. She'd had seven, one died before it was born. We mostly avoided Mum, we knew we'd get an earful about Dad and how she couldn't cope. If we felt sorry for her we'd get more jobs. My older brother started part-time work when he was fourteen, that's when Mum refused to buy any of his clothes. And that became the standard. I knew if I started onion picking I'd have to go without the Levi jeans I wanted.

I called in to see Mr Pipi late one afternoon. He was on the tractor in the onion paddock, turning a row into a wave of earth and onions ready for picking.

'There you go, boy. When you've picked them I'll open up the other rows until we've picked the paddock clean.'

If I could pick and stack a hundred boxes a day I'd earn ten dollars a day, which worked out at four weeks' work to buy Ginger.

That would leave me a couple of weeks to ride her before school started.

Dad dropped me in the onion paddock on Monday morning and headed off to work. It was daybreak. I watched his car disappear through the dust suspended in the damp air and then I was alone. There were no clouds in the sky and no wind. Not even Mr Pipi was up yet. There was only me, a paddock full of onions, and in the distance Ginger strutting around.

I thought I'd get started, get as much work done as I could before it got too hot. It was supposed to be in the high thirties. The soil had a light crust and was powdery underneath. I picked my first onion and put it in the box. The onion tops, with a tinge of green through them, were still firmly connected to the onion: I could pick up the tops without the onion falling off. My first box seemed to take ages, but I didn't have to move far because it was a thick crop. Pretty soon I was kneeling in the dirt, my knees and thighs covered in lumps from the milk thistles.

Mr Pipi and his worker arrived about an hour later. Mr Pipi got straight onto the tractor while his worker followed beside the trailer, putting boxes out along the rows. After they'd finished the boxes Mr Pipi came over to me and said, 'You're working too slow. Here, I'll show you.' He said I couldn't pick quickly if I was kneeling or sitting on the ground. He bent over and started picking the onions in clumps. He gathered the onion tops like he was pulling in a blanket with his fingers; he picked up to eight or ten in one go and put them in the box. 'Do it like that,' he said. 'Don't drop them hard into the box either, I don't want them bruised. You understand?'

I nodded. 'Yeah, I know, I know.'

'Now,' he said, 'when the box is full, give it a firm but gentle push down and heap the box up to a hump, so when the onions settle, the box will be full.'

'Yeah, I know, I know.'

'I know, I know, I know. Is that all you can say? You don't know, that's why I'm telling you. Go back and fill up those boxes you've already done before you go any further, and wear shoes from now on. There's snakes in these crops.'

With that he turned and walked away. I stopped for lunch. Mum had packed her trademark sandwiches – raisin and apple, and Vegemite and tomato – and a drink. When Mr Pipi came back I didn't feel like picking more onions, so I stacked my full boxes. I wanted to believe that the money was mine. I'd picked thirty-five boxes: three dollars fifty. It didn't seem a lot for the work I'd done. I went back and started picking.

Mr Pipi came over, yelling and screaming. 'Don't stack your boxes there, that's the farm road. Stack them in the rows you've picked. Come on, how old are you?'

'I'm thirteen now, Mr Pipi.'

'Well, use your brain. I don't want to be coming over here looking after you all the time. Okay?'

I nodded. 'Yeah I kno—' I stopped. 'Yes, Mr Pipi.'

I rebuilt my stack on the empty section of the row. When I'd finished I stopped and looked across the paddock: there were thousands of onions, probably millions. My eyes followed the fence line to Ginger and then back to the onions. I was a long way off my hundred boxes a day. The rest of the afternoon I concentrated on picking up as many onions as I could in one scoop and tried to forget about Ginger or counting the boxes.

That afternoon I picked thirty boxes – more in less time than in the morning. But I still had only sixty-five for the day. Six dollars fifty.

Waiting for Dad, I gave Ginger a pat and a hug. She rubbed her nose into me and whinnied and nodded. I imagined riding her into the sea with the waves crashing over us, jumping through the breakwater.

ONION PICKING

The next morning I waved to Ginger as I walked into my onion paddock. Today I wouldn't stop for lunch until I'd picked forty boxes. My legs stung from the nettles, but I rubbed dirt into the red welts to stop the itching. I was still picking when Mr Pipi and the worker went in for lunch. I needed another five boxes. After I'd done them I ate my sandwiches. I was starving. It was hotter than yesterday. When I stopped, the sweat poured off my body and mixed with the dirt, making me itchy.

Mr Pipi coming out of the house was my cue to start again. I worked hard in the afternoon, even though my body started feeling like it wanted to go to sleep. When the sun reached the chimney I knew Dad wasn't far away. I packed up. I'd picked forty boxes for the afternoon. Eighty boxes for the day: eight dollars. I had to get faster.

I tried to get Dad to leave earlier the next morning, but he liked his cup of coffee and a crack at the crossword. He wouldn't budge. I had to get a hundred boxes today. Finally he dropped me off and I ran into the paddock from the bitumen and started work. When Mr Pipi arrived I didn't even bother to say hello.

'Look, look,' he yelled, his hands outstretched. 'Your stack, it fell over. Fix it straight away before the onions get squashed, and fix the other stacks as well so they don't fall over. Okay?'

'How did it fall over?' I asked.

'You don't stack right.' He pointed to his worker. 'Joe, he'll show you how to do it.'

Joe didn't speak to me. He just showed me how to place the boxes. Two boxes along, four across – this gave the base. Then the opposite on the next level. I lost half a morning restacking, so I didn't stop for lunch; I ate my sandwiches, raisin and apple, while I worked, and by the end of the day I'd picked and stacked sixty-five boxes. It was okay considering the time I'd lost.

When I woke up Thursday morning my hands ached, they

were red-raw and swollen. Mum said to wear gloves. Dad said to piss on them. The ammonia, he said, would harden them up. I didn't want to piss on them but I relented. I wanted my hands to have black calluses in the lines of their fingers and palms like Dad's.

I started slowly, my hands still aching. It was lonely, but I wasn't in a classroom and I was making money. I loved being in open spaces, except for the occasional dust storms that cut into my eyes. Every day was a different sky and I had time to think. I mostly thought of what Ginger and I would do when I grew up, and was working in the outback and living under the stars.

Even though it was still morning, I stopped and ate my lunch and drank the lemon water Mum had packed for me. I was starting to feel better. I kept going all day and when it was time to finish I worked through until Dad arrived. He built machines and knew numbers and time per product. I needed a system, he said. I had a system: I didn't stop. He helped me stack the boxes. Ninety boxes: nine dollars. Tomorrow I would get my hundred boxes.

I started well the next day. I concentrated on grabbing as many onions in one go as possible. It was hot and windy and my eyes were sore from the dust. The sun had gone behind the chimney as I picked my hundredth box. Dad was late. It was pub night. I decided to stack the rest of the day's pickings. Then I sat under the cypress trees to wait. I was too tired to walk to the road and it was good to get out of the wind for a while. I lay down on the boxes and fell asleep. Joe woke me up, pointed to the road. 'Go, go boy, go,' shooing me like a cow. It was sunset and I walked and hitched the five k's home.

The old man came home a bit after eight with a new neighbour he'd brought back from the pub. He introduced me to Mr McHugh as his number three son. We knew each other, but neither of us said so. One afternoon, Mr McHugh, half pissed, dressed in a shirt and tie and his hair thick with Brylcreem, was down around the pier looking at his new mooring. We were on the pier smoking. He came over and said he'd kick my arse till my nose bled for smoking. He said he knew who I was and reckoned I was a smart arse. Then he started stabbing his finger into my chest. Now, sitting at my kitchen table, he was pleasant and polite and wanted to know all about what I was doing. But I didn't tell him anything and moved away into the lounge room.

Saturday morning I set out to pick a hundred and five boxes. That would give me fifty dollars for the week. After stacking the boxes, I went to Mr Pipi for my money. He counted the five hundred boxes, nodded and gave me five $10 notes. I was rich.

The following week the picking got harder. Mr Pipi had run the tractor over more of the rows, and with a little overnight rain a few days back the ground had hardened. The turned-up onions weren't loose in the ground any more; some were caked in dirt, some I had to dig out with my fingertips. The first things to go were my fingernails and then the tips of my fingers wore thin, until they were sore to touch. The onion tops browned and became frail, and when I tried to pick a lot at once the tops snapped and the onions fell back into the row.

I picked four hundred and seventy boxes that week, but when Mr Pipi came to inspect my work he picked up a box and screamed, 'Look, you're not putting enough onions in the boxes.' He unstacked a couple more and pushed his foot down on top of them. 'Look, they're not bloody full! You're only half filling them, for Christ's sake. I'm not paying for half-boxes.' He looked at me sharply. 'I'll give you eight cents a box.'

'No way, Mr Pipi, you told me not to squash the onions and I didn't. And I overfilled the boxes like you asked. We had a deal.'

He said something in Italian and walked off. I followed him. I had to get my money. I'd worked so hard for it, it was mine and I wanted it.

He went into his house at the back of the property and I knocked on the door after him. His wife opened it and I asked for Mr Pipi. When he came to the door he said nothing, but slowly counted out the forty-seven dollars and handed it to me. Still angry but relieved, I turned and headed home; he yelled out that he wouldn't be paying ten cents a box in future unless they were picked properly. Then he went off in Italian once again.

So far I'd made ninety-seven dollars. I was almost at the half-way mark.

On Monday a man called Roger turned up in the onion paddock. He had a slickback hairdo like Elvis, a wiry build. I didn't trust him. He did give me smokes, though. I wouldn't buy them but I didn't mind smoking his. He said he was a professional picker.

It had rained on the weekend and the onions were caked in dirt. Roger had Mr Pipi redig the onions with the bar to break them up a bit. You beauty, I thought. Finally, I wasn't on my own with Mr Pipi. Roger was an ally, not an enemy. He taught me to pick faster. He told me to concentrate and watch what I was doing, to bend over and reach as far as I could without moving, to move less and maximise my position.

'Start picking on the side of the row, not in the middle, and grab the tops of the onions near the base, using the little finger like a hook. With the rest of your hands grab clumps of tops, and as your hands come together your forearms can gather onions as well.'

I could get almost a quarter of a box like that. If I gathered up a few clumps of dirt in the process I left them there. I didn't go back and I didn't do things twice. I could only gather large amounts occasionally, when the outsides of the row had been picked. I set my picking around this strategy.

The only thing was, now that Roger was here the paddock would run out faster than I'd planned. I would have to work harder to get the money I needed. In the cloggy soil I averaged about eighty-five boxes a day, and on Saturday, back in softer soil, I picked a hundred. Fifty-two dollars and fifty cents for the week. One week to go and I should have the money.

On the last Monday night it was almost dark by the time Dad arrived. I kept working so he could help stack my boxes – that way I could pick more. No matter what I did, I couldn't get more than a hundred boxes a day. And I wanted to ride Ginger home on Friday night. My back ached when I straightened up, but the pain was only temporary. I was used to the heat and my hands didn't hurt much any more. Even the dust in the wind cutting into my body didn't bother me too much. Only my legs hurt. In bed they ached, when I woke up in the mornings they ached, and when I walked they ached.

By Friday lunchtime I had four hundred and fifty boxes for the week, sixty boxes short of my goal, and there was about a day's worth of onions left to pick. I was stuffed. Roger drank a few bottles of beer for lunch. He was a good bloke but he lied a lot. What he said on Monday was different to what he said on Wednesday and different again on Friday. Some mornings he was pissed but he could still work. He was renting a caravan somewhere. It didn't seem much of a life and I was glad I had a bed to go to. I lay down on the empty onion boxes under the cypress trees where the cool offshore breeze was blowing.

The next thing, Dad was waking me. I'd slept for six hours straight. I went to Mr Pipi for my money and said I'd be back tomorrow. He said they were going to process the onions on Saturday and to come Monday. I only had one day left to get the money.

On Sunday morning I heard Mr McHugh in our lounge

room. He'd come to confirm he was going to buy the pony for his daughter, Sonia. Dad said no worries. He said I couldn't afford it anyway. Mr McHugh was loud, laughing nervously; he shook Dad's hand and walked out. I sank on the edge of my bed, listening.

Later that day, a small crowd gathered around the front yard. I went over to have a look. I saw the distinctive colours of Ginger coming around the bend about a kilometre away. I froze. As she got closer I felt sick. Mr McHugh's daughter rode Ginger over to me and said g'day. She said, 'We're calling her Honey.'

I was trembling and sick in the stomach. Ginger rubbed her nose into me and pushed me, like she normally did. Sonia said her dad had promised her a horse if they moved down here, then she jerked the bit hard to the left and rode off.

I walked around the back of the house and there was Mr McHugh, who was in an unusually good mood without a drink, talking it up to my old man. He shook Dad's hand and thanked him. The old man must have told him about the horse.

When I walked back into the onion paddock on Monday morning I looked across at Ginger's empty yard and the dust-blown paddock. There were a few rows left to pick, but my motivation was gone. Roger arrived and said, 'Let's wax em,' and by lunchtime we'd stripped the paddock. Mr Pipi paid us. That's how I found out Roger was getting seventeen cents a box. I looked at Roger but he couldn't look at me. I'd earned my two hundred dollars but I was half a day late.

I walked past the dairy shed. The cockie was sitting on a drum with a bottle beside him, fixing something. He slinked a look at me then returned his attention to what he was doing. I took a deep breath. Dust swirls and roly-poly weed were already inhabiting the onion paddock, Ginger was gone and my childhood was over. I felt different: older, harder, stronger. The sky was a clear light blue; there was a slight breeze blowing and I walked home.

Sonia and I did start to get to know each other after that. We were the only two about the same age in the neighbourhood. She would bring her horse over and we would see each other down the beach. The farrier fixed the hooves and Mr McHugh booked her into pony club. Ginger would have had a different life with me: sleeping under the stars, swimming in the river, stuff like that.

That winter I worked for other farmers picking cauliflowers and cabbages after school for a dollar forty an hour, and when the onion season started I picked a hundred boxes every day I worked until I had enough money to buy a horse. Dad helped me find a little piebald gelding.

A GOOD WORKER

ALTHOUGH I WAS under age at fourteen, I was hired as a live-in farmhand on a horse and dairy property about ten kilometres from home. It was late spring 1973. On my first day my alarm went off at 5.15 a.m. I had a cup of tea with Michael, one of the owners, and walked to the dairy to meet his cousin, Tucker, the other owner. Tucker was about six foot and had a big beer gut, except he didn't drink. He sang a lot, but he could get a bit angry sometimes. He was the oldest of twelve and I knew a few of them from around town.

'Dennis the menace,' Tucker greeted me. 'You really done it this time, you're a bad little egg, boy, a bad egg, now they sent ya down here to work with me, huh.'

'Yeah, but I wanta work on a farm. This is what I wanta do.'

'Kicked out of school at your age – what'd your parents ever do to deserve you?' He concentrated on screwing together some stainless-steel pipes for a second. 'Na, you're not that bad. Not yet anyway.' His mind was back on the milking. 'Get the dairy horse, take Billy and Gidget.' He let go a short sharp whistle and a heeler and a kelpie appeared from the dark, then he yelled, 'Get away back,' and whistled with an upbeat on the end of it and the dogs took off. 'Follow them out and bring the cows in. Quicker they're in, quicker we're out.'

The first twelve cows were in place, Tucker loaded up ten cows with the suction cups and I did two. I kept dropping the cups every time the cows moved. I didn't like putting my head under their bellies in case I got kicked in the head.

'That's Mary Jane, she won't kick ya.' Then I dropped the suction cups into a fresh pile of cow shit.

Tucker started screaming, 'The milk tester wants milk in the vat, not shit, boy. My god, we'll never get our milk passed at this rate.' Then he laughed and started singing, 'There's shit in the milk and a bad egg in the dairy . . .'

One cow lifted her tail and shat all over me.

'Have to keep your eyes open, boy, that apron won't help ya if ya standing under a cow shitting all over ya like a fire hydrant on full bore.' He laughed again.

I didn't.

'See that cow's cracked teats? Put cream on them from this jar before you put the suction cups on and put the cream on again when you take'm off. Watch for it.'

I put the cream on but the bitch kept kicking me every time I tried to put the cups on. Tucker did it.

After about six or seven lots of cows, we had a break. We were both leaning up against the cows' walkway.

'Now, what happened at school? Not that I ever did any good at school, either. Didn't matter I 'spose, I was always coming back to work on the farm and have cows shit all over me.'

'Well, I told the Dean of Discipline to get fucked.'

'Did he?'

'He tried to march me into home room through the school corridors. I refused, said we had to walk, school's rules. He didn't like that. He grabbed me round the neck and lifted me off the ground and marched me into my home room, then he said, in front of the class, did I have anything else to say. That's when I told him to get fucked.'

'Is that the Mr Spain fella who gives out communion at church?'

'Yeah.'

'Is it true he has his hunting dogs at the school with him?'

'Yeah, two of them, and he kept his cat-o-nine tails in his drawer, but the deadly weapon was the plastic pipe under his desk. That really hurt.'

'What'd your old man say?'

'He just asked me over and over did I say it. He said if I told him the truth I wouldn't get in trouble. So I told him I said it and he didn't do anything.'

'Aw well, ya out of there now, so let's get ya moving here, Dennis the fucken menace.'

Tucker rushed over and pulled the cups off one of the cows. 'She's got mastitis. Have to give her some medicine. Her milk's all lumpy; we milk her and throw it out, till she's better.'

After milking, Tucker said, 'You hose down the yard and the dairy shed and I'll clean the machines and shovel all the shit into a sludge pit. When you finished that, go over and feed the poddy calves with the milk in the white bucket, okay. Now, if you want to be a good worker always look about for what's gotta be done. Don't wait to be told. If you can do that you'll always get a job.'

Then it was breakfast at Tucker's mum's: cereal, bacon and eggs and plenty of toast. I was starving by then.

In the early part of the summer I cleaned stables and irrigated between milking. Later in the summer, between morning and evening milking, I was carting hay. Bellin, a farming neighbour's son who was building a truck and contracting business, had brought his team to do most of the carting. Michael – the other owner – Tucker and I used to race them with our own tractor and trailer.

We headed out one 38-degree morning with a hot north wind blowing: rain was coming. Michael was at the back of the trailer, Tucker up the front, I was on the elevator in the middle, and another cousin drove. The elevator picked up the bale and brought it to me. Driving and stacking were the biggest skills. I sent one bale to Michael and one to Tucker. The truck was racing around the paddock. I kept falling over or being hit by the elevator when he turned at the ends. Michael screamed at him, 'Slow fucken down or I'll put Dennis on there and you can come up here. 'Useless cunt,' he said under his breath.

The dust was laced with grass seeds and the fresh hay cut into my bare arms. I strained with every bale. The harder it got, the more pumped I became. Tucker and Michael would bring three or four layers along from each end of the trailer and marry them in the middle.

Building up the ends of the haystack was the first stage of building a secure stack. The last section to go in was the middle. Once the stack gained height, Tucker stood halfway up and I lifted the bales to him; he passed them to Michael. The hay went down the back of my shirt, in my bum, I had sweat and grass seeds in my arse, and I couldn't open my eyes because of the wind gusts coming up from behind the elevator. On the ten-minute trip to the haystack we sat down and tried to recoup before unloading into the stack and heading back out to the paddock.

Tucker milked by himself. The rest of us worked under lights until eleven o'clock. That's when we'd get the last of the baled hay into the stack. I'd have no energy left in my arms and my eyes burned. I earned thirty-four dollars the first day. Not bad for a kid. In a big week I was earning over a hundred and seventy dollars.

More than my old man earned. I was working up to eighty-five hours a week. Michael told Dad I was a good worker. The old man was real proud.

I loved working hard and working with the blokes. Any chance I got I tried to get out of milking the cows. My hands had become calloused from the twine on the bales. I didn't know how I'd go being back in a classroom. The season ended, the men left, and my work ran out.

The following February I went to a farm school in Sunbury, north of Melbourne. The school had an academic and an agricultural stream, but it had once been a boys' home and some of the practices of the brothers and priests remained. I was allowed to bring my horse and my duck to school with me. I wanted to do well and learn all about farming life. I felt good when things went right for me.

On the second day of school we rose at six, put on our work clothes and went hay carting. Rain was coming. The farm had several tractors and trailers. We were split into teams of five for the hay carting. This was something I could do well and I worked long and hard in front of the other boys. Other students were put on cutting, racking and binding. The tractor lights went off at seven a.m. and back on at seven p.m.; we started and finished in the dark.

We ate in rosters. There were twenty of us, fifteen- and sixteen-year-olds manning all the stations, except for a couple of brothers and a priest overseeing us. Some of the blokes really knew their machinery. The competition was fierce. Everyone wanted to be the best driver or the best mechanic, the best welder or the best worker. The litmus test was to back a turntable trailer. Only a few could. Those boys wanted to be interstate truckies.

Later in the year there was cropping and planting to do and in the spring we harvested the grass around the clock again, cutting and stacking it in pits and silos for fermenting. Work came before school. It was as much a practical course as it was academic.

In a normal week we were in the classroom for two and a half days and worked on the farm for the rest, with rostered work shifts every second weekend. Milking the cows had a separate roster. In the morning our first class, English, started at seven, before breakfast, and when it was your turn on the roster you had to go down and milk before class. I found myself reading *For the Term of His Natural Life* walking to the dairy; I couldn't put it down. Rufus Dawes was the most amazing and tortured character I had ever come across. I just wanted him to make it. Our school's most famous old boy was Ronald Ryan, the last man hanged in Australia. He didn't make it and he couldn't give the past student's speech we had at the beginning of each year.

I learned shearing, wool classing, ploughing, engineering, carpentry and animal husbandry. I didn't mind shearing, but I didn't plan a life as a shearer. I preferred working with horses. I was allowed to work with Freddy Mommsen when he came to the school. He was a legendary horse breaker from the Bogong High Plains and he took me on as his apprentice. I had more respect for him than anyone I'd ever met before and he didn't say much.

We started with brushing the untrained horse. I came early mornings and evenings, brushing out his nervousness. Then we put a rope around his neck and pulled it with one hand, motioned with the other hand, and said, 'Come.' Every time we did it we gave him some oats. Soon he was doing it on demand with no rope.

We saddled him and worked him with long reins for hours, one way then the next. I made sure I didn't pull too hard. Freddy said always go soft on their mouths. Finally we tied his front legs up with straps and walked around him. Later we did this with all his legs so the farrier could shoe him. When it came to riding him we put a leather band around his hoof, pulled it up under his knee and tied the band around his bent knee. I put my foot in the stirrup and stood up, making him take my body weight on one side then the other, preparing him for mounting. Then Freddy saddled another horse and held the one we were breaking in close and I climbed on.

Freddy walked us around, then I rode the horse around alone, turning him with my knees for hours. Soon I was riding him all over the property. I jumped him a few times. Then he became part of the pony-club horses to be ridden on weekends. Freddy told one of the priests that I had a good feel for horses and would do well working with them. That was on my report.

The school also had a darker side. I got beaten up and knocked out by a brother once for being too loud in the dormitory. He said he was feeling sick and I woke him. He uppercutted me with no warning, then threw a couple of left-and-rights into my stomach. When I was bent over he dropped his elbow into my back and the next thing I remembered was waking outside at the bottom of two flights of stairs in my pyjamas.

One of the boys snuck out some clothes and I slept in the haystack. The brother laughed the next day, asked where I slept. I didn't tell him. I'd seen worse. He'd given a few good kickings to some of the older boys. You didn't interfere when he lost it. The school wasn't an orphanage, nearly everyone had at least one parent, but I sometimes felt I was floating in a sea of disconnected bodies.

It could get lonely at night and sometimes we would lie awake thinking about our families and girlfriends, if we had them. Occasionally we would hear the training brothers and priests, who were scattered throughout the various dormitories with us, yell and scream in the night. That's when I felt most alone, hearing a grown man scream and cry. The next day they'd be gone. We never asked any questions, you just knew not to.

School overall was a great adventure and ten times better than the Catholic school back home. During boarders' leave, I'd stay and work on the farm and ride my horse and look after the other horses. Sonia would catch the train up to visit me. We'd started writing to each other; it was great to get a letter, and to write and tell her all my adventures on the horses. I had always seen her as a little girl, but she was starting to change.

My two years at the farm school finished on a bit of a sour note. A horse and I had a head-on collision with a shearer in his ute on a farm track out to Emu Bottom. I wasn't supposed to be riding the horse I was on. It ended with its leg bone sheered and dangling. The vet shot it on the spot and the knackery picked it up the next day. The rector told someone he thought I'd been showing improvement. Donald, my duck, stayed at the school to reproduce an entire colony of ducks and I sold my pony to a young family.

A WORKING LIFE

THE DAY I started my factory apprenticeship the reality sank in that I had been born into this life. Born for the production line. It was never a question of if, but what trade I would take up. I didn't think anyone took my dreams of a farm seriously. Dad was adamant I do an apprenticeship as a backup. He was a boilermaker, said he wanted something better for me than he'd had. He thought fitting and turning would give me more options.

On the first day, the new apprentices went on a tour of the workshops. In the machinist department a couple of hundred men wearing grey coats and protective glasses stood by their lathes waiting for the siren to start work. I imagined the next lot of apprentices coming through, looking at me standing next to a lathe. I felt sick. Every factory department we looked into had hundreds of men standing next to their workstations just waiting to die.

You had to clock on to start work and clock off to finish. The office in our section of the factory had a glass front. Nobody left their station without permission, even to go to the toilet. Sirens ruled our lives. At night everybody streamed out into narrow corridors between the saw-toothed corrugated buildings. It was a stampede, and the first time for the day I would see the sun.

When I was a small boy I wanted to be a boilermaker like my dad, but not in a factory like this. I shot through.

I got a job as a jackeroo on a cattle stud at Kinglake, near Yea, about a two-hour drive from home. The property had lush green grass with white timber fences and red and white Herefords dotted across the hillside. It looked like something out of a magazine. The manager told me my duties. 'Son, we want you to break in two horses. The pony is for the owner's grandchildren, so it has to be completely childproof. That's one of the reasons you were selected for the job. The other reason is we believe you're a good worker, so don't let us down.'

'No worries.'

'The horses are broken in on weekends and after work. Right now I want you to work with the leading station hand to shift the irrigation pipes around and follow the stud master's direction when shifting stock. Okay? Any problems, come and see me. Welcome aboard, son.'

About the third day the station hand said, 'We won't be comin back for lunch or smoko today, so make a thermos and some sandwiches.'

I said, 'But I don't have a thermos.'

He shrugged and walked off. He was a big bloke, a redhead, whose face was too big for his eyes. I was sent beyond the green grass and white timber fences to a clearing site full of bulldozers, trucks and chains, a log-clearing site.

At first I loved it. I thought I might get on a machine and learn how to drive a bulldozer. Or how to hook up chains and pull and dig out trees. But the station hand's arse never left the tractor seat and I ran behind the trailer picking up logs for ten hours a day. Some logs I could hardly pick up on the unstable ground. For this I was paid seventy-five dollars a week and I had to pay twenty-five of that for board. If I was employed as a labourer I would have earned more than triple the money. By calling me a jackeroo they were entitled to pay me crap. I later found out they were charging me fourth-year jackeroo board to compensate the station hand's wife cooking for me.

The old man and my uncle came up for a visit. I'd lost weight and my groin felt like it was split in half. I snatched it. I was disillusioned. I realised I'd never get my own farm working on one.

Next was tractor driving on a property in Jerilderie in southern New South Wales. The sharefarmer, David, was a stocky, jovial bloke who had a reputation as an interstate truckie. He was my mate's brother. He gave me board, keep, grog, ten dollars for working all day, and another ten dollars if I worked all night. He was trying to get out of the interstate runs and buy some land. For two weeks I drove around one paddock that was so big, after a few laps I didn't know where I was. I only had the tine marks of the combine to follow.

David hadn't quite finished putting in his crop when a shed he regularly shore in was ready to start, and knowing I could shear a little he took me off the tractor and sent me shearing for two days. He lent me his combs and cutters and I fronted at the shed to shear for the day. The owners were two bachelors. I shore the first sheep badly.

One brother said to the other, 'Wonder if this one might go wool-blind.'

The other brother said, 'See if he can find the chute.'

I improved a little and by the end of the day I had shorn fifty-five sheep. I was wrecked, but I felt fantastic. I went back the next day and at the start of the run I didn't think I'd see the day out. Every part of my body ached. That day I shore forty-eight sheep. The cockies said I'd make a good shearer because I was a hard worker and I learnt quickly. I earned more money in those two days than I earned tractor driving for David in a week, or jackerooing in two weeks, and I was only a learner. I thought this was the best option I'd come across and I reckoned I could build a life around it. The harder I worked, the more I earned. The other thing was, people respected you when you did a hard day's work, even David's wife said I didn't have to do the dishes. The other shearer told me that the shearing season was in full swing in Victoria.

I headed home and called into Sonia's high school, picked her up and went back to her place. I told her about my plans to look for a shearing pen and we had a great afternoon together. She had been out with a few boys, but nothing serious.

While I was looking for a shed I picked up a job loading refrigerated trucks with frozen goods. They said if I stayed I could get a forklift ticket and load the trucks, and then in a couple of years I'd get a job on a big rig driving interstate. Everyone had jobs for me, but I had more ambition. I had dreams.

I'd started ringing shearing contractors as soon as I got back to Melbourne. Grazcos, a national company formed by the Graziers Association, were short a roustabout at a shed in Yarram, Gippsland. I said I wanted a shearer's pen. The bloke said their roustabouts from the year before got the learner's pens, I had to start as a roustabout first. I snatched the freezer job with a day's notice but the boss was so shitty he paid me out on the spot and told me to fuck off.

WARRIGAL CREEK STATION

MY ELDEST BROTHER Neil drove me to Gippsland on the proviso that Sonia and I didn't kiss in the car while he was driving. He hated that. The only time we kissed was when Sonia got out to say goodbye to me at the shed. I knew she'd be safe with Neil on the drive back; even though he was a pain in the arse sometimes, he was a good brother.

My swag slumped to the ground. The noise of four cylinders pinging out of the property was replaced by the dense sound of bleating and shuffling hooves coming from the shed. The smell of sheep shit and piss replaced Sonia's lingering smells. The yards, full of woolly sheep, were on a lean and the fences and posts were knotted, uncut bush timber. I wondered how I would go here.

A slight, hunched, middle-aged bloke with a drinker's nose and red freckles came out of the meat house. He was wearing a slouch hat more in line with a digger's hat than a stockman's. 'Don't think I've seen you before,' he said.

'No, this is my first shed for Grazcos.'

'Well, just hung a sheep for you blokes. My missus does the cookin. Call me Mac. Are ya shearing here, or?'

'I've been shearing in New South Wales and I wanted a pen shearing. They said I had to be a rousie first, but I'm a shearer sort of already.'

'Big money shearing – if you don't drink it. I've seen a lot of shearers over the years. You've got the build for it, short and stocky. Ya don't have to bend as far.'

'What sort of horses are in the yard over there?'

'He runs a small breeding program for quarter horses as well. Since the son took over from his old man, that's all he cares about. He don't like sheep. That Appaloosa stallion,' he laughed. 'Worth more than a Mercedes-Benz car, that horse is.'

I found a hut door open near the kitchen. The room had three boxes of beer, two cyclone-wire beds, one without belongings on it, and a bedside table to share. The floorboards were buckled and the walls were cracked. I put Sonia's debutante photo on the table. This'd do me, I thought, and unpacked.

My roommate turned up. He was taller than me, just. Had round, lopsided shoulders and a bashed-in baby face. His eyes drooped and weren't even.

'Get another room,' he said.

'What?'

'Get another room.'

'I'm already in and half unpacked.'

'Go on, I don't like sharin.'

'Don't worry, I won't bother you.'

'I snore and fart all night and I drink alone when I drink.'

'Well, I won't bother you, as I said. I just want to sleep here.'

'Orright, but don't bother me now you've said it. You shearin here?'

'Na, I'm rousin. I can shear a bit, though. Should be a shearer soon.'

'Not a mongrel roustabout. Suppose this is ya first shed too.

How old are ya?'

'Nearly eighteen.'

'Eighteen! I was thirteen when I started rousin. Still live with ya folks, I bet.' He snickered and left.

I walked through the empty mess into the kitchen, where I heard some movement. Mrs Mac looked up, but continued cleaning utensils in the industrial sink. 'Wasn't expectin many tonight.' She shook her head. 'You never know, do ya. I'm expectin most blokes'll be here in the morning. Don't worry. I got a good feed for ya, roast and ice cream and jelly.'

'I love roast and ice cream and jelly. Have you got any custard?'

'Yes, somewhere, I 'spose.'

'That's a pretty good feed for a Sunday night.'

'I know how fussy you shearers can be, only needs one bloke and one bad feed to stir the pot and they'll sack ya quick. And this is our Christmas money and Mac can't drink a cheque.' She laughed. 'If he thought he could, he'd a tried by now.' Her knuckles were knotted and not all her fingers were straight. She had a purple rinse through her hair and looked auntyish, but her eyes were moist and young.

I sat alone and ate two helpings of everything. I ate that much I could hardly walk. She laughed and said I made cooking worthwhile. I went straight back to my hut and went to bed.

The next morning the empty huts were transformed. Cars were coming in, people unpacking, some going for breakfast, others chatting outside. Everyone was wearing virtually the same thing: blue dungarees that narrowed around the ankles and blue singlets with a patch on the side. I later learned that those patched singlets were called Jackie Howe singlets. Jackie Howe was a gun shearer in the 1890s. He held the blade and the machine-shearing record at the same time. His hand-shearing record had never been beaten.

I had breakfast and headed to the shed. Mr Bell, the wool classer, who was also the overseer, was preparing the contracts on the wool table.

'Ah, you must be Dennis.'

He was a tall man with a thick multicoloured beard. He spoke with a cultured voice and he had a washed and ironed white coat on ready for work.

'Mr Bell,' I said and nodded.

'Thanks for making it on such short notice, Dennis. This time of the year it's hard to fill all the teams. I usually work in the office myself, but I do get out for one or two sheds around this time of year.'

The back of the shearing shed had double doors that opened onto the yard where the sheep were held. The large holding pen had gates into two more pens, and those pens fed the smaller catching pens for the shearers. The floor in the catching pens was slatted so the piss and shit could drop through onto the ground underneath. In the middle of the shed was a wall partitioning off the sheep. The shearers each had a stand with their shearing machines on this wall. To the left of each stand were batwing doors into the catching pens so the men could walk in and get a sheep without having to open and shut the door. On their right or behind them was a chute. When they'd finished shearing they pushed the sheep down it. It was built like a slide and led to counting-out pens. Each shearer had his sheep counted individually.

The diesel motor had a pulley hooked to a shaft near the ceiling. The shaft ran along the shearers' stands and for each stand there was a flywheel on the shaft. Connected to the fly wheel was a down tube with a flexible elbow that locked into the shearer's handpiece. The shearing floor was made of timbered boards that ran out to the back of the shed where the trucks picked up the baled wool. The part of the shed the shearers and roustabouts worked in was commonly known as the board.

In front of the shearers' stands were oblong-shaped wool tables with slatted tops to allow the locks to fall through. The bins the wool went in were behind the tables, and the presser got the wool from the bins and pressed them into bales, which trucks collected at the loading bay at the opposite end of the shed to where the sheep came in.

We had to sign on for a minimum and a maximum amount of sheep to be shorn. There were about nine thousand sheep at this shed, about three weeks' work for six good shearers. Once the shed hands were signed on they were paid until the shed was finished. Shearers, on the other hand, only got paid for what they did.

The presser was tall with a thick moustache. He wore footy shorts and had hairy skinny legs to go with them. He saw me, nodded and gave me a wink. He later told me you needed short shorts because of climbing in and out of the press, stomping the wool. The wool roller was also tall. He was a toothless, long-haired, unshaven bloke of about twenty-five. He smirked: 'You the board boy? New, uh? Spent ten years rousin all through Queensland meself. Not no more, fuck em.' He had a habit of throwing his head back and pushing his hair off his face and behind his shoulders.

I nodded. I wasn't going through the spiel about being a sort of shearer any more. I knew I was back on the bottom. The other board boy came in and Mr Bell called out to him to come over and meet me. Mr Bell asked whether I knew how to throw a fleece. I said I sort of knew. He looked at me for a moment. 'Don't worry too much, Kevin's an expert board boy and he'll show you the ropes.'

Kevin was about seventeen with thick blond curly hair, a little taller than me and skinny. He nodded confidently to Mr Bell. It was as good as done.

'I'm next in line for a learner's pen,' he said, still not looking at me. 'Been rousin for . . .' His eyes rolled up, his chin drifting upward and to the left. 'More'n four years. Don, in the office, and Mr Bell here been promisin me for sure next season I'll get a pen. Only reason I ain't shearin now is I'm too good on the board and they can't replace me, otherwise I'd be shearin me hundred a day already.'

Fuck, I thought, I'm not rousin for four years before I get a pen. Anyway, I thought, I should be better than Kevin at shearing.

'Now watch.' He looked around the shed and poked his chin out like a weightlifter. Then he stopped. 'I've picked up for five on me own at Windouran. All guns too. I could do this shed on me own if I wanted, if I had to. Not interested, though, only cuttin a bloke out of a job by doin that. Should be one rousie to four shearers. Okay now, a fleece is the same as a pegged-out hide. Pick up the back legs first and pull them back over the fleece like you're folding a blanket. Then still holding the leg wool, wrap them around the body of the fleece, pick it up and throw it with a little flick, and it should float onto the wool table upright. Got me?'

Kevin smiled into space. 'Picked up thousands of fleeces, can do it blindfold, can throw a fleece from the board and land it on the table perfect. I'll pick up for the three shearers on this side of the board and you do those three shearers. I'll get your third shearer's fleece for a while if ya need it.'

The shearers walked onto the board with an air about them. The rest of us slowed what we were doing and looked, eyeing off who they thought might be the best shearer and seeing if they knew any of them. The timbered boards on the shearing floor were smoothed by years of wool and lanolin. The rest of the shed was sticky with wool grease. The shearers didn't look around; they walked quietly to their pens, carrying towels, water bags and tool boxes. Except the last bloke, who came in jumping around.

'God I love this place. Smell that sheep shit. Not everyone gets to do that at work every day, do they?'

I smiled.

He nodded, gave me a wink and said, 'Get'ay, son.'

I nodded back and he walked to the first stand. He was on my side of the board.

Kevin had been coming to this shed each of the past few years with his uncle, one of the shearers, who was also on the executive of the Australian Workers Union. Kevin knew the men and gave me the rundown on each shearer. In the first pen was Rick from Yarram – he was quick, a skinny, hyperactive sort of bloke with a Village People moustache. He had a property but was a worker before he was a cocky. Dan drew the second pen; he worked locally with Rick doing two-stand sheds. He was a big bloke with red curly hair and red freckles, a solid and steady shearer. Dan also had a little property outside Yarram.

Reggie, the union rep for this shed, drew the third pen. A big, cranky-looking bastard with droopy cocker-spaniel eyes, he walked with one dropped shoulder and was a slow but clean shearer. In the fourth pen was Morgan, Kevin's uncle, a middle-aged pommy bachelor with a broken back. Morgan didn't drink and he ironed his dungarees. Kevin reckoned he was the cleanest shearer working for Grazcos. In pen five was Archie, a local cocky shearer who did this shed every year. His back was wrecked too but he worked hard and suffered through it. In the sixth pen was Jimmy, my roommate. He hadn't said much except that he'd grown up in the Bairnsdale orphanage. Said he'd been shearing round Julia Creek in Queensland. Told Grazcos he'd shorn two hundred a couple of times.

'When they got to their pens each man hammered nails into the shed poles and hung their combs and cutters. Kevin said they drew lots for the pens and if nobody wanted to go union rep the shearer who drew number one pen got the job. The men were contained, carefully unpacking their sharpened tools, preparing like athletes before a race. Their towels and waterbags were hung strategically for time saving. Rick hung his waterbag in the pen, above the unshorn sheep. I asked him why he did that.

'I look at the sheep and pick out which one I'm gunna do next,' he said. 'I can see what sheep I've got and work out when I'll shear the roughies and the gooduns. So I'm drinking while I'm planning.'

Dan hung his waterbag on the same hook as Rick's. 'It's outa the way there,' he said. I looked over to Rick and he was smiling.

I asked Kevin why Morgan had a foam water cooler beside him and not a waterbag hung somewhere. 'Morgan, he don't worry about racin, he can stop for a few seconds and have a drink. And he don't like the taste of bag water, especially when the bag's new. As well he likes drinkin out of a clean cup.'

After the men had set up their tools, Reggie, the union rep, called for a show of union tickets. I didn't have one. Morgan pulled out a butt of tickets from his bag. 'Had a ticket before, Dennis?'

'Na,' I said. I hoped I wasn't in trouble.

'There you go, son, your first AWU ticket. Mr Bell'll deduct the money from your pay. A couple of things: don't lose it, keep it on you when you're at work, learn the rules and follow them. Remind me later to get you our award and rule book.'

Rick yelled out, 'Yeah, ya still not allowed to bring a stallion or a bull camel onto the property. Now, don't forget that.' Everyone laughed.

Reggie said, 'Fact is, no one in the union office knows nothing about shearin to update the book. It was a shearers' union, ain't no more.'

My father had got his first union ticket boilermaking at the Newcastle dockyards. He was apprenticed on a warship near the end of World War II. They had to put more than a million rivets into the ship. He's had a union ticket every year since. My mum's dad, Pop, was a member of the railway workers' union in Newcastle when Chifley, a future prime minister, was a train driver a few stations up in Bathurst. Pop lived with us for the last ten years of his life. He reckoned the big strike of 1917 was about the new American style of work they tried to introduce. They brought in work sheets and timed everything a worker did. Time and motion, he called it.

Dad didn't agree, he said it was progress. Dad built machines for mass production. He could speed up or slow down a machine depending on how skilled the workers became. Pop said in the old days the workers were craftsmen. Now the machine was. Dad would always say, 'They still need someone to put two bits of steal together, don't worry about that.'

It was eight-fifty in the morning and Reggie waited till each man gave him the nod, then he went over to Mr Bell and said the men were ready. When Reggie was back by his stand Mr Bell took an umpire's whistle from the pocket of his white coat and blew it. The shearers turned, rushed through the batwing doors into their catching pens and pulled out their first sheep.

My three shearers finished at virtually the same time. I grabbed one fleece and took it to the wool table and threw it. Before I got back Kevin had pulled my other two fleeces away from the stands, to avoid the shearers trampling them or kicking them clear. I went and picked them up one at a time. The second fleece I put on the floor near the wool table and the third fleece I waited to throw. When the table cleared I began to throw, but Kevin had thrown another fleece under mine from behind me and I panicked and only half threw mine. It went partially on the table, over the wool roller, and the rest landed on the floor. The wool roller kept skirting the fleece on the table as if it hadn't happened. I stood there waiting for a bomb. He shook his hair back over his shoulder, didn't look at me or speak. Mr Bell was also a picture of intense concentration, grading the wool as if nothing had happened.

'Wool away, wool away!' Rick screamed. He was standing in the pen doorway with a fresh sheep and I hadn't picked up his last fleece. I ran over but Kevin beat me, picked up the fleece, tucked it into his belly, stayed bent and picked up my second fleece, while I stood there looking at him. Mr Bell yelled out, 'Dennis, give him a hand, don't just stand there.'

Kevin went harder. He ran to the wool table, opened his arms, dropped the first fleece he'd picked up and simultaneously threw the second onto the table. Then he got the broom, started from my end, and in a mad flurry swept the entire board, leaving a mound of locks in a pile near the wool bale positioned on the side of the work floor. Mr Bell yelled, 'Pick the locks up, Dennis, and put them in the bale.' I knew that was coming.

Three more fleeces came off close together. I got two and Kevin got one. I threw my first one and most of it got onto the table. The wool roller said, 'Don't try so hard, just a little flick, they're small fleeces, you're splitting the fleeces cos you're throwing too hard.'

'Dennis.' Mr Bell walked over and pointed. 'Pick up those damn belly wools strewn across the boards. You're supposed to take the piss stains out of them first – put the stained wool in one wool pack and the belly wools in the other wool pack. Kevin's done all his.'

I started to do as he asked but had to leave for more fleeces coming off. I bunched the belly wools up under the wool pack as the run progressed and did a couple when I could. Three fleeces came off at the same time again. I went one, two, three and pulled all the fleeces back. Picked the first fleece up and went to throw it. Kevin threw a fleece from five metres away before I could throw mine. I dropped the fleece I was carrying and grabbed the second fleece. This time I threw it as soon as the fleece on the table had been skirted. I put the third fleece next to the table. I looked at the clock – six or seven minutes till smoko.

'Sheepo, sheepo,' Dan yelled. That was the signal his pen only had two sheep left in the catching pen. The presser, who also did the penning-up, was out the back. The press had a mechanical fault and he and Mac were fixing it. Mr Bell yelled over the noise of the engine and the revving handpieces. 'Dennis, Dennis, put some sheep in the pen until the presser gets there, quick.' I ran through the batwing doors. Kevin had already ducked in and jumped the pen railings and was pushing sheep in. I started helping him, then I heard another shearer scream, 'Wool away, wool afucken way.'

Shit. I ran out. It was Reggie. Luckily he'd picked up his own fleece and thrown it. He laughed. 'You'll get the hang of it, son, don't worry.' My legs were sticky from sweat; tomorrow I was going to wear shorts for sure.

The whistle blew at twenty-seven minutes past nine for smoko. The shearers had three minutes to finish off their sheep. After the bell went, shearers couldn't pull another sheep out of the pen. Four shearers got a catch, a sheep before the bell went, so I started on the belly wools. I had about thirty to do. When I'd finished that I swept the board and picked up my locks. Smoko was from nine-thirty to ten. I got to the teapot about thirteen minutes to ten. Tea and toasted sandwiches with cold sausages. I was starving and I loved cold sausages. Then I rolled some smokes for the next run.

About five to ten I heard a machine going. I raced back to the board thinking they'd started. It was Kevin. He was shearing a sheep for his uncle. Everyone had one eye on him because there was nothing else to look at. Mr Bell came and stood next to me.

'They call it barrowing, Dennis – that's when a roustabout is learning to shear. A rousie can start a sheep for a shearer, any shearer that'll let him, at five minutes before starting time, to learn. You can do it too. Reggie's someone that likes to teach young chaps like yourself. I think he'd like a good student. Also, don't forget you can finish the sheep off at the end of the run as well. As long as the shearer does the roustabouting for you while you're shearing their sheep. Have a go in a few days, when you get the hang of things.'

Kevin was good, real good. Fuck, I could be rousin for years, I thought. I'd better start practising as soon as possible.

As the clock ticked on to ten Mr Bell blew the whistle and the second run began. The whistle would blow again at exactly three minutes to twelve. Lunchtime. I had two hours to survive.

Rick could shear a sheep in two and a half minutes and Dan a bit over three. Rick was so fast in and out of the pens I couldn't pick his fleece up and sweep his board before he got back, so I copied Kevin. He would pick the fleece up and give the board a swipe all with one action, pushing all the locks away from the stand. Then he'd sweep around the shearer later.

The wool roller was fast. He and Mr Bell skirted the full fleece, rolled it so the shoulder of the fleece was upright, and then Mr Bell picked a staple of wool out of the fleece and gave it a flick with his finger to test for breaks and evaluate the tightness of the crimp. The tighter the crimp, the better the wool. I knew that because I'd learned it at school in wool classing. Then Mr Bell put the fleece in the appropriate bin, marked A, AA or AAA. While he was doing that the toothless wool roller skirted all the fleeces without missing a beat.

About an hour into the run the men stopped to change their combs and cutters. Some smoked and squatted and Morgan always lay down to rest his back. During the mini-break I was pulling the piss stains off the belly wool when a burr pricked my finger. Without thinking I put my finger in my mouth and sucked it. It tasted terrible. Morgan spotted me and laughed. Rick saw it too; he was upright with a fresh sheep between his legs, smiled, sucked hard on his smoke, threw the butt down the chute, bent over, exhaled and started shearing. I was barely making it through the runs, catching up in the breaks. By the end of the day I was stuffed. After work I had a shower and lay on my bed until teatime.

Jimmy sat on his bed and drank a few bottles. He had shorn about ninety sheep for the day, a lot less than his predicted two hundred. Then he started talking to me. 'Yeah, learnt farmin work and that at the orphanage, hey. Me mum put me in for a while. She had twelve kids, ya know. I was her favourite, hey. Shot through when I was thirteen. Hitchhiked to Queensland on me own. Worked in the sheds ever since. Not like you, still suckin on Mummy's milk, aren't ya?'

I was too tired to answer.

'I got me first learner's pen and that round Hughenden and Julia Creek. You wouldn't last. Ya too soft. No one likes ya here, ya know. The manager's daughter reckons you're ugly too.'

I said, 'I don't even know the manager's daughter. I don't know anyone.'

'She came into the shed today. That's where I was last night. Mrs McDonald knew me family. Is that a picture of ya girlfriend? She's all right, seen better. I got a sheila and that back in Queensland. She's better looking than your one too. Anyway, I'm starvin.'

I felt sorry for him and just listened.

We went for tea and this time there was a room full of men. Reggie was late, but Kevin reckoned he drank about five bottles between knock-off and dinner time. After dinner I went straight to bed. Every day was the same. Sleep at lunchtime, and early to bed after work. By lunchtime Friday, for the first time, Kevin hadn't picked up one of my fleeces. I asked Reggie if I could shear a sheep for him.

He showed me how to check the handpiece and make the best setting with the comb and cutter. I pulled a sheep out before Kevin realised, one that Reggie had picked, and I started shearing.

I looked behind and Kevin was racing. He was too late – by the time he started I had the belly wool off. Reggie, kneeling far enough away not to get hit if the sheep kicked the handpiece out of my hand, yelled, 'For Chrissake, slow down.'

I'd nicked the skin on the belly in a few spots and there was blood everywhere, but it was only superficial, didn't need stitching. I was a bit out of practice, that was all. I couldn't help looking around at Kevin.

'Stop fucken lookin where Kevin is, will ya. Ya head'll fall off in a minute. I'll have to put blinkers on you, I can see that.'

The bell went for the start of the run and Reggie took over from me. I had finished the long blow, a bit over halfway.

Kevin arched his back when he finished, pushed the sheep down the chute, walked over the fleece, gave the handpiece to his uncle, picked up his fleece and threw it, all in one continuous action.

He didn't pick a fleece up for me for the rest of that day. About five minutes before the last run ended, Mr Bell offered me a lift to Melbourne and a return trip on Sunday night if I wanted to go home. I took the offer.

I got home late and went straight around to Sonia's. She lived in the side room of the house and her window was partly hidden by a travelling vine. She'd left the window ajar. I tapped it and whispered her name. She put her hand out the window and I held it. She had her little bag of clothes and a neck-to-ankle flannel nightie on, even though it was warm. We walked across the paddock to my place and lay in bed and kissed until our lips hurt. Her skin was soft and goosebumped; her breasts were full and pear-shaped. We fucked slowly, exploding inside and straining to hold our silence.

The next day we went around to Tucker's house. His bitch Gidget had pups – she sat in her box with her swollen nipples while some pups fed and some played. One smoke-brown-coloured pup sat and stared at me. It was bold and courageous. I called him Smokey and took him with me.

The second week of shearing, Jimmy started to struggle. Once, when he pulled a sheep out that wouldn't stop kicking, he hit it a couple of times with the tension nut of the handpiece and started swearing. After he threw the sheep down the chute he ate another spoonful of Bex powder out of a bowl on his stand.

Reggie said you saw a lot of Queenslanders eating Bex. Morgan reckoned it used to have cocaine in it.

Jimmy would wash it down with a swig from his beer bottle. No one knew if it had beer or water in it. I think it was water. He was literally frothing from the mouth when Mr Bell said, in a sober voice, 'Clean em up, Jim. That's just not damn good enough,' and walked back to the wool table.

Jimmy yelled out, 'Need a fucken hard-hat in this shed with all the bombs goin off. More snipers round ere than Gallipoli.'

I was going good now. Kevin would even talk to me when we had a few seconds to spare. Leaning on our brooms, we'd look at how different shearers took the belly wool off or went up the neck, where their hands were on the handpiece. Every time I barrowed a sheep for Reggie I concentrated on not looking at Kevin, until near the end. Reggie said, 'Work around the sheep, don't go draggin it around you, you'll be dead in a day. And watch the end tooth of your comb. Keep it full. That's the difference between the guns and the rest of us. Keeping that comb full.' He was always saying that.

I'd check on Smokey during lunchtime. He had a box, a blanket, food and water. Thankfully he slept a lot and Mrs Mac gave him plenty of pats. During the lunch break, after eating, everyone usually went back to the shed early and slept on the floor. I went up, rolled my towel as a pillow and lay down. Rick started talking to me, rolling onto his side and propping his head on his hand. 'So ya wanta shear, save money and get your own farm, hey. Is that it?'

I nodded. 'Something like that.'

'Forget it. You'll never do it, son. That many young boys, including me, have had the same dream. It's a cunt of an industry, ya know. Can't get a full year's work, travelling all the time, payin for your tucker in a shed and payin to keep your missus at home. You're greasy every day and your back'll ache for the rest of your life. In a couple of years it'll be all you can do and you'll be trapped in it, like the rest of us silly cunts.' He lowered his voice. 'Do you wanta be runnin in and an outa those pens draggin 200-pound sheep out when you're Reggie's age? I know he's a good bloke and he says he loves it but he's quit shearin more than twenty times. He can't get out. Stay home with ya little girlfriend and get a regular job, one what's got holiday pay and sick pay. I've heard there's some jobs that have even got superannuation. That's the future. Get out of this dog's job while you can.'

That was the same advice the old fitter and turner gave me at the factory. I figured anybody in the one job too long would say that.

'I don't want to shear forever,' I said. 'I just wanta do enough to get my farm and maybe do a bit of shearing to supplement my income, like you. I can do it too. I'm a good saver and a good worker, you know.'

Rick smiled. 'I know you're a good worker, we're all good workers. So fucken what?' He was up cleaning his tools now.

What could I say? A few minutes lapsed. He stopped cleaning his tools, knelt back down beside me and put his hand on my shoulder. 'Son, the only reason I got a farm is I married a widow who owned the property, that's all. And I still gotta work. Shearing gave me nothing. Remember that. And I can shear a bit too.

I don't want to ruin your dream, son, I'm just telling you the way it is. I married into it. That's all I'm saying.' Then he loaded his handpiece and turned it on and off a few times, oiling it.

I hadn't planned on marrying a cocky's daughter. I already had Sonia. I'd just have to work a bit harder, that was all.

After work Reggie's room was the drinking room. He would drink his five or six bottles of beer before tea. Dan always stayed back, saying, 'I'll just have one more,' and he'd end up drinking about the same as old Reggie. He may as well have lived with us because he never went home. Jimmy drank in our room, alone. As the shed progressed, so did his drinking; some days he would drink up to five bottles before tea as well. Morgan didn't drink. He didn't understand people who drank one bottle after the other. I didn't drink the first week. In the second week I had a couple with Jimmy.

My mother had always drilled into us, 'Don't end up an alcoholic like your father.' She'd especially say it after they'd had a fight. She must have said it at least twice a week for my entire life, and if I went home tomorrow I bet within a few days she'd have said it at least two more times. It was on her mind that much I reckon she kept forgetting if she'd said it or not, so she'd say it again with the exact same anger in her eyes and worry on her face. Then she'd go back to whatever she was doing, usually cooking.

People said she couldn't cope because my dad was a drinker. But his drinking didn't really bother me that much. He worked six and sometimes seven days a week, so we didn't see him that often. He reckoned he was just a square peg in a round hole. The time my dad's drinking bothered me the most was when we came home and my mates saw him drunk on the couch. After that I never let anyone upstairs if the old man had been drinking too much.

On the second Saturday at the shed, I turned eighteen and we went to town for my birthday. The Yarram Show was on. We went to a few shooting galleries and wandered around checking out the local talent. I woke up early on the Sunday, lying on some stinking blankets in a small room with no lights or windows. My eyes adjusted and I could see some gaps around the tops of the walls as daylight came.

I heard keys rattling first, then the door being unlocked. The big cop let me out, said I threw a few swings at him, but they were going to let me off this time. I apologised. He gave a laugh and I left.

I got back to the shed and checked that Smokey was okay. I was glad Mr Bell went home for the weekend. I thought if no one knew about it then maybe I'd get away with it. Men don't like someone who can't handle their grog.

At the start of the next week, Mr Bell came onto the board to speak to me. He leaned over to beat the noise. 'We've got an unfortunate situation, Dennis. Mac has injured his back and he can't kill the sheep for the cook. Do you have any experience killing and skinning sheep?'

'Yeah, no worries.'

He beamed. 'I thought you might have. Can you do it after work? And don't worry, you'll be paid for it as well.'

After work that evening I killed, skinned and hung a sheep for the cook. Mac was there giving some pointers and he showed me some shortcuts as well. He had a bottle going and asked if I wanted one. I shook my head – not after the weekend, I thought. Kevin came and watched. Mrs Mac had saved my dinner and extra sweets, then I went to bed stuffed. It's hard work punching the skin off a sheep.

Jimmy came in from doing his washing. He softened a bit towards me, started talking about Mrs McDonald's daughter, said how much he liked her; he wished he had a girlfriend.

I never said, but I had the biggest loneliness inside me

sometimes, especially when I woke up in that cell. I went to sleep patting my pup.

The shed came to an end and Mr Bell said I'd done a good job, and if I stuck at it I'd get a learner's pen in time, but I had to be patient. Then he said to report to Lal Lal Station out of Ballarat. Morgan said I was lucky to get a Christmas shed after only my first shed with the company. The cocky shearers went back to their runs, Reggie went back to Jerilderie, and Morgan and Kevin went to the Western District. I never saw or heard of Jimmy again. Mr Bell bought a nut farm and moved his family to Queensland.

'Good luck, son,' he said before I left. 'And remember, grog ruined more men than shearing ever did.'

LAL LAL STATION

THE OVERSEER RANG the bell out across Lal Lal Station at about eight-thirty in the morning. Six shearers, in various stages of faded, patched, repatched and sewn-up dungarees and singlets, lurched forward in grease-soaked shearing boots and dragged out their first sheep from the pens opposite their stands.

I was boxed in down the end of the narrow board when the number six shearer came off first. The board was damp and slippery with wool grease. It was December and freezing around Ballarat. I picked up the fleece, ran flat out back and forth down the board, didn't slip, beating every shearer. I threw my fleece; no Kevin, I relaxed, and then sped back and pulled four and five's fleeces out of the way. Picked them up, threw them, swept the board and skirted my belly wools.

'Wool away,' number two yelled, and nodded towards me to get his fleece. The other rousie was holding his first fleece, waiting at the table. I rushed down and pulled it out of the way. Number six finished first again; I ran and picked the fleece up and took off, but four was close behind. I turned sideways and ran in behind him as he went into the pen. I beat three. Two was right in my path and he jumped into the pen and I ran headfirst into one.

'Sorry.'

He caught me, rotated me from the shoulders without stopping. 'Steady, boy, steady.' He grabbed a sheep from his holding pen and dragged it out across the board to his stand.

Six was coming off first every time. As the run went on, four was closing in and nearly finishing at the same time. I was sucking for breath. I started picking six and four's fleeces up and tucking them into my belly and walking slightly bent to the wool table. That worked for a while. The other rousie wasn't helping much, he seemed a bit lost. Half the time they were picking up his thrown fleeces from the floor around the wool table because he couldn't throw straight. I picked up the broom and swept the whole board. Picked up his belly wools and skirted the piss stains and threw them into their bins. Said, 'Hey, what about your belly wools, mate?'

He lifted his head up, gave me a dirty look to start with, then smiled. His name was Simon. He was about fifteen or sixteen, from Glenroy. At smoko I met Robert Chirnside, the wool roller; he was the son of a wealthy squatter's family in the area. The overseer, Mr Smyth, was also the classer. The presser was a local. Mr Fisken, the owner, had come to welcome the chaps. He was over forty; his chin was slightly raised and he had thinning blond hair. He was broad-shouldered and his jodhpurs hadn't seen a saddle for a while. His fashionable denim shirt and big buckle on his belt complemented his hunting jacket. He was standing looking at the tally book posted near the first stand.

Shearing in the first pen was the union rep; he was in his late forties, ran in and out of the pens. He was from an old whaling port. They called him Captain Ahab. He had twenty-two sheep for the short run. In two was Haveachat, a little nuggetty bloke from Ballarat. He had shorn twenty-two sheep as well. In three was Barnesy, a lanky local cocky's son who was third in line for the family farm, so he had to shear for a living. He had twenty-three. In four was Keith Viking from Creswick. I'd heard them talking about him at Warrigal Creek. He was not only a gun shearer, he was a gun spud picker as well: he had picked over a hundred bags of spuds and shorn over three hundred sheep in one working day. Not many men could do that. He had twenty-six. At that rate he'd shear more than two hundred a day. In five was Harold. Short, old and slow, he had shorn thirteen sheep. He would just get his hundred. In six was a bloke whose eyes were completely bloodshot. He had twenty-six as well and was on target for two hundred a day.

Mr Fisken looked proudly at his shearers' tallies and said, 'Yes, it looks like Viking may well ring the shed again.' He went over and chatted to the men, particularly the tall, rangy Keith Viking, then left.

Mr Smyth, at smoko, said, 'Give young Simon a hand, will ya, he's a bit lost with the pace of the men and the narrow board. And go easy on him.'

I called Simon over and showed him how to pick up a fleece and said, 'You can stay up the easy end till you get the hang of it. Then we'll rotate. This run you get Captain Ahab and Haveachat and I'll do the rest.'

'I'm not doin this for a livin, ya know. I'm only here cos the old man made me come out with Harold when I got kicked out of school.'

'What are you going to do?'

'I was plannin to be a jockey. I been doin track work in the mornings for the old man, that's how we know Harold – he likes to get down to watch the horses when he's not away shearin. Anyway, I got too big. Now I've taken up boxing.' He let out a left and right from under his chin, then he weaved his head. 'No worries,' he said, 'I'm faster than these old codgers as well. This isn't me first shed either, so don't think I don't know what I got to do. Hey,' his eyes lit up, 'maybe we could do some sparrin tonight. I'm quick.' He laughed and threw his head around as if dodging a punch.

That night we walked up to the huts together. He had a few drinks with Harold and I played with Smokey, and after tea I was in bed, rooted.

At exactly seven-thirty the bell rang for the start of the first run on the second day. This time Simon was on the job and I developed a system for the boxed-in end of the board. I picked up both Viking's and Bloodshot's fleeces and every second time I picked up Harold's with the other two and walked to the wool table carrying three fleeces. Captain Ahab and Haveachat were shearing about forty-six in the standard two-hour run. Barnesy was getting forty-eight and Viking and Bloodshot fifty-two. Harold twenty-six.

Simon and I were working well together. Sometimes I'd slap him across the face when he wasn't looking and he'd instantly shape up into a Johnny Famechon pose – he had a similar build too. But I think he already liked partying too much.

After lunch we were sitting down on the board, rolling smokes. The headline on last month's paper sticking out of a slat on the wall had an article about the dismissal of Gough Whitlam the year before. The shearer in three, Barnes, started it.

'Kerr had no choice. He couldn't sack the opposition. Whitlam was sending us fucken broke.'

Harold, at the end of the board, was on his feet. 'Malcolm Fraser's the greatest slime to ever enter politics and he had no right to block Supply. We were in opposition for twenty-three years. Twenty-three fucken years. Fraser hates workers. Big business can't stand the thought of working people running the country. That's what it was about.' Harold was red in the face, old and old-fashioned; he had a few strands of white hair brushed back, his hands went in and out of his pockets, then he switched to fidgeting with his fingers in front of his rotund belly.

Barnesy, a quick talker, sounded like he knew what he was talking about. 'For fuck's sake, Harold, Whitlam —'

Harold started edging his way up the board. 'Whitlam,' he cut in, his voice lifting. 'Yeah, Whitlam was elected. Do you know what that means?'

The shed went quiet. No one moved. I was frozen in my spot. I kept my head down, turned towards the two men.

Barnesy exaggerated every syllable. *'As-I-was-saying, he-was-fucking-the-country-and-had-idiots-as-ministers.* That's why you were in opposition for twenty-three years. Jesus, Harold, look at the facts.'

'Facts, facts.' Harold's voice was searing. 'The only fact I know is that those with wealth and power think they can break the law when it comes to working people. You think you're part of it, don't you Barnesy? You think because you came from a bit of land and you're ambitious, you're the same. Look at yourself, son, you got sheep shit all over ya. Your arms are sticky from sweat. You've got a rash from the burry sheep and you go home on weekends to help your brother. But you walk around like you're part of it. Son, you're a fucken shearer.'

'Harold, communism failed.' Barnesy was sarcastic. He yelled the next four words out slowly: 'It. Didn't. Fucken. Work. Money makes money. That's how it works, and it's been working pretty well in this country for years. And you're still dirty on me for not going on strike when they sacked him. That's what this is about. What was the fucken point? What? You don't have a family to feed. A farm to keep. Kids at school. Food to buy. It's just the races for people like you.'

Harold was calm. 'Give it a break. Commos! It was about *democracy*. It was about the people choosing. Not big business making the rules. And as far as you being too miserable to lose a day's pay, you're the one still talking about it.'

Haveachat intervened. He agreed with Harold but he was Barnesy's mate. 'Leave it alone, fellas. It's over. Fraser's a slime of a man, we all agree on that, and Whitlam's gone, so for fuck's sake move on.'

It was two minutes to one o'clock and Harold shuffled back to his stand, unhappy with the way it had ended. Barnesy seemed removed. The bell went to end that round and start the run. The arguing stopped and the shed had an uneasy quietness. No matter what happened, work came first.

Wednesday was pub night. Haveachat, Viking and Robert the wool roller met us at a pub near Dunnstown for a few drinks. Viking lived up the road in Creswick, Haveachat lived in Ballarat, and Robert lived in Skipton.

Haveachat said to me, 'What'd you think of the blue yesterday?'

'Don't know. That Barnesy seemed to know what he was talkin about.'

'They shouldn't put them together,' said Haveachat. 'Anyway, Harold's nearly had it. He's over sixty, you know. Not many shearers still going at that age.'

'Why didn't the other fellas say something?'

'Well, Bloodshot don't like Barnesy.'

'Why not?'

'Well, if you shut up, I'll tell you.' Robert was still with us but Viking had started a drinking school with some others now. 'Barnesy's a farmer through and through. He don't say it but he's a Lib. And Bloodshot is like Harold. He hates the cockies, reckons Barnesy's a bigmouth – always talking about big ideas but he has to front up and work with the rest of us every day.'

'What about Viking and you?'

'Well, I agree with Harold, but me and Viking work with Barnesy and he's a good bloke, works hard, says what he thinks, and that's it. He gets us a few cocky sheds when things are quiet. He could do em on his own but he always includes us. He's loyal like that.'

'What about Captain Ahab?'

Robert said, 'Captain Ahab usually has a drink with my father after our shed's finished. He likes to rub shoulders, so to speak, with the property owners.'

'Is he a Lib too?'

'No, he's a member of his local Labor Party branch.'

Haveachat, with a few drinks under his belt, asked Robert why he was out in the sheds.

'I don't mind admitting we're a bit cash-strapped at the moment, and I don't want to be a burden on my father. I'll make my own fortune in time. But I like mixing with you chaps. I like getting down with working people.' He wasn't so drunk that he didn't realise what he'd just said. He went a little red in the face. 'I mean, I like working too.'

He changed the subject. 'What about you, Dennis, do you like working for Grazcos?'

'Yeah, why?'

'Well, they're owned by the Graziers Association. Local contractors and shearers hate them. They've ruined a lot of runs. You don't see any show shearers working for Grazcos. I know some shearers that wouldn't work for Grazcos on principle.'

Haveachat said, 'Wait a minute, you can't work for someone who hasn't got the sheds. Anyway, it was those show shearers that brought the Kiwis and the wide combs over here.'

'That's a bit rich, don't you think? The union totally supports the show shearing, and so should we. Those men are staunch men. They don't think you Grazcos guards are too hot either.'

'Well, they shear on the weekends and the award says in black and white, no shearing on the weekends.'

Viking came over. 'Settle down there, Haveachat. I think it's home time, boys. See you fellas bright and early in the morning.' He grabbed Haveachat's arm and laughed as they went out the door. Haveachat was still trying to get his point across, now to Viking, but he wasn't listening either. We headed back to the huts.

The rest of the week the shed was uneasy. No one showed a close allegiance with either Barnesy or Harold except for Bloodshot, but that alliance was well forged prior to this shed. Barnesy lifted his work rate and was edging around fifty a run. Bloodshot lifted into the mid-fifties every run. He would never let Barnesy beat him. I watched each shearer closely. I wasn't game to ask anyone if I could shear a sheep for them so I tried to learn as much as I could by watching. They were the best shearers I'd seen. Captain Ahab said always bring the handpiece back quickly. Haveachat said don't push the sheep out the chute, walk it and conserve energy. Barnesy only took the wool off he had to. He wasn't there to be a pretty shearer. Viking had rhythm and long strokes. Bloodshot concentrated on every blow; he had the longest blows I'd ever seen. In the lambs, Bloodshot and Viking shore just over eighty in a run.

The shed finished ahead of time. The team shore eleven hundred sheep a day, and Bloodshot rang the shed by two sheep from Viking.

Mr Smyth told me to report to Ulonga Station on the seventh of January. It was on the other side of Hay, on the One Tree Plain in New South Wales. Most of the team would be there.

Mr Fisken came to shout a few drinks. He loved mixing it with the men. Bloodshot and Harold declined but took their share for travellers. Fisken particularly liked talking to Viking, I think because he was a local boy who'd done well. He was a great worker. All these shearers could push their bodies and their minds to levels I'd never seen before.

It was Christmas 1976 and it had been a year of finding my way. I knew what I wanted. I wanted to be master of my destiny, create my future. I wanted to be part of life, I didn't want to be stuck in a corner and watch life go by, and I didn't want to read about it. I was in a big team now, heading to the outback after Christmas, and I was sure I'd be a shearer soon.

I headed down to Apollo Bay to see Sonia. She was there for the summer with her folks and I went to their camp on the foreshore. This was our place. It was fantastic swimming together and sleeping in the tent in the afternoons. I wanted to be single and follow my dreams but I didn't like the thought of anybody else being with her.

ULONGA STATION

LEAVING THE WAVES, parties, green hills and rainforests of Apollo Bay – and Sonia, seventeen and beautiful, with my mate Ethan hanging around her – I hit the flies, dust, 40-plus degrees, and deserted-looking huts at Ulonga Station. At the cattle grid on the edge of the property I got out to have a look. The sun hurt my head. Flies buzzed around my dashboard and crashed into my windscreen. The place looked too empty. Maybe there was a back station or something, or I'd got the wrong date.

There was a car behind the kitchen. Relieved, I walked in with Smokey following me.

'Don't go bringing your dog into the kitchen, ya hear me, and don't expect miracles here neither. The town's ice factory is broken down and this shed's got no electricity and only two kero fridges. So don't try puttin grog in em. My meat goes first. Got that?' The cook was short, fat and mean. Her lipstick overreached her lips and her makeup looked like spack filler.

'What about some cans?'

'No. I told the Grazcos man I wouldn't come here again unless I got more fridges than last time. And look at it, still no fridges.

If any you blokes complain, I'm snatchin it. I'm not cooking through a heatwave without decent refrigeration again. I'm a chef. I shouldn't have to put up with this.' She gathered herself, aired her sweaty armpits and said, 'Name's Launa, son.'

By this time we were standing outside. She went back into the kitchen and I went looking for a hut. Bloodshot and Harold turned up, and a baldish bloke in a red panel van.

That evening Launa made a salad with cold meats. It was good too. The balding bloke walked into the mess, got some food, sat down, smiled, ate his food and read the Sunday paper. I followed him back to his hut and started talking.

'I'm Dennis from Werribee. I was at Lal Lal but I been down the beach with me girlfriend up until a couple of days ago.'

'Bernie, Bernie Bourke.'

'Where you from?'

'Balliang, near Bacchus Marsh.' He turned and went into his hut. I stood there for a few seconds, peaked into his room to see if he was coming out. I yelled, 'Balliang, that's not far from Werribee.'

'No, not that far.' He didn't come out. I went back to my hut, not wanting to look lost.

Bernie had a fridge, a fan, bedspread and sheets, a side lamp to read by, a radio and the Sunday papers. I had a sleeping bag and Smokey.

A little while later, Bernie appeared at my hut. 'Where'd you get to?' he said. 'I was trying to find this for you.' He handed me a brand new waterbag. 'Soak it in hot water tonight to get the bag taste out of it and fill it up early tomorrow morning. When you get to the shed hang it somewhere where the breeze can cool it. It's going to be a hot couple of weeks. Do you know how to drink from it?'

I wanted to say, Out of the top where the hole is, but that

seemed too obvious. I said, 'Not really,' to be safe.

'Never hold the bottom of the bag when you're drinking. The oil from your skin rots the bag. Hold the top of the bag and it'll last, and next time you're in town buy me one and we're square.'

I thanked him and went and soaked it straight away.

Harold was out the front of his hut. He looked my way and nodded, so I went over and sat on the shaded step. 'Where's the rousie from Lal Lal?' I asked.

'His old man got him some work in the stables for a while. Didn't want to come up here. Think I made a mistake too.' His grey gabardine pants were ironed, his white singlet was spotless and his black leather shoes polished. He had white powder under his arms and I could smell men's cologne. 'It's hot, maybe too hot.'

'How'd you end up with Barnesy?'

He smiled remorsefully. 'Barnesy. Barnesy's all right. He was half right.' He looked away. 'The track's been my life. Always loved the races and a bet. I've gambled a small fortune on certainties. Barnesy's gambling that if he works hard, takes risks and does the right thing he'll make it. And look at him, thirty-eight, thirty-nine, and still breaking his back at work. If you don't make it early it's nearly impossible to make it later. You can't keep working hard like that all your life.' He turned and looked at me. '*That* is a certainty.'

Cars kept rolling in until around midnight. That's when my tiredness beat the heat and I fell asleep.

I woke up feeling like I had a hangover. The heat had flattened me. It still felt over 40 degrees – I'd never known such a hot sun so early in the morning.

At breakfast most of the blokes from Lal Lal were in and around the kitchen. Haveachat rubbed my hair up. 'This'll test ya, boy, this heat.'

I said, 'Where's Barnesy?'

Viking said, 'Cocky shearing round his home and planning how he's going to make his first million.'

I looked for Bloodshot. He wasn't up yet. Captain Ahab had finished breakfast and was outside smoking his pipe, talking to the cocky.

I headed up to meet the overseer and sign on. Bill Draphine was an old cocky-cum-shearer from down the Western District of Victoria. 'How'd ya be, boy?'

'Yeah, good.'

'You'd be Dennis.' He grimaced, looked down his list and ticked me off. I signed on. 'Ya reckon you could go out the back there and push those sheep into the pens? The shearers'll be a while at the swarm, I reckon.'

I went out the back of the shed and started pushing sheep into the catching pens. Outside, the ringer was pushing hot sheep into the pens I'd just emptied. About eight o'clock the rest of the shed hands arrived. The wool rollers were burned-out old shearers. The classer was a part-time opal miner called Wally, a skinny, intense bloke. The other board boy, Ben, was a sixteen-year-old local.

I finished and went back onto the board. 'Good on ya, boy,' Draphine said. 'Now just check there's nothing in the counting-out pens, will ya.'

'Like what?'

'Like drums or sticks. And make sure the gates're shut too.'

I climbed out every chute; there was a drum of petrol in one pen and some timber and wire for fencing in another, but all the gates were shut properly. I went back.

'Now, go over to the cook and see if she's got a bone for me dogs, quick like.'

I ran over and asked Launa for a bone. She smiled, grabbed

some chops from the stove, handed them to me and nodded.

I thought I'd sit things out for a while – every time I finished a job Draphine would give me another one. I gave his dogs the chops and went to the toilet.

When I got back I said, 'When do you think I can get a learner's pen?'

'Jesus, boy, ya just started as a rousie.' He turned towards me. 'Most rousies work for a year or two before they get a pen. Just depends. Let's get this shed under our belt first and then we'll see how you're goin, eh, what about that?'

Wally had all the rousies and wool rollers washing the shearing board and cleaning the shed. 'No rousie'll be sitting down on my shift,' he said.

The shearers arrived. They marched in laden with tools, fans and other gear, bolted their fans to the overhead drive shaft, hung towels, hammered nails into the timber beams for their tools and needles. One of them told Wally the rousies weren't here to clean the cocky's shed. Wally smiled insipidly and mumbled something back. That saved us from any more crap jobs.

The sheep that came in from outside heated the shed up, and whatever edge off the heat the morning gave, by nine o'clock it was gone. The heat was weighing me down; I felt the energy draining out of me, as if I was bleeding to death. I didn't know how they were going to shear. Draphine pulled up next to me. 'Keep the water up, boy; you can blow up in this sort of heat, specially at the start of the hot season. If a shearer blows up, their thermostat goes haywire and they're never the same. Wrecks em for life.'

About nine-fifteen the bell rang to start the shed, and at nine twenty-seven the smoko bell went. Foxy, an Aboriginal shearer, yelled out, 'That's how long a run should last.' We laughed. They'd shorn between three and five sheep each, except for Harold. He changed his comb and cutter after the next starting siren blew, while everyone else rushed to get a sheep. Then he went into the pen and came out without a sheep. Went to his bag and took some tablets. Then pulled a sheep out and shore it.

During the next run most of the shearers stopped on the hour for a fifteen-minute break, except for Bernie Bourke and Harold. Bernie kept running into the pen. He looked funny with his tennis headband and wristbands and roundish body. His right hand never stopped pushing his handpiece while his left hand moved and turned the sheep around. Nothing bothered him except getting that next sheep. When I picked up his fleeces he looked to be in a trance.

Harold had shorn two sheep. He was having a run of bad luck. First he had Draphine replace his down tube, then his handpiece. Draphine, a good shed mechanic, replaced the insides of Harold's handpiece quickly. Then Harold walked into the pens and didn't come out. I picked up a fleece and threw it and came back. Harold still wasn't out. I went in and he had fallen. I put my hand out and pulled him up.

'You okay?'

'Fine. I slipped on the sheep shit, that's all. Pull one out for me while ya there, son.' Harold was panting. I dragged a sheep out onto the board for him. He gathered himself, took a couple of deep breaths as if he was going underwater and said, 'Okay, give him to me.'

After lunch I went back to the shed and looked on the tally book. Haveachat was the union rep for this shed. He could only get about twenty-eight sheep per run because of the heat, the wrinkles and the dense wool. Viking in two was getting about thirty-three a run. He nodded to me when I picked up a fleece.

In three was Fox Kennedy, a local Aboriginal fella; he was a happy sort of bloke. He had a sinewy, muscly frame and he worked hard in the heat. He was difficult to understand because he talked so fast. He was shearing twenty-six a run. In four was Bernie Bourke. He was shearing thirty-four a run and ringing the shed. He didn't drink or smoke and thought sex was overrated. In five was Knight, I didn't know where he was from. He had a huge gut but it didn't slow him down – he was fast when he got going but he stopped for long breaks on the hour. He was getting thirty-one a run. Harold was in six. He had twelve for the run. I hoped he would improve once he got himself right. Bloodshot was in seven. I said hello to him again, he didn't even look up; he just lifted his eyebrow to scare me off. He was shearing thirty-two, thirty-three a run and like Knight and Viking sat down for long spells on the hour. Captain Ahab was in eight. He was holding twenty-eight a run, the same as Haveachat. It was a shed to survive, not race, in. They went blow for blow at Lal Lal.

Ben, the other rousie, and I waxed the shed. We spent half a day at each end. One end was close to the wool table and the far end had no wool packs for bellies and locks.

At night we put our beds outside and slept with our sleeping bags over the wire frames – the mattresses were too hot. Smokey was great. He hid under the huts and slept all day. After dinner I brought him a bit of mutton and a few bones to chew on and played with him on my bed. Ben loved Smokey too.

The second night, Ben woke me up. 'Grab Smokey, grab Smokey,' he said. 'There are pigs scavenging about.'

I sat up and felt around for Smokey. I found him on the end of my bed, asleep. Ben reckoned that the pigs' razor-sharp tusks would kill him straight away. At the same time, Smokey woke up and started barking and the pigs squealed off. It was about three in the morning and it was still hot.

Each morning I woke to the heatwave. A few days in I asked Captain Ahab if I could shear a sheep for him but he said I'd blunt his comb and it was too much hard work in this heat. Towards the end of the run he yelled, 'Dennis,' and waved his head to come over. He handed me the sheep on the long blow. 'Finish him off for me, son.' Ben was doing one for Foxy.

Captain Ahab said, 'Never stop the handpiece from moving. That's what's making you money.' I was going as fast as I could, trying to improve. 'Slow down, slow down. What are you doing looking at Ben? Well, look at him then, he doesn't rush his strokes. He runs his blows out. He's gunna be a good little shearer, that boy.'

I didn't like that. He couldn't see my talent. I didn't want to learn off someone younger than me and I wanted my own style. How could I be better than someone if I copied?

Ben was good, better than I was and two years younger. Fuck, I hated that. I felt like I was too old, like I'd missed my chance. I'd only met two rousies and they were both better shearers than me, and I thought I was pretty good.

After that every sheep I shore I slowed down and concentrated on just filling up the comb. I decided to perfect every blow. I wanted that next learner's pen. The sheep were covered in burrs and even though I was only shearing half a sheep a run the lanolin getting into the burr-scratches on my hands and arms stung like shit.

Bernie Bourke developed pus-infected knees from the burrs. Some thought they were yolk boils. His legs were dotted with red pockmarks and pussed sores. At night he bathed his knees in metho to try to dry them out. I suggested pissing on them. He just looked at me for a moment. Each morning he bandaged his knees tightly. During the run, if the sheep kicked or pushed into him, Bernie'd scream with pain.

Picking up his fleece, I said, 'How's your knees?'
'Sore.'
'How do you put up with the pain?'

He shrugged and didn't answer for a minute. 'The more it hurts, the harder I go.' Then he smiled. 'That's what I do when I sometimes feel dizzy.'

'What?'

'Go harder.'

He wasn't cool in any way. He didn't care what anybody thought of him, he didn't care how hot it was, he didn't care how bad the sheep were. Bernie Bourke was a machine. His goals were to watch a test match at Lords, pay cash for a house, and see the Cats, the Geelong Football Club, win a grand final. I asked Bloodshot at smoko what his goals were. He lifted one eyebrow and tilted his head slightly towards me. That was his answer. Viking choked on his smoke when I asked him, and the team laughed. I didn't ask that again.

The next run, Harold was bending over on his stand for a few minutes after every sheep. His portly belly squashing his lungs made him suck harder than most for air. He walked to the pen and bent over the batwing doors and had another rest. Earlier in the week he was hiding that. Then he went in and didn't come out. Bloodshot followed and didn't come out either. I waited. I would have gone in except for Bloodshot being there. So I went into the next pen not to embarrass him. Harold was down again. He came out and sat the run out.

Harold hadn't shorn over sixty sheep in a day yet, which meant he was earning less money than the rousies, and today the town temperature was 47 degrees. After the third sheep, Harold slipped again and half fell on the board. Rather than get up, he slumped to the floor. Bloodshot called Draphine and they brought him some cold water. He sat there, his short arms looking puffy and his face ashen. He watched the other shearers, then stared out the chute. He wanted to get up but he couldn't.

Bloodshot stopped and talked to him for ages. Then I saw

Harold nod reluctantly, and he and Draph helped him to his feet and took him over to his hut. He lay down and Launa brought him some watermelon. Draph asked if there was anyone he could call at home. Harold said there was no one.

At the end of the day, Bloodshot stayed behind. The shed was quiet, the shearers were gone, and the light on the board had dulled with late evening. He undid Harold's handpiece, opened his toolbox and laid out an oily cloth on Harold's stand. He carefully dried Harold's used tools and laid them on the cloth, oiled them and folded the cloth twice over the row of combs. He took Harold's unused combs off the hooks on the pole, carefully oiled them and placed them in the cloth as well. Then he packed them all in the bottom of Harold's box. He cleaned his mug and placed it neatly in the corner. He oiled his cutters and wrapped them in another cloth and placed them flat next to his clothed combs. He tightened the screwtop lid on the Staminade bottle, placed it in the other corner next to his screwdriver, needles and waxed cotton. He closed the lid, locked it, and wrapped Harold's sweat towel neatly around the box. He hung his waterbag off the handle and took it over to the hut.

That evening, Draphine and Bloodshot drove Harold into the hospital for a check-up and then booked him into an air-conditioned room in a hotel. His bus left for Melbourne the following morning.

Despite the persistent heat, the wrinkly sheep, burrs and dense wool, the other shearers fronted every day. Four 2-hour runs between seven-thirty in the morning and five-thirty at night. The men were pale at breakfast, slept at lunchtime, and lay on their beds drinking at night until sleep time. Draphine said the shed was due to cut out on the Thursday, since we'd lost Harold.

Thursday morning before lunch, he started going around having a quiet chat to the blokes.

'I'm going to Maude,' Ben told me.

'How do ya know?'

'Draphine just told me. Where're you going?'

'Haven't heard yet.'

Ben came up to me at lunchtime and said, 'Well, where you going?'

I shrugged. 'Hasn't told me yet.' I didn't see the need to worry. They wouldn't have sent me four hundred kilometres for one shed.

Outside, it looked like the heat was about to break. The sky was blackening and the air had become steamy. During the third run we were all melting in the humidity, but the race was on to beat the rain. We didn't. By the time the last sheep went down the chute, the rain had started and it was torrential. Wally made us wash the board, wash the wool tables and clean the shed.

I thought, Fuck it, why hasn't Draphine told me where I'm going? I wanted to know so I marched over to him. 'Draph, where am I going?'

'Gunbar Station, son, in February.'

I was relieved.

Draph gave me my cheque. 'Call in and see the Grazcos man in Hay on Monday, he might have a bit of work for you here and there until Gunbar starts. If I don't see you before, I'll see you there, son.'

'No worries.'

We packed during the downpour of rain.

Ben yelled, 'Well, are ya goin out to Maude as well?'

'No, I'm going to Gunbar.'

Ben stopped. 'We're all going to Gunbar after the next shed.'

Draphine had conned me: he didn't tell me most of the men had another shed before Gunbar.

The black-soil track was soaked and soggy underneath the surface. Bernie Bourke put his snow chains on, yelled, 'High gear, low revs and follow my tracks,' and took off cutting through the soil. I had Ben and a wool roller from Hay with me. One was pushing the car from behind and the other was on the passenger side, trying to keep it in Bernie's tracks and stop it sliding into the table drain. But we slid from side to side like we were on ice. By the time we hit the bitumen, all my clothes were wet and my car was covered in mud, inside and out. The only one to love it was Smokey; he was jumping and barking and his eyes were wired, taking everything in.

Smokey and I camped on the Murrumbidgee River on the outskirts of Hay. We had a few weeks to wait until Gunbar Station started, and I was hoping to pick up some other work before then.

I rang Sonia. She said she was going to be a nurse and her parents were pushing her to go out more. They said she shouldn't spend the best years of her life sitting around waiting for me. They said I was good but I wasn't around. I said I'd try and get home in a few weeks. She'd stayed down the beach for a few weeks after I'd left. She said Ethan had called in to see her brother (they'd gone to school together), and he was good fun but it wasn't the same after I left.

I told her how Harold snatched it and how Bernie Bourke had rung the shed only because Viking and Bloodshot thought it was too hot to work hard. I said one day it got up to 47 degrees. I told her Ben, the other rousie, could beat me at the moment but I reckoned I could catch him. I told her what a bastard the classer was. She said Ethan had been given some tickets to a concert and he'd asked her to go. No worries, I said. I asked, 'When's it on?' She said it was last week but she couldn't contact me. She said it wasn't that good without me. Then her mum said she had to get off the phone.

Smokey and I went adventuring down the river and we did a few pub crawls with the boys. On a lazy day Foxy and I went drinking in the Caledonian Hotel in the centre of Hay. We left after a solid session and I got into the car and backed straight into the Hills hoist, knocking it out of the socket. I was stuck there with the socket jammed under my differential, revving the head off the car, going nowhere. We pushed it off and Foxy ran in and told the pub owners we'd just seen a red Cortina run their clothesline over. I wanted to tell them the truth. Foxy said, 'Na, insurance, insurance'll pay for it.' But I knew I got caught at everything I did.

We went round to the RSL and the police came in and got me. The red Cortina had had an off-duty cop in it. I had to go back and own up to the lady who owned the pub and pay for the clothesline.

GUNBAR STATION

GUNBAR STATION WAS a huge property between Goolgowi and Merriwagga, north of Hay. The shed and huts were fifteen kilometres in from the main road. In some places they had dogs tied to the posts to keep the cattle in, rather than gates. On a lead, in the sun, with half a roo thrown their way and a bowl of water was their life.

This was a fourteen-stand shed, the biggest I'd worked in. That meant over twenty-eight men in the team and we signed on for forty-five thousand sheep. And it was still hot.

Draphine was the overseer, Wally was the classer, a big man called Greeny was the presser, and Schultz, an ex-pastry cook, was in the kitchen. They said he was a perfectionist and could get a bit cranky sometimes, but his cooking was the best going. The core of the Ulonga team was here, along with some local Hay shearers.

I walked across the claypan to the shed. Morgan was among a group. 'Where's nephew Kevin?' I asked.

'Well, he's having another try at school. He can't read or write and he's been invited to be part of a pilot program. He'd love to be able to read.'

'Didn't know that. Say hello for me.'

'Oh, he'll be back.'

I ran and caught up to Viking and Haveachat. Haveachat was union rep.

'How come?' I asked.

'I nominated. Just won too.' He looked at Viking when he said that.

Viking reckoned, 'Need to keep the shed on an even keel with this many blokes. Big sheds like this can get outa hand quick like.'

Everyone set their stands up and we organised the wool bins and tables, filled the catching pens and checked the counting-out pens. Then Haveachat yelled and waved his hand for people to come and sit down.

'I want to have a bit of a meeting with you fellas and give ya an update on the union and how things are going.'

I squatted next to the other rousies. Everyone was listening.

Haveachat was a little bent over, his finger pointed as he looked over the men. 'Okay, listen up, listen. Had a talk to old Don the other day.'

'Who's Don?' someone yelled out. I didn't know either.

'Don McIntosh, the branch secretary down in Victoria. He reckons the word is, Fraser's gearin up to get us. They reckon Fraser and the Libs think, with public feeling high against Labor, this is the time to go after us and break the union. They think Whitlam turned a lotta workers away from Labor.'

I looked for Bloodshot's face but I couldn't see it. He had his head down between his knees and didn't flinch.

'Big business and the big cockies reckon now's the time. They reckon the union can be broke.'

There were a few laughs and people started talking among themselves.

Haveachat started getting louder. 'And it's not just us either. They want the wool stores, the meat works, the lot. Now we need to be vigilant. No ticket, no start. We don't want the Kiwis coming in using their wide combs. We don't want people shearing on weekends and we don't want people living in fucken caravans and not using the huts.'

Men were talking over one another. Haveachat was almost yelling. His voice was excited. 'We spent a hundred years fighting for everything we got and we got fuck all, really. But we have to protect what we got or we'll end up with nothing.' He was full-blown yelling now. 'They spend millions trying to invent machines to get rid of us. They never think to spend one fucken cent to make shearin easier for us.' Then he said proudly, 'And they can't invent a machine to beat us.' The men smiled. They were proud of that.

One bloke started talking above the noise about a shed where the Kiwis loaded up two handpieces, one narrow and one wide. Then when it was safe they'd pull out the wide one and use it. Another bloke jumped in to speak and Captain Ahab yelled out, 'Let's get to work, otherwise we'll be here all day.'

The first bloke, Eddy, a cranky bastard from Ararat who loved being cranky, pulled his ticket out and waved it. 'I got a paid-up right ta speak. I move a resolution to send a vote of support to the AWU branch secretaries and that we form subcommittees in each area and start patrolling sheds. Now I want a seconder.'

Morgan, an executive in the union, said, 'You can't do that.'

'The fuck I can't.'

I looked around. Morgan was not popular. He seemed a good bloke – quirky, but he knew his stuff.

'The resolution's on the table,' Eddy said. 'I want a seconder.' The shed went quiet. He yelled louder. 'Have I got a seconder?'

Morgan went to speak. Haveachat intervened and said he'd bring it up at the next official union meeting. He looked at Morgan and Morgan nodded. Then the place erupted; everyone had an opinion and Viking yelled out, 'Anybody wants to know anything, ask later.'

Everyone got their tickets out and showed Haveachat. He ticked their names off a list. One rousie didn't have a ticket and Morgan organised one for him on the spot. Draphine rang the bell and went out the back to pen up. He seemed pissed off and didn't care that not everyone was ready. It was a hairy start to a shed.

I said to Bernie, 'What's wrong with old Draph?'

'He wouldn't like the men getting stirred up like that. The blokes in the office always blame the overseer if there's trouble in a shed or men go on strike, reckon he can't handle em.'

The catching pens were behind the shearers, which made our job easier, and the counting pens were under the shed. The wool table and wool room were opposite the shearers. There were three board boys. We split the team into five shearers at each end and the rousie in the middle took four. Each run we rotated. There were several belly-wool and lock bins around the board and we had a lot of room to move between the shearers and the wool table.

The first week, the men shore just over eleven thousand sheep. Haveachat in one and Captain Ahab in two were holding forty a run. In three was Knight, he was holding forty-two a run. He never chased anybody, he just shore for himself. Bernie Bourke in four was slaving out forty-six. Morgan was in five, his back wasn't holding up, but he was still getting his thirty a run. I thought maybe it was his pommy accent that people didn't like. Viking was in six, shearing about forty-three a run, but he hadn't cranked up yet. Bloodshot was in seven. His eyes were real bad and he was holding forty-three as well.

In eight was Monahan from Albury, a big redhead. He was shearing forty every run – he reckoned that was the maximum he could shear before the tax became too much. He wasn't doing one more sheep than he had to. He said to me, 'You wait till you've got a wife and a few kids, see how easy it is. I hate, I fucken hate, shearing.' And he meant it. His face went sour when he spoke. I squirmed in my stomach. I could see he was trapped. I hoped I wasn't fooling myself about shearing. I didn't want to be trapped when I was his age.

Foxy was in nine, he was getting thirty-five a run, and in ten was Tumbarumba Dave. He had a farm but it wasn't paying, so he had to get back out and shear to keep things going. A second wife and family didn't help at his age. He was holding thirty-eight a run.

In eleven was Hollywood, another local gun shearer. He was getting forty-six in a good run and less in others – he was smooth and rhythmical when he shore, a natural. In twelve was Taffy, a Welsh migrant who loved the outback and seemed to love the life of a shearer. He was getting thirty-seven a run, working hard for every sheep he got. No one seemed to mind his accent. It was more lyrical than Morgan's chopped words. In thirteen was cranky Eddy. His back was wrecked and he was getting about twenty-five a run. And in fourteen was Lewis from around Deniliquin. He wasn't really part of the team or any group – he didn't say much and had a reputation for being hard. He was holding forty-four a run, just off the pace.

At night there were several camps. The locals from Hay – Knight, Hollywood and Foxy – drank together. Bloodshot drank with Viking, Haveachat, Captain Ahab and cranky Eddy. Lewis drank alone, Bernie Bourke and Taffy sat together and talked sport, Morgan and Tumbarumba Dave bunked together. Wally polished the stones from his prospecting, and the other rousies and I went round the camps listening. I usually ended up with Bernie and Taffy.

Knight didn't like my pup and he and Hollywood usually

changed the subject when I arrived. Even though I got on with Haveachat and Viking's crew, they usually went quiet when I went in there too. I thought it was Bloodshot. Lewis from the fourteenth stand also hated my dog so I stayed away from him. He'd beat the shit out of you if he felt like it. Haveachat and Viking told me to stay away from him, especially if he'd been drinking and more especially if I'd been drinking.

Smokey went wherever I did. Haveachat bombed me a few times for his barking at night and Lewis complained that I had him in the hut with me, which was against the rules. I had to put him two hundred metres away from the huts.

I said, 'But he'll cry and yelp all night.'

'Well, pet dogs are no good in sheds, boy,' Haveachat said. 'Get rid of him, give him to a station hand. He's a fucken working dog, for Chrissake.' He was getting cranky. The pressure, I reckoned.

At night I tied Smokey up, then went and got him and put him in my bed. Everyone got off my back after that.

In the second week, the competition in the shed went up a notch. Bernie Bourke was still in front, mainly because he never stopped. Bloodshot and Viking were shearing over forty-eight a run now, but I didn't think that would be enough to catch Bernie, who had too much of a lead. Hollywood shore over fifty some runs but fell back in others. Lewis had stepped up but he was still only getting forty-seven. One afternoon Knight shore a hundred sheep in the last two runs for a bet – forty-eight in the third run, fifty-two in the fourth. He won a black jellybean off Hollywood. He couldn't straighten his back afterwards and his knees buckled under him. He walked buckling and limping like a cripple across the long claypans to the huts. He was thirty-nine.

I was shearing a sheep for Viking before the bell. The sheep were hard to drag out because they were so big and strong but there were no wrinkles on them and it was easier to push the comb through them than through the sheep at Ulonga. I asked Viking what the differences were. 'These are South Australian merinos and those mongrels at Ulonga were more the Peppin strain – wrinkly, and the wool was denser, plus they were full of burrs and it was fucken hot there, boy, don't forget how hot it was. Mind you, these sheep are cutting a lot of wool too.'

I finished in about seven minutes and tried to push the sheep down the chute but it baulked at the darkness and steepness. My back ached; I pushed the sheep harder but it got its front hooves stuck in the edge of the chute. Viking came by and nudged it with his hip and it went down.

The other two board boys, Ray and Mick, weren't interested in shearing. Ray was that lazy, every run he'd go to the toilet, leaving Mick and me to pick up for seven shearers each, and with everybody pushing hard that was tough. Draphine went up to Mick and said, 'I'm going out the back to pen up some sheep. If ya give that Ray a floggin when I'm not around I'm not going to say anything, you get my drift?' And he nodded repeatedly and looked at Mick until Mick nodded back. Then Draphine went out the back.

Ray was quick to make his move. 'I've got to go to the toilet.'

'You're not going to the toilet during the run no more.'

'You can't stop me from goin.' He turned and started walking.

Mick bulldogged him to the floor and they ended up under the wool table. Nobody stopped them. They'd been given the drum and knew it was coming. Ray was strong, but eventually Mick got on top of him and hit him properly a couple of times. The sweat on their naked torsos made the wool locks stick and they looked like half-plucked chooks. Most of the shearers slowed down to watch the fight, but nobody stopped. Knight picked his own fleece up and threw it on the wool table. He said the rousies were a bit busy at the moment and everyone laughed, but it wasn't funny to us.

Ray went to Wally to put in a complaint, but Wally said he never saw anything. He went to Haveachat, but he reckoned he never saw anything either. Ray didn't go to the toilet during a run again and he said he was going to get all of us.

That was a Friday and he was heading home to Hay for the weekend. As he walked across the flat between the shed and the huts he said, 'I'll be bringing my gun back to fucken shoot youse.' He was wild; Foxy said he'd always had a bad temper and could go right off. Ray thought the whole shed was against him. It was.

The cook snatched it as well. That was a real blow. Draphine was in there for hours trying to talk him out of it. Schultz was the best cook in the industry. He was in his late fifties, always wore a chef's hat and a white coat buttoned up to the second-last button. He made all his own cakes and even made ice cream. But as the shed progressed so did his drinking. In the evenings he was smashing plates around. He wasn't angry, he'd just lost his touch. Some nights he could hardly walk. Then he started turning up pissed in the mornings. The blue started over the hut keeper.

In the first week, the shearers'd had a blue with Draphine. Knight and Hollywood had blued with Haveachat, saying that, with more than ten shearers, the rules stated the contractor was obliged to put a hut keeper on. Haveachat said they hadn't done that in years but they insisted, so Haveachat had to go and fight it. Grazcos said no and Draphine had to sort it out. Turned out Hollywood and Morgan had also nominated for the rep's position. Morgan was trying to keep his presence up because he wanted a job in the union and Haveachat had only just pipped Hollywood, the New South Welshman. That's what some of the fellas said, anyway.

The men won and Draphine overrode the office by getting the station to pay for it. The hut keeper's duties were to sweep out the huts and do the shearers' washing (he wouldn't do the rousies'). Schultz also used him for peeling all the spuds. Knight jacked up again, said it wasn't the hut keeper's job to work for the cook. Haveachat had to tell Schultz that if he wanted a helper he had to pay for one himself. Schultz was a contract cook. By this time he wasn't just drunk, he was in the horrors. Cooking for about thirty blokes was big money. He said he couldn't put up with the undermining that was going on and if he didn't get the hut keeper back he was going. A taxi from Hay picked him up.

He'd been earning over thirteen hundred dollars a week, or something like that. The shearers were earning about fifty cents a sheep. That weekend it was help yourself in the kitchen. On Sunday afternoon a bloke from Merriwagga, who also worked as a shearer and a wool presser, turned up to finish the shed as cook.

On Sunday night Ray came back with a .22 bolt-action rifle.

I said, 'What's that for?'

He said, 'You'll find out in about five minutes' fucken time.'

He put a bullet in the slot and pushed the bolt in and down. Mick moved in and smashed him with a right hook to the cheekbone and another on the nose. Ray went down and the tussle brought Wally out of his hut. He confiscated the gun. Ray, covered in blood from the nosebleed, got up screaming, 'You pack of fucken cunts . . .' He sobbed out the next 'fucken cunts'. By now there were a dozen men around. He seemed to be looking up at the growing crowd. He sniffed and wiped the dripping blood from his nose. Then he started to cry. No one spoke. His face was wet and smeared red. He walked off into the darkness, sobbing. I heard him until he was out of range.

Draphine drove him to the manager's house early the next

morning, about fifteen kilometres away, rang the Grazcos man in town and Ray's mum. She came and got him.

That left us a rousie down. Wally took a wool roller off the table and put him on the board and we managed without Ray for a while. With one man missing and the shearers shearing close to five hundred a run, the production line started to slow and clog up with fleeces. The shed hands had to process five hundred fleeces in a run, one hundred and twenty minutes. We had to pick up the fleece, throw it, sweep the shearer's board, skirt the dags and sweat stains off the fleece, and roll the fleece for the classer – every fifteen seconds. That had to be done for two hours straight every run.

Wally began losing his cool every time I threw a fleece badly, because he and the wool rollers had to straighten it out. Sometimes I threw the fleece a few feet from the table because I had to race and get another fleece from the shearer's stand. Despite the fleeces banking up, Wally stopped classing, came onto my board and grabbed me by the arm, squeezing his fingernails into my flesh. Through gritted teeth he said, 'Stop throwing those fleeces from the middle of the board or I'll get two new rousies. Ya got it?'

I had no allegiance to him. But I wasn't going to let a shearer walk onto a fleece.

After lunch a new rousie turned up and we got back on track and Wally's stress levels went down.

I had stopped barrowing for Viking once he got serious about his shearing, but Eddy let me barrow for him and I was starting to shear a sheep in less than six minutes. Eddy said I was nearly ready for a learner's pen. The top boys, Viking and Bloodshot, were cutting Bernie Bourke out by about three sheep a run, which meant about twelve sheep a day. Bernie Bourke didn't have the rhythm of the truly gun shearers – he was all guts. He still had a lead of about eighty sheep from the first week's work. On the last day, after leading for the whole four weeks, he lost by two sheep. Viking rang the shed.

Draphine came up to me before the last smoko and said, 'Windouran Station out of Moulamein, and you're the only rousie to get a follow-on, so keep your gob shut.'

On their way out, Haveachat and Captain Ahab nodded. 'See you at Windouran.'

After we'd washed the board and cleaned up I packed my bag, threw Smokey in the car and collected my cheque for five hundred dollars. I'd earned over eight hundred but had to pay tax, and I'd drawn some money on weekends. Draphine said Windouran was starting in late April. I had to ring the office to get the actual starting date. 'You got a good cheque there, put it straight in the bank.'

'A month away, that's no good to me. Where are the other blokes going?'

'Nowhere, it's the off-season. You're an ungrateful little bastard. That's the only shed going and you're in the team and whingeing.'

'Draph, I got plans, plus I'm still paying off me car. I can't afford to sit around for a month.'

Smokey barked and jumped around when we drove past the dogs tied to the gatepost. I headed straight back to Melbourne to see Sonia.

WINDOURAN STATION

IT SEEMED LIKE my shearing future had stalled. I didn't want to hang around taking bits and pieces of work. Draphine reckoned I was getting all the off-season sheds and I should be grateful.

My month off was okay. Sonia was working. She was training in the city and she had to live in. I picked up a few days' work with the old man, cleaning up the factory he was working in, and a couple more days putting tomato stakes in the ground – enough money not to spend my savings. Once I put it in the bank I wouldn't take it out.

I had suggested Sonia and I split up. I said we were going in different directions. She said there was nothing between her and Ethan. I thought I'd rather end it than endlessly wonder. But the next weekend she had off we went to the movies, then mid-week I went to see her and she snuck out for a while. Mostly we spent our time fighting and making up. We never mixed with anyone, only more recently with Ethan. I agreed not to get jealous.

That was hard. I had an image that was burned into a reminder button in my head. She got drunk one night and told him she loved him and kissed him in front of me. I know people say you speak the truth when you're drunk, but I'd said plenty of things I didn't mean when I was drunk and plenty more sober. And I liked Ethan too, he was a good bloke. But I didn't like him so much that I wanted to share Sonia with him.

People said Sonia and I met too young. Her folks said that too. There was one good thing about working hard: when I went to bed my brain crashed. When I wasn't working I couldn't stop thinking at night.

Windouran was a five-stand shed. I was the board boy; Gannon, a trainee wool classer, was the wool roller, Greeny the presser, Wally the classer, and Draphine the overseer and penner-upper. The shearers' swarm finished early and they were on the board at about eight-thirty in the morning.

Captain Ahab was in one and the rep, Haveachat in two. Viking three, Bloodshot four, Bernie Bourke five. This was Grazcos' guard team. It was late April now and the weather had cooled from the January heat. The shearers were ready and fit and were up in the shed quickly.

They looked keen. In the first hour before smoko they shore between twenty-two and twenty-three each. Haveachat and Captain Ahab started racing each other from the beginning. At the end of each run we rousies were twenty fleeces behind. They were stacked up on the floor next to the wool table. The boys were shearing a thousand sheep a day. I worked my guts out. After about four days Haveachat and the Captain were shearing between forty-nine and fifty-two a run, Viking and Bloodshot were getting up to fifty-four a run. Bernie Bourke was getting fifty.

After lunch we were all lying on the board. It was quiet without the machines roaring and sheep being pushed around the back pens. It was about 28 degrees, clear skies and no wind.

The conversation turned to the Kiwis. There had been a team of them over here working for a while; a couple of the cockies had encouraged them to come over. A few rebel cockies. Wally laughed. 'Relax, boys, they won't get a hold here.'

Bernie Bourke said, 'They've been in Queensland for a while.'

Wally returned sharply, 'Yeah, and they haven't been as big a problem as people thought.'

'This is different,' Viking said. 'It's not the Kiwis looking for work. It's the cockies recruiting them for our work.'

Wally didn't answer that. No one did.

Gannon was listening to every word that was said. He was at the wool table picking through some fleeces and pretending to concentrate on what he was doing. He'd been splitting his spare time between Draphine and Wally. After work he'd go networking and at dinner he'd sit with Wally, away from the men. He wanted a run classing. He reckoned he wasn't far off getting his own run. Said he might give me some work when he was overseering, depending on if I caused trouble or not.

We roomed together but he didn't like to be seen to be friendly with me because he wasn't supposed to mix with the men. I seemed to be the only one he wasn't allowed to mix with. The idiot sat in Viking's hut every night drinking with them. Gannon was a sort of skinny, good-looking version of Frankenstein, except he had long hair. He thought he was so shit-hot, the best wool roller for Grazcos. I was always asleep before him because I worked a lot harder than him during the day. He worked a lot harder at night being a suck.

Haveachat came up to me while I was walking from the shed and bombed me for my dog barking. He said I got told every shed.

'Smokey loves you, Haveachat.'

He laughed. 'Keep him fucken quiet, all right?'

The men were drinking in Viking's room. I could have gone in but there wasn't much room and they didn't really like rousies hanging around listening. Plus Wally was there, along with Greeny the presser. And Gannon, of course. It was the place to be.

Bernie Bourke rarely left his room looking for company. I usually visited him. We got talking about a lot of things. I asked him if he had a farm at Balliang.

'No, my old man worked in the mill all his life. I still live at home with me folks.'

'Are you going to buy a farm?'

'No, that's work, Dennis. Shearing's enough for me. I don't want to buy a job. I'm saving to build my own home.'

'How much are you going to borrow from the bank?'

'Nothing. I'll pay cash when I got enough. The banks are cunts,' he said with unusual venom. 'Trouble is, the prices of things go up quicker than I can save. I'm going to save a hundred thousand dollars and build a house with that.'

'I want a farm. Wheat and sheep in the bush. Not the outback, though.'

'That's a lot; I reckon you'll do it too, Dennis. You got that determination.'

About two o'clock on the Wednesday afternoon, Haveachat nicked a belly. The guts started oozing out of the gash. Haveachat was shaking from working so hard. He was in front of Captain Ahab by two sheep and he didn't want to stop and give up his lead. He asked if I could sew the little ewe up for him. So I did, but the guts still oozed out in the yard and Draphine came in and said, 'Better go and fix it, boy.'

Wally gave me the cold tea left over from smoko. 'Pour that on the guts and it should shrink it a bit before you push them back in.' I slid down the chute and caught the sheep. I put the pain of the sheep out of my mind and did what I had to do. Her stomach was covered in dust and she was fretting badly. I sat her up on her bum as though I was going to shear her and pulled her over to the fence and poured the tea on the guts and waited. Draphine came out and held her while I pushed the soft stomach lining back into her belly. We had to lie her virtually on her back. Once I had the gut in I sewed tight stitches because the gut could ooze back out of the smallest hole.

Draphine shook his head. 'Don't go doin their dirty work any more, okay? Now Wally's not too happy with ya. You being out here instead a doin ya job, so he'll probably chip ya, just be ready for it.'

There was wool everywhere when I went back inside and the last run had just started. Wally was pissed off and so was Gannon; they'd worked right through smoko and they were still behind. I was stuffed. Haveachat was back into it and Captain Ahab had him by just one sheep. Haveachat said thanks and reckoned he'd fix me up later, but he never did. At knock-off time he and Captain Ahab were level, and Gannon and Wally and I were forty fleeces behind.

Viking rang the shed, with Bloodshot second, Bernie third, the Captain fourth and Haveachat close behind. Haveachat couldn't believe he'd shorn nearly two hundred a day and come last. Bernie Bourke got the biggest cut-out cheque because he didn't drink. The others averaged four or five bottles a night. We were there fourteen working days and the boys shore a bit under fourteen thousand sheep.

At the cut-out Draphine said, 'Boonoke Station in a few weeks, boy. You right for that? And leave that fucken dog at home, will ya?' Draphine wouldn't be there, but he said if all went well he'd see me at Tubbo Station in June. 'Now, on ya way.'

'What about a learner's pen, Draph?'

He looked at me and shook his head. 'I've spoke to head office and I told em I've got a fella out here who can't wait to kill himself.'

BOONOKE STATION

HOME FOR TEN days, another big gap between sheds, then off to Boonoke. There was a swaggie camped in the table drain on the road past the entrance to the station. Gannon and I travelled with Greeny the presser to the shed. Gannon didn't have a car or a licence and my car had broken down. From the glow off the swaggie's fire I could see the outline of his hat and turned-up collar. The other side of his face was shadowed.

The Boonoke shed was an old, hundred-stand, handblade shearing shed from before the turn of the century. It was on a famous sheep property out of Deniliquin, originally owned by the Peppin brothers, the name given to the wrinkly sheep throughout the Riverina. The Falkiner family purchased it next, and more recently it had been taken over by Rupert Murdoch. Back at the turn of the century each of those stands would be full. Now, with machine handpieces, we were using about sixteen shearers and the place trained property owners' sons, employing them under the jackarooing system of apprenticeship.

I roomed with Hobbsy from Ivanhoe, a town a couple of hours' drive past Hay. He was a big, unshaven, unwashed red-headed seventeen-year-old, a left-hander who could really shear. He'd come down to the big drink-ups we'd had around the river in Hay, but I hadn't got to know him until now. The roo shooters from Ivanhoe had picked on him because he was big, young, and his old man was the local copper. But he wasn't really a fighter. We weren't instant friends but I warmed to his sense of humour.

Hobbsy brought flagons of brown muscat to drink. The stuff blew my head off. Life was one big party for him. All of a sudden I cared less about saving money, getting a farm and making it. I thought of what Harold had said back at Ulonga. 'Gambled on certainties.' I wasn't sure what he meant. I knew it was more than horses. I could still see him slumped on the board.

Hobbsy and I worked well together. When we were barrowing for the shearers he was faster than me, but our friendship wasn't competitive, we were just different. The jackaroos working on the property didn't earn much money; they'd all been to exclusive private schools in Sydney or Queensland and were studying at Dookie Agricultural College. We were friendly enough with each other during work, but we didn't mix outside. The one time we did get together for a drink, we went and made a bush camp away from the station, but Hobbsy and I ended up in a fight with them, as I knew we would. They were three or four years older and punched the crap out of us. It was a drunken brawl over girls. The jackaroos got the girls. All I remember was going down after a king hit.

We shore about two thousand sheep a day at Boonoke and were there about eight working days. I should have guessed something was up. As the shed progressed, Gannon started having breakfast before me and dinner after I'd finished. The last few days, he was in the shed before I got there and he stayed after I left. He walked to the shed and back with Greeny the presser. Sometimes the blokes talked to me and sometimes they didn't. I preferred being with

Viking and the boys. My plan was to get my own run anyway. I didn't want to spend my life in a hut.

At the cut-out Greeny said I wasn't his responsibility and left me behind. Gannon couldn't look at me when he got into the car. By the time Greeny left, the other lifts had gone. The presser was usually the last to leave a shed because he had to bale the wool up. Greeny could have told me earlier. Bernie had offered me a lift, he might have known something. Standing at the huts as they drove off, I thought of Draphine. I missed him. I'd never tell him that. He didn't get this shed and was sitting down himself.

I had to hitch into Deniliquin, where I saw a few trucks ouside a servo and asked for a ride back to Melbourne. I thought if Greeny had dobbed me in for something, maybe I wouldn't get a follow-on to the next shed. The only thing I could think of was when Hobbsy and I got barred from the Conargo pub the week before for pissing in the gutter. The manager might have had a go at him and the Captain because I was in their team and they liked drinking with the cockies in there. Gannon had told me that Greeny had more influence with Grazcos management than the overseers and classers did. Greeny would have told him that. I thought it was self-promoting gossip.

I was getting sick of this. I wanted more than meeting a few blokes in a shed, going from one place to the next and putting up with the likes of Greeny. Sometimes I reckoned I drank because life was too slow. I was impatient, I couldn't wait for things. I was always in a hurry and I didn't trust anybody. I had to make it happen. Waiting made me tense and my stomach locked up. Waiting – I never got used to it. Waiting for Dad to come home, waiting in the car at the pub, waiting out the front of class for the principal, waiting for my parents to find out what I'd done this time. I couldn't wait, I was no good at it.

I didn't know why I was like that. I thought about it often.

Hobbsy let life come to him. Bernie Bourke knew what he wanted and seemed unfazed with his lot in life. I think that's what I liked about Bernie. He accepted his life and who he was. Harold had gambled on certainties and now it was too late for him. Barnesy was gambling on hard work. When would he find out if his gamble had paid off? Was I gambling on a dream that didn't exist? Was I fooling myself?

TUBBO STATION

DESPITE EVERYTHING, GANNON bunked in with me at Tubbo. Greeny was in with the Captain. I liked the Captain a lot better when he wasn't with Greeny. Gannon was shocked that I was pissed off with him for what happened at Boonoke. Reckoned it wasn't his fault and he had to get home.

Greeny had given him the flick for sure. Gannon was a huge drinker and a pest when he got pissed. He really shit me sometimes. He wanted to be my mate when it suited him. The thing I liked about Gannon was that he was so cocksure he was going to make it, but even I could see he was never going to make it.

Twelve shearers signed on at Tubbo, in the Riverina. The Victorians came up first and the Hay boys afterwards and that's the way it stayed. In one was Taffy the Welshman, who'd been at Gunbar. Bloodshot was in two, Haveachat in three, Viking in four, Bernie Bourke in five, the Captain in six. Seven was Hollywood. Tumbarumba Dave and Foxy were in eight and nine, Knight was in ten, Morgan was in eleven, and in twelve was Bill, another pommy. He said he'd been sent to Australia from England as an orphan after World War II.

Draphine was the overseer, and this was Wally's last shed classing for a while – he was going back to his claim in Emerald, Queensland. He loved it there. Ray, the rousie from Gunbar, was at Tubbo too. I'd heard Draphine hadn't wanted him back after Gunbar, but had to take him because the shed was organised by the Hay division of Grazcos and Ray was part of that team of workers.

On the board before the bell rang, Ray and I glanced at each other and nodded. Hobbsy was the other board boy.

It wasn't long before Knight came up to me and said, 'There's been a few complaints about your dog already, son. He's too close to the shed and his fucken barkin's gunna drive people mad. Do yourself a favour and take him home, eh.'

I ended up tying Smokey round a tree about four hundred metres from the huts. Draphine started taking him during the day and working him. Reckoned he was a beauty. Said he was smart and sharp, but I already knew that.

After lunch I went straight back to the shed for a lie-down. I saved a half-full wool pack and lay on it, rolling smokes, digging burrs out of my hands with a shearer's needle, and listening. The conversation broke up into small groups but the issue with the Kiwis always came up, and with it the idea that we workers from the wool industry should break away from the AWU and get our own union. Hollywood reckoned the Kiwis had shorn in some sheds around Hay. Haveachat said they'd been doing a bit of work around Moulamein and shearing the lambs for half-price. I listened but I didn't really understand it all. You couldn't say much anyway, only the better shearers spoke – except Bernie Bourke, he never said much.

These sheep had corkscrew burrs. The corkscrew burr is small and black and sits on the wool rather than in it, but when it connects with your skin it burrows in straight away. It has a fishhook tip and I've seen it go right through a hand. The trick is not to pull it out straight because you end up breaking the stem off and pushing the hooked tip down further. You have to dig under the hook. If you didn't get it quickly, Haveachat always reckoned, it was better to leave it and try a poultice.

I couldn't get a corkscrew out and after work Knight made up a poultice for me. Sugar soap and kero, mixed together into a mash, put on a spoon and heated with a lighter. Knight claimed his poultice would draw a train ten miles, it was that good. He was a bit of a bush doctor. Bernie Bourke said he used Magnoplasm. I asked him how he made it up. He said he bought it at the chemist. When the poultice was hot enough Knight put it around the corkscrew, wrapped my hand with elastoplast, and melted the adhesive with a lighter so it stuck better. Then he got out his shearing kit and sewed up the elastoplast. He told me not to touch it for a week. Wash in it, but don't take it off.

Knight was the rep in this shed. He was a good bloke and always treated the rousies well, no matter where they came from.

Gannon, who knew everything, told me there was some bad blood in the shed. 'Morgan and Knight both wanted the rep's job. Knight got it cos Morgan's not popular with the blokes.'

'Why is that?'

'Don't know, think everyone reckons he's using his position on the executive to get on as an organiser, so he's not fair dinkum.'

'He'd be all right at it.'

'Listen, listen. The other night, apparently, Bloodshot went into Hollywood and Knight's room and they snubbed him. Fuckin snubbed Bloodshot, can you believe it? Listen.' He was starting to emphasise every word now. He was half pissed. 'Listen, Hollywood reckons Bloodshot went into a shed after they'd black-banned it. Can you believe it? Bloodshot doing that?'

'Well . . .'

'Listen, fucken listen, will ya.' Some dribble came out the side of his mouth. 'No fucken way would he do that. No fucken way. Anyway, that's why Bloodshot picked up the pace. Him and Hollywood are going for it. Everyone reckons Bloodshot will beat him cos Hollywood's too fat and hasn't got the heart.'

'Hollywood's got —'

'Hollywood might blow up taking on Bloodshot but he's got balls.'

I finally got a word in. 'Hollywood's smarter than the others. He's not sucked in by the racing.'

Gannon didn't answer me. He thought he knew everything. He was so smart he couldn't even get off the wool tables.

After work Hobbsy and I trained Smokey to sit, and stay, and to get away back. Even though Hobbsy liked him, Smokey only took orders from me. And even though the blokes hated Smokey's barking, they respected his skill as a working dog.

A few days into the shed, an organiser from the New South Wales branch of the AWU turned up. It was time to renew our union tickets. Morgan objected, saying this was the Victorian Riverina branch's territory. A union meeting was called after lunch for all members. That included us. At lunchtime I yelled, 'Hey Gannon, you can't go to the meeting cos you want to be a boss.'

'Get fucked, you little arsehole.' He sniffed, snickered and kept eating.

Most men sat on the floor, some leaned against wool tables. Bernie Bourke and Taffy had the best seats on the wool packs.

The organiser started. 'Fellas, we have a situation where it's time to renew tickets.'

Morgan intervened with a point of order. 'This is designated Victorian Riverina territory. The revenue belongs to Victoria.' He looked around, but he got a blank response from the men.

'I think you'll do a good job on the executive, Morgan,' the organiser continued, 'and I know you're coming up for re-election. I have tickets here to sell and it's that time of year.'

Then it started. Bill the pommy said, 'What're you going to do about the Kiwis coming over in droves?' And Taffy waged in about the showers at some shed he did past Booligal. Knight stood up. 'I don't give a fuck where the ticket money's going as long as we get a ticket. Last I looked on the map, we were in New South Wales, not Victoria, and I move we buy these tickets.'

Hollywood backed him. People had the right to speak for and against the motion. Morgan had another go, said he could get tickets from Victoria here in a few days, before the shed finished. No one cared enough. Finally it was put to a show of hands.

I found it really hard because I had to put my hand up and vote when I didn't really understand it. Did I vote for Morgan because I liked him or vote for the organiser? I voted for Morgan. The vote went against him and we all bought New South Wales union tickets.

That didn't end the meeting. It erupted with problems that hadn't been resolved. The organiser had to go, he said, to write out a list and give it to Knight. And he left.

That night Gannon gave the daily run-down. 'Well, Knight and the organiser worked together for years. Knight arranged a hit on the Victorian branch, that's why he wanted the rep's job. The New South Wales branch was part of the left and the Victorian branch was part of the conservatives.'

I said, 'That'd be right. Who's telling you everything, that arse Greeny?'

'Can't say.'

'You can't say. I heard you'll be wool-rolling for the rest of your life and I'll be getting a learner's pen soon.'

'You? Who told you that? I might be going to Queensland with Wally to start up there.'

We kept on drinking and then went to bed. The next morning, I woke up on the floor. I said, 'How'd I end up here?'

Gannon sat up in bed. 'You got out of bed and stood at the back of the hut and said something about a race and going flat out, then you ran full bore into the door and knocked yourself out cold.' He was laughing. 'I tried to wake you. I thought you'd killed yourself. The noise would have woken some of the blokes for sure.'

'I feel okay.' That was strange. I got dressed and went for breakfast.

Bernie said, 'Did you here that noise last night?'

Taffy said he did. I couldn't remember a thing. But Gannon would tell everybody because he was a bigmouth.

Later in the week, I was looking at the tally book and Bloodshot asked me in his sarcastic voice, 'How many did you get?' That meant 'Fuck off.' So I snuck out between the shearers and rousies that were gathered around the tally book and left. The question was, would Hollywood round up the alcohol-fuelled Bloodshot before he blew up? It was blow for blow at the moment. Hollywood had great rhythm and Bloodshot had precision and he was relentless. No one took any notice of Bernie Bourke, but he was in there shearing forty-eight a run. Bloodshot and Hollywood were getting in the high forties and low fifties, but as usual Bernie had been going flat out from the bell on the first morning.

We were there three and a half weeks and Bloodshot, who got fitter and meaner as the shed went along, had Hollywood by six or seven sheep on the last day. Hollywood won the politics after work and Bloodshot did his talking at work, but in the end Bernie Bourke rang the shed by one sheep.

Draphine was a busy bloke this shed and he worked Smokey a bit in the catching pens. He came up to me at the last smoko and said, 'Ring head office when ya get home.'

'What for, what have I done?'

'Nothing, nothing.' He shook his head. 'Can't you just ever do what I say without so many questions? Just ring head office when ya get home, okay?'

'Yeah, okay, but tell me why. Why can't you do that, eh? Is it about Smokey? Have I got a learner's pen?'

'Jesus, get yourself some combs and cutters for Greystones Station in July. I'll see ya there.'

I didn't believe it. I wanted to get excited but I was too scared in case something went wrong between now and the start of the shed.

It was starting in two weeks. They knew how to keep you poor in this game. Two weeks on, one month off, three weeks on, three weeks off. But the season proper was starting, so I expected more regular work. I told Gannon I'd be at Greystones and if he was there he couldn't bunk with me cos he was only a mongrel rousie.

I headed back to Sonia's. She and a friend had rented a flat. It was a five-hour trip and I'd drunk a bit by the time I got to her place so I decided to sit out the front for a while before I went in. It was always on my mind that I might see something I shouldn't. I wished I wasn't like that. Then I'd put her through an interrogation anyway.

GREYSTONES STATION

I DROVE OVER the cattle grid onto the property and thought, No more roustabouting for me. I felt I'd waited a lifetime for this moment, and now that it was almost here I was scared. Scared I wouldn't measure up to the other men.

Greystones Station was outside Bacchus Marsh. It was July 1977. Up on the hill the lights were on in the squatter's bluestone mansion. The shearing shed and huts were down in a valley, a couple of k's off the main road. It was a wild, windy night. I could see some lights in the huts but no signs of welcome. The married shearers in the team would arrive early tomorrow morning. I walked over to the kitchen – no sign of life there either. The concrete huts, damp with condensation, had the standard two beds, one small bedside table, and a low-watt globe hanging in the middle of the room. I put my swag in the corner of a hut and my blankets on a bed. In the half-abandoned camp, I grabbed Smokey, put him on the end of my bed and tried to sleep.

The cook's banging and the gusting winds woke me. The sky was full with heavy, low-lying purple clouds. Maybe the wind would win the battle and blow the rainclouds away. Shearers won't shear wet sheep, but I could hear the sheep were in the shed from the huts so I knew we'd get a start today. It was early, but I headed over to the kitchen anyway to see if I could get some breakfast.

The cook nodded. 'G'day.' He was a small fat bloke, wearing a stained white apron. 'I've put a few different things on this morning. Till I know what the boys like, you know.'

'Oh yeah. Don't worry about me. I eat everything anyway.'

'Not everyone's that easy to please, son. Name's Graham.'

'Dennis.'

We shook hands. 'Where you from, Graham?'

'Uh, I'm from all round, you know. Had me own pub in Hamilton for years.'

'What are you doing out here then?'

'Women.' He chuckled sarcastically. 'You know, fucken women.' After a pause, he said, 'You want a bone for your pup?'

'Yeah,' I said. 'Thanks. It'll give him something to play with during the day.'

I'd heard of Graham. Good cook, they reckoned.

I was starving. I ate bacon and fried eggs and sausages and a chop with some spaghetti. Then I sat watching the others. Old, young, bald, curly-headed, fat, skinny men: they all straggled in and out of breakfast. Nodded to each other, but no conversation. I passed the time guessing what job went with what body. If they were dressed for work I could tell straightaway. The wool presser wore footy shorts and a singlet. The wool rollers, usually old shearers, were fat and couldn't do up their dungarees. The board boys were young, had a full crop of hair, jeans, tee-shirts and gym boots. That was me until a couple of weeks ago, but it felt like years.

The shearers, all shapes and sizes, wore dungarees with stretch belts and Jackie Howe singlets. Jackie Howe was held in higher regard in shearing sheds than Don Bradman was in cricket. I wondered how many sheep I'd get today.

The shearers' most notable physical identification was the smooth lumps on their knuckles. I looked at my own knuckles and clenched my fist. I couldn't wait until I had the knuckles of a shearer.

Draphine was cutting a track between the shed and the mess and from his hut to the back of his ute. 'Thank Christ ya won't be askin me for a pen no more.' He was carrying toolboxes, handpieces and down tubes, emery papers and glue for the grinding wheel. The overseer in this shed was also the expert, the person responsible for grinding the shearers' tools. Some experts ground tools too severely, wearing them out and costing the shearers money. Draphine had been a shearer, so he was better than most.

The camp was busy. Smokey jumped around barking, just going mad with the other dogs in the camp and the barking sounds coming from the shed. He was as excited as I felt. Draphine's hollow-gutted working dogs followed him everywhere, barking at anything. A motorbike bringing another flock to the yards echoed in the valley. Cars were arriving, ute doors slamming, men's voices criss-crossing the camp. The kitchen flywire door banged with workers going in for breakfast and the last lot coming out. The smell of dogs, the shed, the kitchen food, and the killed sheep hanging in the meathouse signalled the first day of shearing.

I was up in the shed with the rousies getting ready when Draphine yelled at me to go to the swarm. I hadn't forgotten, I was just too nervous about shearing. They couldn't start until I was there.

The swarm was in Viking's room. I walked in. The room was layered with smoke. Haveachat laughed and rubbed my head. 'Well, you've made it to here.' Viking smiled and said, 'Great-coloured braces, boy.' I'd heard that belts and sweaty singlets hurt your back so I had braces and flannels. I had all the right gear. The men smiled and Bernie moved over for me to sit down. I didn't say much, I was too nervous.

The purpose of the meeting was to elect a union rep for the shed and draw lots for shearing stands, a process that involved picking numbers from a hat. It was an eight-stand shed. Laurie from Hamilton, in the Western District of Victoria, drew one and became the rep. He was big, with a big mouth, but he was a good-hearted bloke, they reckoned, and a good shearer. He'd shear forty a run in these small-framed, straight-necked ewes.

Viking drew the second pen. The lines on his face looked more deeply etched today and his eyes were puffy. I thought he'd been drinking a bit. If he pulled up okay, he'd shear fifty-plus a run in these sheep. Haveachat drew three. He'd shear his forty-five. Bloodshot was in four and looked better. Not only his eyes, his face looked shiny. I wondered if he'd treat me differently now I was shearing. Tumbarumba Dave drew five, happy to be in good sheep, not so happy to be six hours away from home. In six was Stan, an unusual bloke. I'd never seen him before. He was small and talked out the side of his mouth. He seemed very suspicious of the other men, told me to watch them, they'd stab me in the back quick as look at me. Bernie Bourke drew seven. I was glad he was next to me. He would get his forty-eight a run. As the official learner, I was in pen eight. It was a standard contract in all sheds that learners were guaranteed the minimum wage of a roustabout – a hundred and twenty-five dollars a week after tax, the equivalent of about sixty-five sheep a day. Although if I sheared more I'd get more.

The official duties out of the way, the mood changed quickly when Laurie said the Kiwis had taken the Mortlake area. Haveachat had heard they were breaking our no-work-Saturday rule around Ballarat. The Kiwis were scabbing on us, fucking up our work. And the squatters were pushing them along behind our backs.

Viking said, 'Well, let's get up there and get started, we can't solve anything here talkin about it. Draph'll be having a cow worrying about the cut-out and the next shed. Laurie said he'll make sure he doesn't go too heavy grinding our tools.'

With that we headed to the shed. My moment had arrived. I walked up the incline to the corrugated-iron shed. I could hear Draphine yelling, 'Get a way back. Get a way back. Fill it up of course. It's a big shed, so pack em in fore it rains.'

I had new pants, new shirt, new combs and cutters, new waterbag and a clean towel. I looked new. I was new. I had no real smell about me. Bernie Bourke had his faded and thin flannel shirt; the others had stained and faded thick blue singlets, patched and repatched with broken stitching over the shoulders.

Bernie Bourke was putting a nail in the post for his towel, so was Haveachat, so I did too. I watched and copied everything they did. That's how I learnt to shear. We got our needles out and threaded them, ready for sewing any deep cuts we made in the sheep, then put them within arm's reach. I oiled my down tube, put my comb and cutter on, and hung the spares on a nail. Then I pretended finishing a sheep off, reaching for the needle or a new comb and cutter, or my towel. Everything was in place to save time, and as Haveachat kept saying, time was money.

I'd barrowed for these shearers. Now I was one of them, sort of. They reckoned it took five to seven years for your body to adapt to the work. Bernie Bourke and I were penmates. There was one pen of sheep for two shearers. We had no sheep in our pen. Bernie Bourke just yelled, 'Sheepo,' and the penner-up filled our pen. Viking came over and told me to put my towel above the pen door so I could wipe the sweat off my face without stopping. Bernie had his hanging off the wall next to him.

Everyone tested their handpieces, turning them on and off several times, tightening and then loosening the tension nuts. The gear was ready. The other men were ready. I was scared.

Draphine told me to take it easy, not to try too hard. I turned the machine on and dislocated the handpiece from the down tube to warm up the cogs and drive shafts. The machines hadn't been used for a year and needed warming up first thing in the morning, particularly in July in Victoria. The cocky was out the back, peeking through the wool room. You could always pick em, they wore those fancy shirts, moleskin pants with big buckles on their handmade leather belts.

At 8.35 the bell rang. Shearing began.

Draphine sat in the corner on an upturned ten-gallon drum with a folded wool-pack top to cushion his arse from the rim of the drum. He leaned over with his elbows on his knees, smoking and watching me. I grabbed my first sheep.

'Use the weight of the sheep to your advantage,' Draphine coached. 'Lean back when you're pulling them out.'

I dragged the kicking sheep onto the board. She threw her head around, pricking my legs with her stunted sharp horns. Positioning her next to the down tube on her bum so she was sitting upright, I stood behind her and tightened my legs around her body and pulled her front leg back up behind her head. This gave me good access to her belly wool and also calmed her down, but her hooves stank – they were caked in squashed sheep shit and mud. Pulling the wet, grease-stained rope that turned the handpiece on, I put the first blow down the right side of her belly, breaking out the wool with my forearm. The wool felt soft; the smell of the sheep was strong and the lanolin sticky. Her stomach veins protruded from her see-through skin. Her cold snotty nose wiped across my armpit. The rousie went along picking up the belly wools that came off first, putting them into the wool pack at the end of the board.

'Keep the handpiece moving – that's what's making the money, boy. Keep the comb full of wool and a smooth action. Don't start jabbing.'

I did one full blow round her crutch.

'Watch her nipples, watch her nipples, the cocky'll have no lambs next year if you keep knocking em off.'

The sheep was twitching. I think she could feel my nervousness. Her legs were all skin and bone and wool, no fat or meat. I had to be careful. The wool on the legs is sticky – easy to get a tooth of your comb under the skin. She was still on her bum but leaning back to the right. I put her right leg between my legs and leaned her backwards. She settled. I put three full blows down her leg, with the last going to her spine.

'Shearing's about rhythm, son. Move and work in and around the sheep; keep the sheep calm so it's manageable.'

Holding her nose with my left hand, I moved my right leg in between hers. I put two blows in, cleaning up the wool on her head, and put my first blow up her neck. The handpiece revved at 3400 revs a minute. Pushing the machine up the neck without seeing it made both of us nervous. Using the end tooth of my comb, I felt the wrinkle in the middle of her neck and pushed.

'Power and precision, boy. You need fine hand skills. Feeling the skin and the end tooth of the comb is critical. Concentrate. Concentration.'

My arm was buried in wool. With one full rip the neck of the fleece opened up. Good, I had no nicks. Two more blows up the neck and around her ears, trying not to nick the ear. A cut ear bleeds badly.

'Use your body, tuck your elbow in. Keep control. Always keep control of her.'

With my left elbow I held her neck and jaw in place while I pulled her front leg up with my left hand. Three quick blows around her shoulder and I was turning her over with my hips and legs until she was lying on her back, ready for the long blow. With each blow on her back I rolled her, until I had one blow over her backbone.

'Stay calm. Stay in control of yourself. If you can't control yourself you'll never be able to control a sheep. Don't start hitting them, it's a bad habit to get into. Cockies hate it, and other shearers don't like sheep bashers.'

Her legs were kicking but she was powerless on her side. I had my leg tucked into her shoulder and one behind her arse, locking her in. The wool rolled off her body like a mat. I felt excited. The sheep was relaxed. I looked up along the board, and the wool was rolling off the other sheep into small mounds. I leaned her head back; she was limp in this position, but my back took all the strain.

'Use your brains, boy. Always use your brains. Your back won't last too long with the strain of a sheep's weight on it like that.'

Putting three blows down the other side of her neck, I straightened up, then cleaned up her other front leg. She sat upright and I leaned her body back into mine. I started the last side, the whipping side, each blow travelling out to the end of the last leg. After eight to ten blows down the last side I was finished.

'Never push a sheep down the chute,' Draphine yelled. 'Their hooves get caught on the wooden lip in the front and it puts too much pressure on your back. Walk it out – it's got legs, let it use em.'

She scuffled to get her footing on the greasy board and then jumped out down the chute, and my first sheep was in the counting pen.

Draphine looked at my sheep through the window on my stand. 'Not bad. See the comb marks on her body – won't get much more wool off in a blow than that, I don't reckon.'

But I had only put a couple of blows on the next sheep while Draphine wasn't watching when blood started squirting from the stomach. I'd grabbed a stray wether in the flock of ewes and cut half his pizzle off.

I grabbed Bernie Bourke. 'What'll I do?'

'Leave it. Can't sew a pizzle. They don't need it except for pissing.'

Draphine was sitting back on his drum. 'You shoulda seen the piss stains on the belly wool when you were pulling the sheep out, boy. Keep your eyes open. Have a quick look and brush your hand over the belly before you put a blow in next time, eh.'

I struggled through the first day, shearing some sheep well and making a mess of others. Some got away from me and others kicked me out of place. At smoko I sat by myself, thinking about ways to improve. All in all I was feeling okay until the last run of the day, when fatigue set in and I couldn't straighten my back. I started getting rougher with the sheep and losing control of them.

Draphine went off. 'Slow down, slow down. Take it easy. Have a rest, for fuck's sake. You're getting paid anyway. You've got the rest of your life to kill yourself. You don't have to do it on your first day.'

As the days and weeks went on in the shed, I went backwards. Every morning when I woke up I couldn't move my body. Every muscle hurt just getting out of bed. I needed time for my body to heal but there was none. I had reached exhaustion and mentally it became hard to motivate myself. With every sheep, I wanted to quit. But I'd wanted this job so badly, and I didn't want to fail.

On the last day of the shed I woke up and blinked. My eyelids were the only part of my body that didn't hurt. I was scared to move. It was light enough to see the outline of the other huts through the window. My alarm went off. I attempted to take my blankets off but my arm refused. It took ten minutes to sit up.

I didn't think I could face another day.

Eventually I put my wet, greasy dungarees on my warm skin.

I'd run out of clean clothes but I had made it to cut-out day.

I thought, Is this it? The reality of doing this for the rest of my life started to sink in. The rousie thought I was moody because I didn't talk in the morning. But I was too fucked to talk, I just wanted to survive the day. No one talked much in the mornings anyway. Not in winter, when it was still dark and cold.

I loaded my comb and cutter up, picked out last night's tools from the dirty water can and washed them. The noises in the shed had started: the diesel engine, the back gates banging with the last of the sheep being pushed into the shed. The dogs barked, and a truck rolled up to load the wool bales.

The first run got my body working again and heated up my wet dungarees, but the pain seemed permanent. I wasn't trying to keep up with the clock any more. I was lucky the sheep were small, straight, fine-wool merinos. The sticky lanolin in the wool made them more difficult to shear on cold mornings, but when the lanoline warmed up later in the day they shore a lot easier. Draphine had predicted an eleven o'clock cut-out. Almost to the minute, after two and a half weeks, the last of about twelve thousand sheep went down the chute. The shed was empty. Gone were the noises of the engine, the belt flapping, the handpieces and down tubes screaming, the sheep, the dogs, men yelling and joking. It was quiet. I felt hollow and battered. I had waited for this moment for so long and now it was over I was disappointed. The work had been so much harder than I expected. One or two days' shearing are a lot different to a lifetime of shearing, I knew that now. But at the same time I was proud of myself for having survived.

All that was left in the shed was the smell of sheep shit and lanolin. I liked the smell of sheep shit and lanolin.

The presser was out the back finishing off baling the wool when one of the station hands came in to see me. 'That dog of yours is a natural and all. Did you know he rounded up them sheep after we let em go? He's got it. Those working dogs need their guts worked out, know what I mean? No good as pets or nothing. That's what makes a good working dog, working their guts out early, when they're young. Do you wanta sell him?'

Draphine came in looking for me and interrupted. The station hand left. I wasn't selling Smokey.

'Stay away from that Stan fella, he's got a gun in the back of his ute and he's talking funny. Don't tell im you got a follow-on neither. Ram shearing at Mungadal Station for you, boy.'

I didn't want to go at first because I knew how tough the sheep were. Young and fast men got picked first. There were no places to hide old men in a shearing shed. The slowest shearers were usually last on and first off.

What I did like were the boundaries in a shed that the squatter couldn't cross. Yeah, I liked that. And shearing was better money than jackarooing and factory work. The more sheep I shore, the more money I could earn. I liked that too. Jackarooing was a real dog's job – seventy, eighty hours a week for fifty dollars. In the factory I watched the clock. In a shed I raced the clock, always trying to squeeze one more minute out of the day.

While Draphine made up our cheques the union rep did the room inspection. We had to pay for any piss-stained mattresses. I was rapt. I'd beaten the rousie's pay with my first cheque. Viking had rung the shed, with Bernie Bourke close behind.

In my rear-vision mirror I watched the little village of huts get smaller until it disappeared behind a hill. Smokey sitting in the passenger seat and a stubby of beer between my legs, I was headed in to see Sonia and then back to the Riverina and the outback.

Sonia and Ethan's relationship seemed to have developed in my absence but Sonia didn't appear to see it. Strangely, I wasn't jealous this time. It quickly became her and him when the three of us were together, and I was the third wheel. I thought it was my fault because I didn't go to restaurants or concerts. I had never seen *Mash* or *Happy Days*. I didn't know the main bands people listened to. I couldn't really fit into the conversation. In the sheds we listened to Slim Dusty and Johnny Horton, Charley Pride and Johnny Cash, but Sonia and Ethan listened to different music.

The upside was that I was free. Not tied down. I had several thoughts about the whole thing. First I thought that she stayed with me out of loyalty and she didn't know how to end it. Then I thought that maybe she couldn't get Ethan to be her boyfriend and she didn't want to make a move and end up with nobody. Or she loved me and liked Ethan's company. But I didn't really know.

MUNGADAL STATION

I CROSSED THE Murrumbidgee River into Hay late in the afternoon. It seemed that for me, all roads led back to this town on the edge of the never-never. Hay was a sparse town with harsh, uncompromising conditions that produced hard, uncompromising men. Not bad men, just tough. In the past I'd felt like an outsider, mixing with the drifters, shooters and young rebels. They didn't intend to live past thirty. Getting old wasn't in the plan. The end was almost mystic, something like this: on a Harley, drugged, pissed, naked, in a head-on with a Mack truck at two hundred k's on the One Tree Plain road to Booligal.

The One Tree Plain was arid. Temperatures in summer topped 45 degrees for weeks on end. This was different. It was early August and the sun was soft and the breeze was mild. I'd never seen Hay like this. There was an upbeat feel about the place, a healthy bustle down the main street, and the land had a tinge of green on it, almost lush. The river was running and the sunsets spread out across the horizon in a nightly display.

After getting supplies I camped down in my spot on the riverbed. Sunrise woke me early. I felt good except for my kinked neck and a hip that was sore from the seatbelt buckle. The morning was on the warm side, with a light breeze coming across the river. I could smell the eucalyptus from the gum trees, and the rustle from the treetops made me feel protected from the higher winds. I sat and watched the river for a while, a chance to think a bit and relax. I started a small fire, boiled the billy and cooked up some baked beans. I dished some out to Smokey before they were too hot and ate the rest with a cup of tea, then headed out to the shed.

Mungadal Station on the Murrumbidgee River was five kilometres from Hay. The shed and huts were a couple of gates off the main road. A few trees surrounded the huts. These huts were infamous among shearers: run-down tin shacks with no electricity. The wire on the beds almost came through the thin rubber mattresses.

Draphine was out and about, seemed pretty happy. He always arrived early. He had a farm, a wife and a son, but his son was grown up. I think the farm was just a bit of a fill-in for him. Anyway, he was busy looking after me now. He was heading up to the homestead and said he'd catch me later.

'Don't get into no trouble. Get plenty of rest, boy, cos you're going to need it tomorrow. There's some big rough bastards to shear up here.'

As soon as I was settled I headed back into town. I ran into a girl I'd met at one of the river parties.

I said, 'Hi, Julia. How ya going?'

'Good, good, where have you been?'

'Back down to Victoria. And now I've got a learner's pen around here.'

We went for a walk and she said she'd see me that afternoon down at the river. When I saw her coming I got out of the car to greet her. She grabbed my hand as we started walking. It felt good but she was holding my hand wrong and I wanted to change it. I thought if I pulled away she'd think I didn't want to hold her hand, so I stopped to look at the river and then pulled my hand away and put it around her shoulders. She wasn't good at looking at me. She always seemed turned away from me. Then she turned and kissed me. I could feel her breast on my arm and on my chest. We knelt on the ground, kissing. 'Not here,' she said. 'Someone might come.'

'Do you want to go back to Mungadale? I've got a bed there and no one's around yet.'

She nodded. 'Okay,' she said, but reverted to being side on when she spoke.

Driving out to the shed I didn't feel right. She seemed to want to have sex with me, or do a lot more anyway, but I felt awkward and as if in a hurry. A car was next to one of the huts. The shearers would go ballistic if they knew I had a woman here. I pulled up near the door to my hut and went in first. Then I called Julia in and shut the door.

The room was musky and there was horsehair sticking out of the mattress. The corrugated iron was rusty and the old boards were rickety. We got onto the bed and I lay down beside her. I was used to Sonia. It was more natural with her. Julia wouldn't make the first move so I had to. I went to kiss her but now she wouldn't kiss me. I started rubbing her arm and shoulders and she didn't resist. I touched her breasts. I kept my hand there and tried to kiss her again but she still didn't respond. Then she rolled her head over and kissed me. I wanted something else but I wasn't sure what. I took her top off. I undid her bra. She had beautiful soft plump breasts and I kissed them. I waited for her to touch me; I figured that came later. With minimum movements she took her knickers off.

I ripped off my shirt but I hadn't undone the buttons and the collar got stuck over my head. The buttons on my miller shirt snapped, then I couldn't get the sleeves off. I felt retarded, like I was trying to get out of a straitjacket, and she was lying there half naked and ready to quit at any moment. I wanted it to be natural, like with Sonia. I busted my shirt sleeves to get them off and Smokey started jumping and barking. I kicked him. I pulled my pants down but I couldn't get them off either, my boots were in the way. I felt like I was on a timer and I had to move fast. I wanted to feel her skin on my skin. She looked soft and warm lying there. I wanted to lie beside her so we could touch each other, but she opened her legs instead. I felt two jet engines ignite inside of me. Lying down I climbed between her legs, my hands holding my body away from her.

She was hot and wet. My cock exploded before I got inside. Under pressure, I couldn't control myself. Julia grabbed a towel and wiped us down.

That was it. She got dressed straight away and sat on the edge of the bed. She didn't say anything; instead, she started playing with Smokey.

The following morning the shearers met in Hollywood's hut to draw for pens and pick a rep. I sat listening. You couldn't say much in a shed until you could shear a bit.

The shearers talked about the usual things: other sheds, shearers, cooks and pressers. The men were saying that British Tobacco had bought Mungadal – a lot of overseas companies were buying up the big stations. The squatter was changing. He had always worn moleskins and riding boots, now there was a new type: invisible, who wore suits and lived in the city. And the new managers were stingy, ruthless union haters.

Shearers hadn't changed, not in the last fifty years, anyhow.

Knight was saying he'd heard of some Kiwis working for forty dollars a hundred sheep. We were on over fifty.

Sid laughed. He was the shearer who owned the car that had been here the day before. 'Cou-couldn't push a wide comb in these mongrel bastards. Like to, like to see em up here, uh, uh, uh, like to see that.' Sid's head shook when he spoke.

A local Hay shearer jumped up, whingeing, 'They can have em, fucken lot of them. It's a cunt of a job anyway – if it's not fucken burrs cutting into you or the heat burning you up, it's wet weather starving you out, just for dirty stinking mongrel sheep.'

After the draw the men straggled in groups of twos and threes to the shed. Draphine pulled up beside me and said, 'No women in the huts, boy. Got it?'

'Yeah, okay.'

Draphine winked and walked off.

The fine dust underneath the frail crusty earth stirred with every footstep. The morning sun's rays broke over the shearing shed's skillion roof, exposing dust particles in the air. Summer was close, and up here in these sheds that was hot, real hot. The yelps of a dog being trampled under the sheep screeched out over the camp, mingling with men yelling instructions and whistling, sheep bleating, and the diesel engine starting up. Mungadal had come to life.

I was walking with Sid, trying to get to know him and test the waters a bit. I said, 'Gunna try and get me hundred in these.'

Sid looked at me, dirty-like, and said, 'I know who you are, boy. Don't worry bout that.' Then he started yelling, 'Dun nuthin, dun nuthin. There's a fella in there, doesn't go round talkin about it. You know his name, doesn't go round talkin about it. Works harder than you, boy. Doesn't talk about it.'

'Bernie Bourke, you mean?'

'Yeah, yeah, Bernie Bourke. Ever worked up through

Queensland? No, you haven't. Bernie has. Wouldn't drink lemonade unless it was over 45 degrees. Ever been to Quilpie, Cunnamulla, Blackall or Longreach? Ever shorn in a hot run? No, you haven't. You been nowhere, nowhere, boy. In the '56 strike I never went out. Sat down for the year. We starved but we never went out. Lived on spuds. You wouldn't last, wouldn't last. You're all talk, boy. Been around a long time, thirty years. Seen blokes like you come and go.'

Knight turned and smiled. I looked at him, hoping for a wink, but I wasn't a rousie any more. The other men didn't say anything. Didn't look, just kept walking. Sid was saying what they were thinking, speaking for them. I took it. He could have just told me to get fucked – would've been quicker.

This was another mixed shed – four Victorians and four local Hay blokes – and Draphine had his work cut out making this mob a team. Some of the Hay boys' mates were sitting down because we were given pens ahead of them. They reckoned we'd taken their work. I was especially hated, not only for being single and taking a married man's job, but because I was a learner and a Victorian.

Draphine rang the bell at nine o'clock for the start of the first run. We were into stud lamb rams – I couldn't believe it. I had a chance to shear my first hundred sheep in a day, and at double the pay – the price for stud shearing – I could earn the equivalent of shearing two hundred a day. I would be making four or five times my apprenticeship money. I couldn't keep my brain quiet.

Bernie Bourke was in the first pen and union rep. Knight was in two. He would shear his mid-forties. He could unload his hand-piece at five-thirty at night, wash his tools, walk to the huts, have a shower, get dressed, drink up to eight bottles of beer and make it into the kitchen before the seven p.m. deadline. He was a gun at that. The only thing I ever saw Knight get really narky about was women. He'd been married before. Done the lot.

Hollywood was in three, still dirty on Bloodshot. It was a feud that wouldn't go away. Hollywood was smart and a good unionist but he put a lot of energy into hating Bloodshot. He'd shear his forty-seven, forty-eight a run.

Sid was in four. Sid would bust his arse and get his twenty-two, twenty-three a run. He jabbed and poked his way through shearing a sheep. He was a battler and starting to get old, a skinny bastard. Sid grew up in the Creswick orphanage, now he lived somewhere on the coast – Torquay or somewhere like that. He always dressed like he'd made it. He only shore in the main part of the season now.

Bloodshot was in five. He wasn't talking or mixing and he looked even worse than usual. His eyes were broken. I reckon the drink had him. He didn't shake, and his olive skin and jet-black hair made him look better than he was. I didn't want to end up like him. He had made his name in roughneck sheep around here, in the Riverina and in the St George district in Queensland.

In six was Foxy, the Aboriginal shearer. He'd get his thirty-five a run. Stevens was in seven and was my penmate. He said nothing in the swarm, nothing on the way to the shed, and nothing while we set up our tools. He had a family and was always looking for other jobs but this shed was local for him. Not a big drinker, he hated the big-noting shearers and the drifters that shearing brought into Hay. He'd shear his thirty-eight, thirty-nine a run.

I was in eight, the learner's pen. I hoped to get my twenty a run when we got out of the studs and back into the normal sheep.

At smoko Bernie Bourke walked over to the tally book hanging on an old post in the shed. I was there studying the form, seeing if anyone had two-for-one'd me, or if I was near anyone. Half an hour wasn't much time for the other men to put a big gap between them and me so my tally didn't look too bad. Bloodshot and Hollywood had shorn nine each, Bernie Bourke and Knight were on eight, Stevens had seven, and Foxy and Sid had six. I had five, but I reckoned I could do better next time. I felt like a movie star when I saw my name up in the tally book. I was there with Bloodshot and Knight, Bourke and Hollywood. People I looked up to.

I had a bad case of what was called sheep shit on the brain. I wasn't as burned out as I'd been at Greystones. I reckoned I needed three days on and one day off to rest until my body recovered, but it didn't work like that. At least now I knew I was going to wear out as the shed went along.

Bernie Bourke said he'd never seen a learner in a team shearing studs before. The local boys sitting by their pens, eating during their smoko, looked accusingly at me. That was the first time they'd acknowledged me — just because some of their married mates were sitting down in town while I was working. They saw me as a rousie who was taking a real shearer's job. Married men were fucken whingers. It was my pen now. One worker, one household: that was the rule, and I wasn't breaking that.

Shearing contractors had to give learners a chance. If they didn't they'd run out of shearers. Some shearers wanted to come and go and then wanted the best of everything. The shearers who were loyal and could shear got work. I was loyal.

Draphine came onto the board through the presser's room. He'd been talking to the manager outside. Managers couldn't bomb us, so they rarely came onto the shearing stands. The gentlemanly squatters often came onto the board and would say hello. The shed, during shearing time, was ours. The squatters and jackaroos penned up the sheep and loaded the bales onto trucks, and that was about it. The rest of the work belonged to us.

Draphine was heading towards me. It didn't look good. He

started screaming, pointing and gaining everybody's attention. His feet thumped down walking across the wool room to the shearers' board. The other shearers, rousies, wool rollers, jackaroos, the presser, even the classer, all stopped and looked up. I caught a glimpse of the manager, who was standing with his arms folded on the loading platform outside the presser's room, watching.

'Did you cut the balls on one of those rams, boy?'

'Yeah, but I didn't think it was that bad. Didn't need any stitches, Draph.'

He screamed, 'You didn't think it needed any?' Now he was throwing his arms around. 'You didn't think it needed any! Why don't you go and tell the fucken manager that, then? The ram's balls are draggin on the ground out there.'

'Draph, it looks worse than what it is, I'm telling you.'

The shed boss never bombed you in front of the other men. Most times the overseer would be waiting for a shearer in the catching pens and bomb you, discreet like. Everybody knew when someone was getting bombed, but it happened one on one. Not like this.

'You little fucken arsehole. Sew up your mistakes.'

Stevens, my penmate, went red when he saw the manager nod. 'Who does he think he is? What are you doing, Draphine?'

The men close by patted me on the back. Others, further down the board, nodded, and some caught my eye and smiled. I was in. Draph was a genius. And now I owed him one.

During the last run I stood up on the hour to change my comb and cutter. My comb was blunt even though there wasn't much dust in these sheep. My sweat was blinding me and my back was at breaking point. I unscrewed my comb, put a sharp one in, but I was shaking too much to get my cutter under the fork that held the cutter in place. My skin was clammy. I kept telling myself to slow down, slow down, take deep breaths: breathe, breathe. I got my cutter in, screwed it down, oiled the top and looked around at the other shearers.

Hollywood and his mates had stopped but Bernie Bourke kept going, so I did too. I had twelve sheep out for the hour, on target for twenty-five for the run. I had to get a sheep out every five minutes and get a sheep before the bell went at twenty-seven minutes past five, three minutes before the end of the run. I had to have my sheep on the board when the bell rang or I was disqualified. I'd shorn five sheep the first run, twenty-one the second, and twenty-two for the third. Getting two for one meant I was earning a dollar a sheep. At this rate I'd soon be out of debt for my combs and cutters and clothes.

At the ninety-minute mark of the last run I had eighteen sheep out. I had to do the next six sheep in less than twenty-seven minutes and get the seventh sheep on the board before the bell rang. Four and a half minutes a sheep plus the catch, and after changing my cutter I was forty-five seconds behind. I hadn't shorn that fast all day.

I smashed through the batwing doors and grabbed a sheep, reversing out of the pens. I was looking for small necks, small horns; clean-faced, runtish types. I only had time for a quick scan to memorise where they were in the pen, I couldn't keep searching for them. Taking all the good ones is called pulling the pen. Blokes who did that were well known, and I didn't want a bad reputation. It would only give my penmate a licence to shaft me.

I pulled a good one out at 5.09:45. I almost made up the forty-five seconds I lost changing my cutter, but I was still behind the cycle of four and a half minutes per sheep I needed to get my tally for the run. Down the chute, and I was back in the pen by 5.14. Four minutes fifteen for that last sheep. Now I was beating the clock. I shore the next two in eight minutes and forty-five seconds. The clock read 5.22:45. I was fifteen seconds in front.

I dragged out a little bastard with awkward-looking horns. He was kicking so badly I couldn't get my first blow in. Nearly hit his groin. They were dead in about two minutes if you hit them there. It was 5.22:55. I'd lost ten seconds getting him on the board. I had four minutes and five seconds left.

I got his belly wool off, cleaned around his crutch with one blow. I was trying to concentrate on a full comb and thinking how much money I was making, despite his kicking and my back aching and the sweat dripping into my eyes, stinging and blurring my vision. A blow over his balls – didn't want to cut another one. Draphine would cut mine out for sure if I did.

I put one front leg under my leg. I pressed my hand into his hip and pushed out his hind leg, three quick blows and a glance at the clock: 5.24:40. A minute and forty-five seconds gone. I was behind, thanks to this fucking little bastard. I stood up, moving into shearing the neck, and my back got a moment's relief from the pain. One blow around the brisket and I headed up these twenty-centimetre wrinkles. I couldn't see the comb. Concentrate, I told myself, keep the handpiece flat on the skin, the comb down, so you don't cut one. I had to watch the carotid artery. It would be easy to put the comb through his neck when he was kicking like that.

My hand was under his jaw, trying to stop his horns from hitting my knee. Shearers' compo was half a rousie's pay. Couldn't afford that. I was leaning over, with all his weight on my front leg, shaking. I glanced at the clock. At the same time the ram shook his head and I broke out of the first blow up his neck and clipped off the skin on two of my fingertips.

My fingers were throbbing with every pulse, and the lanolin stung like metho on a sore. There was no blood. It was just white. I turned him around for the long blow. He was kicking me out of position. The rousie poured some water over my fingertips. It didn't help.

Kneeling into his guts, I looked behind me. The team was quiet. A couple of blokes looked across. Everyone was concentrating, trying to get the catch. The ram tightened his body as though he sensed victory. It was 5.25:10 – another two minutes and forty seconds gone. I was losing it. I started the long blow, using all my strength to block out the pain, focusing on the end tooth of my comb. I kept repeating full blows, full, even blows. I put one over his backbone and I was on the last side. Now, at 5.25:35, I had a minute and twenty-five to go.

A blow down his cheeks and I was onto his neck. I couldn't bend him and he slipped back into the wall. The down tube that drove the handpiece was in front of me instead of behind me, and was pulling the handpiece back and forth every time it swung. I just kept shearing: concentrate, concentrate. Watching the end tooth of my comb. I gave the ram a big heave-up to do his front leg. His head flopped: 5.26:13. Forty-seven seconds left. I could do it. I could make it.

I couldn't straighten my back. I knelt with one knee on the board and kept coming down the whipping side. Don't stop. Concentrate, concentrate. Nothing else mattered: 5.26:30. Thirty seconds left. Draphine went by and grabbed the ram's legs and pulled him back into position. I was on the last leg. I kept shearing. I couldn't afford to take my eyes off the comb. One bad blow, one mistake, and I'd miss the catch. I put one blow over his arse: 5.26:53. Seven seconds left. Nudged him down the chute, put one foot into the catching pen, grabbed a leg and pulled him onto the board: 5.27. The bell rang. I had the catch. My first twenty-five for a run.

I relaxed a bit and slowed down while shearing the last sheep. The pressure was off. I was shearing up the neck and the little ram got his back hoof in behind the down tube and kicked; my handpiece went flying and I lost my footing on the greasy board. Doesn't matter how tired you get, every sheep is fresh. I collapsed onto the out-of-control ram. His wool was all over me. The rousie put some wool over his eyes and he quietened. My handpiece landed on my comb, snapping a tooth off. There went eight bucks, sixteen sheep. Sitting on the bastard, I changed my comb. My back felt like it was going to snap, and the throbbing in my fingertips had spread into my head, creating a dull thud with every pulse. My forehead was itchy from sweat rash. Stevens missed the catch and came over and finished him off. I was stuffed.

I grabbed my towel and newly broken-in waterbag – the water didn't taste like a sack any more – and headed for the showers. The generator was on for hot water. The union rep made sure no one stepped out of line and hogged it. Afterwards I sat in my room. I felt sick with exhaustion and bloated from drinking too much water. Most of the shearers, and the occasional favourite-of-the-day rousie, congregated in Knight's room. He wasn't the gun but he was popular. He was always telling stories and cracking jokes.

I was in bed by eight-thirty. My head hit the pillow and I was gone for four or five hours. I woke up with a thumping pain in my arse. It got so bad I had to get up and walk about. I didn't know what was worse, the pain in my arse or the rest of my aching body.

In the morning every part of me hurt. Getting out of bed, I was in so much pain I thought I might've broken my back. This was my second shed and I'd been feeling like this every morning so far. I didn't know when I was going to come good. Draph reckoned it took five years until your body hardened to the work.

I ate like a horse at breakfast – cereal, bacon and eggs, chops and sausages, spaghetti and toast – and headed over to get ready for another day. I was looking at the tally book when Bloodshot mumbled, 'How'd ya go?'

I said, 'All right, but I worked that hard I think I blew me arse out.'

The rest of the team had arrived and laughed. One of the men said his arse once ached until it bled, then the pain went away. He had piles. I asked Bloodshot when the pain stopped.

'Never.' He shook his head and walked away.

Mungadal finished with Bloodshot ringing the shed by a dozen sheep, ahead of Bernie Bourke. Bloodshot was majestic in rough sheep – his hand moved slowly and the wool peeled off effortlessly. He pushed with power and precision through what most shearers agreed were the roughest necks on the roughest sheep in Australia. He was a master in a field where physical and mental heroics in terrible conditions went unnoticed by the outside world. These were body-hardened men. When they slowed down they knew reputations, loyalty and years of hard work wouldn't get them the next shed. I looked at the men differently now. I saw them as men without futures.

Bernie Bourke was relentless. Hollywood had started having a go, but pulled back when the pressure was on. He was probably the best shearer and ten to twelve years younger than Bloodshot, but I think part of him saw the futility of it all. If it came easy enough he'd do it, but he wasn't giving the squatter his heart and soul, even if it meant being beaten by Bloodshot.

The local shearers were heading out near Maude, and we Victorians were going to Booligal Station for crutching. After packing our cars the next morning, we huddled together looking at the fiery red ball emerging on the horizon of One Tree Plain. We seemed a small outfit in the largeness of the outback, but at that moment every small detail around us appeared strangely significant. The damp dust stuck on our boots, on our tattered and stained work clothes that hung untailored, on our scruffy duffle-coats and faded parkas draped around hunched shoulders, on our swollen and gnarled hands and stubbled, rough faces. I could feel a unity between us come alive with the sunrise, replacing, temporarily, the riffs and bruising encounters that defined our friendships.

What a morning. What a sight.

BOOLIGAL STATION

BOOLIGAL STATION WAS a four-stand shed on the outskirts of the last town before the bitumen ends between Hay and Wilcannia. The size of a property was gauged by the number of stands in the shed. Four stands was small.

We met the quietly spoken overseer in the mess; he was also the wool classer. He'd been working in Queensland and said the Kiwis were moving into Longreach and picking up a lot of sheds around Julia Creek and Hughenden. Apparently the graziers were using the Kiwis as strike-breakers and had flown planeloads of them into town during the last dispute.

'Some of those Kiwis are tough bastards too,' Bernie Bourke said with a nervous smile.

A brown paper parcel was waiting for me in the mess. The rest of my dungarees, flannels and boots had arrived from Milro, an ex-shearer who made shearer's clothes and boots exclusively. The leather boots were exactly as they looked in the catalogue. I loved the earthy smells of brown paper and leather. The dungarees were double-lined around the knees to take the punishment from the burrs on the sheep, and the Jackie Howe singlets had a thick sewn patch on the left side.

Sid, organising the draw for the stands, drew the first pen and the rep's job. He started reminiscing about being rep at Toganmain Station thirty years ago, when he stuck it up them in a dispute for extra money over uncrutched dirty sheep. Then he started on about the 1956 strike again. 'We went out for ten months. Ten fucken months, boy. Not a sheep, not a sheep was shorn.' He was shaking his head and getting excited. 'They, they tried to cut our pay. We showed em, we showed em.'

'You showed em what?' I asked.

'We, we, showed em we'd never give up. And we, we, we won. We, won, that's what happened. That's what happened. We woulda fucken lost with the likes of you.'

Bernie Bourke laughed, said, 'Come on, finish the draw, Sid. Otherwise we'll be here till Christmas.'

We headed across to the shed. Bernie Bourke was in two, Bloodshot was in three, and as the learner I had the last pen. There were a few contract drovers and a worker-manager on site, but no homestead or squatter, which made me think it was a back station to a bigger property. The Lachlan River ran through this part of the land, giving the place character and feeling. It meant we had a few trees around the shed and the huts, and somewhere to explore after work.

But we weren't happy with the built-on-stilts shearing shed. With no sheep storage in the back of the shed, the sheep we were about to shear were housed directly under the catching pens. The sheep in the top pens pissed and shat on the sheep underneath. When we dragged them onto the board we ended up with sheep shit and piss all over our clothes. By smoko we were wet through and stinking.

We were crutching but the sheep were in bad shape: the wool around their arses had flystrike and dags. It was boring, hard, heavy work picking up, dragging out and pushing down the chute seven hundred or more full-grown merino wethers in a day. It was a lot less money per sheep than shearing.

The first blow was around the inside of the sheep's back legs. Then it was an effort to lean the sheep back and shear a small, neat circle around its arse so the shit didn't stay on the wool and attract flies. It was dirty work when we got into the maggot-ridden sheep. Ploughing through a plague of maggots eating into the meat of a sheep was like cutting chaff. I was concentrating on my work when I noticed a green, butter-like paste smeared over my arm and handpiece. I had gone through a puss-infected boil.

Bernie complained about the piss and shit on the sheep's backs. The classer said that was only the case with the sheep that had been housed under the shed overnight – a couple of hundred sheep, about an hour's crutching for a team of four men. After the first run the rest of the sheep would be clean. Considering there was no sign of rain, he said he'd see what he could do about the sheep not being housed under the catching pens overnight. While we were all together he said the manager put a complaint in about too many cuts on the sheep.

Bloodshot shook his head and said, 'He should concentrate on looking after his sheep better. These are in bad condition, maggot-infected bastards.'

'Just watch it, that's all I'm saying. They're his sheep.'

Sid fired up. 'What about, what about a bit of support for the men? These, these, these sheep have been presented badly, fucken badly. What's wrong with these cockies? Too many cuts? They go mulesin them after we're finished. Cuttin ten-inch strips of flesh off the poor bastards. What's a matter with, with em?'

The overseer said, 'Look, we're only here for a few days. Let's just get into these sheep and get out of here as quick as possible. If we aren't finished by the end of next week you boys will more than likely miss a pen shearing lambs back at Greystones. There's good money in them lambs and you don't want to go missing that because of this shed. Come on, get into em. Get out and make some money, boys. Let's go.'

Why was it always us who had to make the sacrifices at work, to get work? I thought. How come we always had to fuck ourselves over for the job?

At the end of the day I stood up and looked at myself. My fingers were taped where I'd nicked the skin off my fingertips. My wrist, suffering a touch of tendonitis, was bandaged for support. My arm was wrapped where I had a large, ugly, purple-reddish boil – the doctor said I'd contracted scabby mouth disease from the sheep at Greystones. Maggots covered the bottom of my new pants and boots and there was green pus smeared on my skin and new clothes, and on the board where the rousie had tried to clean my stand with a handful of wool. I was also nearly green with sheep shit. And I could feel a rash on my forehead from wiping the sweat off with the towel. I didn't know who to feel more sorry for, the maggot-ridden sheep or us. I couldn't wait for the showers, the huts and a drink.

Wednesday night was town night. Garth, the old wool roller, came with Sid and me. Bernie Bourke didn't drink, and Bloodshot didn't go to town. Sid drove. I was rapt when I heard the old pub had burned down. We went there when I was at Ulonga and we could only get hot beer. It had been nothing more than a shanty; the fridge didn't even have a back on it. It sold bottled beer at room temperature. The new pub was a one-room portable, but it had a fridge and beer on tap.

We sat by ourselves for a while before a local shearer came over. Then a red-faced fat loudmouth joined us. He had the insignia of Dalgety's stock and station agents on his shirt. Dalgety's managed properties for city squatters. A handmade leather belt with big cow horns etched into the buckle held up his moleskins. Out of tiny lips surrounded by fat red cheeks he blurted, 'Where are you boys from?'

Sid poked his chin out, looking real proud, said, 'Booligal, Booligal Station – crutching the big bastards out there at the minute.'

'Shearers!' The fat bastard's face turned sour. He pointed at us with his short arm and puffy hand. 'Shearers, they're making a fortune now. Running the poor cocky dry. They don't grow the wool, or look after the sheep or the land, for that matter. They do nothing. Fucking nothing, except make all the money.' His face turned redder and his right cheek started twitching as he talked faster. 'They just come in, make their fortune and go. Fucken bastards, they are. Always going on strike over nothing. Nothing. You blokes better watch it, things are going to change.'

The local shearer looked down into his beer and mumbled from behind his orange moustache. 'Them shearers' huts round here was going to the pack, that's for sure. The squatter's not looking after the quarters like he used to. And I guess there's too much sugarbagging going on.' Sugarbagging is when shearers take their tucker to the shed and travel back to their homes at night and the huts don't get used.

A cocky, overhearing the conversation, threw his hands in the air and laughed. 'You're the worst at it, mate,' he said. 'You never stay in the huts no more.'

The shearer looked at the school of drinkers and said, 'I know. I know I'm as much to blame as anyone. We don't go using the huts no more. When you live up here and all, and you got a missus and a warm bed back in town, why would you stay out in the huts with a bunch a pig-ugly shearers like you blokes?'

We all laughed. Mainly because the local shearer was one hooked-nose, hollow-gutted, flappy-eared ugly fucker. And we all had to be better looking than him.

Old Garth, a broken-down shearer who had grey bushes growing out both nostrils and ears, eyebrows he could use for a comb-over, a fat gut, and a face that had got off skid row twice, paused and drew a wheezy, emphysemic breath. 'I reckon I'm better looking than your missus, anyhow.'

We were on the floor laughing. But Fat Bastard, still listening, started frothing from the mouth. 'You blokes can't take anything serious. You want five-star accommodation for two or three weeks of the year. What about the poor cocky?'

Sid had had a few beers by now and I could see a spray coming. I ought to be able to pick when Sid was about to go off – I'd copped plenty when he'd been half pissed. 'Why, why don't you sh-sh-sh-sh . . .'

I didn't think he was going to get it out.

'Sh-hut the fuck up?'

Fat Bastard began walking off, backwards. 'Your days are numbered. We'll get you. We'll get you. Alexander Hay – he'll get you. Stitch you blokes right up. You won't be laughing then.'

Alexander Hay was in the paper and on the TV every second week. He was a spokesman for some right-wing organisation closely linked to the Graziers Association, and they were after us. They bullshitted that the economy couldn't sustain workers' extravagant wages and conditions. They blamed workers for a failing economy. No one was standing up for us, putting our point of view across. I hated them: Alexander Hay, Malcolm Fraser and people like Fat Bastard.

The old cocky didn't agree. 'A lot of us aren't happy with that Hay bloke neither. He don't represent us. Don't want another Hitler on our hands, do we, ay? Na, don't you boys go listening to that fella too much, he's all piss and wind. Mind you, the unions are having too much to say in this country at the moment. They need taking back a peg or two. Everyone needs a fair go but you don't need a union to tell you what you're thinking, and that's what's happening. The workers are all right and that – it's those flaming unions what's the trouble.'

The local shearer reckoned that with only one room in the pub and the cockies and the workers having to drink in the same bar, the tension always went up a notch or two when a few blokes got half pissed. Sometimes the bar was like trying to mix milk and oil.

We finished off our rounds, bought some travellers to drink on the way home and headed back to the huts.

On the way home, Sid drove into the wrong property. I tried to tell him but he wouldn't listen, kept saying, 'Cut-out, cut-out, tomorrow.' He bombed me all the way home. 'By, by, by the way, your fucken dog's barking is driving us crazy. You have to shut, shut, shut the fucker up at night.'

Garth, the old wool roller, insisted on having his say too. Sid treated Garth differently, probably because he was an ex-shearer. Garth took an emphysemic breath. 'Dogs aren't a good thing for shearers to cart around, you know. They're trouble, know what I mean?'

I said, 'You've got a dog, Sid. A mongrel corgi at that.'

'That, that, that's different. Don't bring my dog into it or I'll kick you out, kick you out, right, right now.' He looked mad enough to kick me out so I shut up to make sure I got home. I swore I'd never go with him again.

I was heading back to Melbourne the next day and I started thinking about Sonia. I wondered whether she was with Ethan now. Maybe I should have fought for her. I'd given up too easy. I'd just rolled over. But I didn't think a bloke should have to fight like that for a girl. And maybe she was trying to make me jealous. Maybe she wanted me to stay home with her and get a regular job. Maybe she was using Ethan, keeping him interested to get me back on track. Why couldn't she just ask?

No, I'd seen the way her face lit up when she saw him. The way her parents' faces lit up when he came with me to her place. I couldn't work out why she kept saying she wanted me. Maybe she didn't think she was good enough for him. Ethan's family were rich. His old man drove a brand new Mercedes and I'd heard he had big shares in the stockmarket. I thought the stockmarket was a stockyard in the city until I asked Bernie.

The cut-out came late in the afternoon. Everyone was going back to Greystones to do the lambs but I had to go to a learner's shearing school. I protested. I wanted to go to Greystones but Grazcos said no.

Later we heard Grazcos was going to lose the shed. Grazcos was blaming our militant attitude. They always did. Unless we let them walk all over us, they called us red raggers.

It was always a battle. Sid reckoned things had never completely healed between some of the pastoralists and shearers after the '56 strike. It was more than that, I thought. We were under attack for being workers. The rules of engagement were being challenged. Our award was under threat. There was less middle management on a property than in a factory. I never met the owner of the factory I worked in, and there the managers looked after the workers. It wasn't like that out here – the manager's sole responsibility was the station and the sheep. That's what was different.

Some station hands liked the shearers and some saw us as invading their territory. A lot of them stood up for the cocky and the squatters, even though they were the lowest paid of us all. They saw themselves as somehow equal, through the shared hardship of the land and the heat, because they stuck it out in the one place. And that put them above us itinerant shearers. Except the cocky bought a new car every year and his children would go overseas for a year after secondary school. And the station hand's children would become station hands, or cooks.

Contract musterers were a breed of their own. Local shearers often resented outside shearers. Victorian shearers were resented anywhere outside Victoria, especially in Queensland. Usually, if you dug a little, it was ex-Victorians that resented Victorians the most.

The groups could get confusing. There were the right-wing Liberal squatters and right-wing Labor cockies; old soldier-settlers; the middle-class Labor supporters; the conservatively dressed, plum-in-the-mouth squatters who I'd hate just looking at. The most irritating and frustrating type was the right-wing conservative shearer. They were usually the most aggressive haters, especially of the union and the organisers, even though they were in the union. They had to be. Didn't make them bad unionists in a shed, because they followed the rules. But for me only two categories counted. Those who had land and those who didn't. The rest was bullshit.

Heading out the gate at Booligal, I pulled over to look at a sunset I knew would only last a moment. There were a million little tufts of cloud all tinged with changing colours. I pretended for that moment I owned the sunset, like at night when I owned the night skies and during the day when I owned the wind.

As a kid, one of the lessons the nuns taught us was that the poor would inherit the earth, but I knew that wasn't true; that was only a story.

SHEARING SCHOOL.

I TURNED UP at Coburg Wool School in Melbourne's north with eight other learners in September 1977. The school was sponsored by the Wool Board and the government, to prove they were doing things for working people. I didn't want to be part of the sham, helping suits in offices keep their jobs, and I didn't want the blokes to think I was scabbing it in a learner's team. That's how they thought of learners' school.

The school promoted the tally-hi shearing style, regarded as the most efficient way to shear sheep. In my roustabout days I'd picked up a bit from every shearer and tried to fit the style to my body type. A tall, long-armed shearer can do things a short-armed bloke can't, and vice versa. But it didn't matter which way I shore, my legs ached more than my back. My legs always ached.

The country newspaper *Stock and Land* turned up and did a story on the shearing school and I got my photo in the paper. The secretary of the AWU came down to have a look. After a week at the school we went out to a sheep property in Gisborne and shore there for a week. I hated the highbrow squatter that owned the place. It was cheap shearing for him. He wanted to be friendly. Fuck him, I thought. We all got a little sheep in a box as a memento for our time there. His wife did the cooking and I complained. They hated me but I loved stirring. You could back it in someone was getting something out of it. And anything that had school in it I didn't want to be part of.

Mum said Sonia had been asking where I was. I called her to see how things were. She was expecting me, so I went over to her flat in Cheltenham. She was upset I hadn't called.

So it was the trying-to-make-me-jealous strategy. I said I'd thought it was over, that she and Ethan would have been together by now. She got angry and hit me.

She didn't want to split up but she did want to go out more when I was away, just with a group of friends. She asked whether I'd seen anybody else. I thought about it, but I hadn't really, so I said no.

BARUNAH PLAINS STATION

BARUNAH PLAINS WAS out from Inverleigh, in the Western District of Victoria, on the Hamilton Highway. The squatter's palace had the lot: botanical gardens for a front yard, a huge bluestone mansion, stables and courtyards. Down the valley were the shearers' huts. They were in reasonable condition, made out of timber, with little verandahs on them. The shearing shed, up on the hill above the huts, was a huge, half-bluestone, half-corrugated-iron shed.

'G'day, boy, how was Hay?' It was Graham the cook.

'Yeah, yeah, got through it all right. You know what it's like up there. The locals hate you, the cockies hate you, the sheep are rough, the huts are crappy and it's fucken hot.'

'How was Sid?'

'Drove me crazy half the time.'

'You got home all right then? He didn't leave you at the wrong shed, ay?'

'News travels fast down here. Anyway, I'm starving. What's for breakfast?'

'It's all there. Help yourself.'

Bacon and eggs, chops, snags, spaghetti, scrambled eggs, toast and cereal – this bloke was a gun cook. The shearers had him ranked second-best in the sheds. Old Schultz, if he was sober, was still regarded as the best cook going around.

The swarm lasted a while. I was glad to be back in the team. Captain Ahab said the Kiwis around Mortlake were cutting into a fair bit of our work. 'The cockies are loving it. They think they've got us on the ropes. Apparently at one shed they shore the lambs for nuthin to get the shed. Dirty bastards, and they pulled their wide combs to do it.'

I asked, 'What's pulling your comb?'

Viking laughed. 'Tell the boy what's going on, Haveachat, will you? We don't want him going on the other side. He might reckon it's a good idea. Let's go, boys.'

Haveachat nodded, jumped on me and said, 'Come on, boy. I'll tell you all about it at smoko.'

Taffy the Welshman drew pen number one and was the rep. He was a rock-solid unionist. His trademark homemade leather patch was strapped to his side. He was shearing about thirty-seven, thirty-eight a run in these sheep. They were big, straight, wild Ropel wethers. Ropel was a growth hormone placed behind the ear in the form of a pellet. It sent sheep mad. The wethers kicked and twisted.

Haveachat in two was getting his forty-three, forty-four a run and cruising. Viking had the third pen. He was shearing around forty-eight, forty-nine a run. Captain Ahab drew the fourth. He was shearing about forty-three.

In the fifth pen was a bloke from Ballarat who could only manage twenty-five a run. He didn't talk, just stared at everybody. Haveachat reckoned he hit the piss that hard he had to be locked away. Reckoned he was a good bloke before that. In the sixth pen was Mr Forty-a-run Monahan from Albury. I'd last seen him at

Gunbar Station. He still hated shearing. Bernie Bourke was in seven. He was getting forty-five to forty-seven a run, but it wasn't the tally that separated him and Viking. Bernie Bourke was in his prime and savage. Viking was past his and eloquent, if you can call a shearer that.

I was in the eighth pen.

The owner walked in and onto the board. He stood in front of me with his legs apart, cracking his whip on his leather boots. I had an instant surge of rage and wanted to smash him. I was coming down the last side of a sheep as fast as I could. I pushed the sheep down the chute and charged forward. If he gets in my way I'm going through him, I thought. He moved one step ahead of me. Draphine was leaning over the rail at the back of the pen when I smashed through the doors. He said, 'Steady, boy, steady.'

The squatter wasn't watching when Bernie Bourke moved into the pen and he got swiped. I laughed. Bernie just kept shearing.

At smoko I told the blokes what happened. 'He won't be coming down our end slapping his whip on his riding boots for a while.'

Captain Ahab didn't like what I said. He thought the squatter was all right. Then he got a bit spiteful towards me. 'We get work every year off him and he creates jobs for a lot of people. A lot of workers rely on him for their income.' He was staring at me and his voice was severe. 'And he doesn't let them down, boy.'

Haveachat lightened things. 'You're only brown-nosin cos you get free drinks off him at the cut-out.'

Captain Ahab was always invited up to the house for a drink after the shed was finished. He squeezed his beady little eyes, looked at me and started on me again. 'You're in my territory, boy, so none of your troublemaking ways down here.'

'What's that got to do with anything? I haven't caused any trouble.'

'I know you got yourself barred from the Conargo pub.'

I hadn't been sure if they knew about that or not – so that was why Greeny had left me behind at Boonoke. Pack of bastards.

Changing the subject, Viking said, 'Now, have you educated the boy on those wide combs yet, Haveachat?'

Haveachat laughed, asking the team, 'You reckon he wants to use them?'

'Come on, stop fucken around and tell me.'

'Well, pulling a comb is when you heat up the end teeth of your comb and pull them out, widening them. You can take in more wool with each blow. Only scabby bastards use them.'

Bernie Bourke, who tended to talk in facts, chimed in. 'They used wide combs in the thirties before the squatters outlawed them. Reckon they didn't do a good job – left too much wool on the sheep, and the shearer had to do a second cut to get it off. The wool off the second cut of a fleece is useless to a farmer, so they made a lower rate for the wide comb and it wasn't worth using them.'

Captain Ahab said, 'Read your award. Our rate per sheep is based on the width of the comb. The wider comb is illegal now.'

Haveachat went on, 'Now they want em back, but they don't want to change the award.'

'But it's more than that,' Taffy said. 'It's the conditions that go with the award. Once the award is gone there're no rules. A lot of young blokes think they can come in, make a quid and get out, so they'll do anything. Live in crap huts, caravans; reduce the price to get the work. Like the Kiwis do, and we're left with nothing.'

Viking finished the conversation off. 'So don't give up conditions other men have spent lifetimes achieving. Got that, boy?'

That night I came into tea half pissed. Captain Ahab was still there, holding a newspaper with Malcolm Fraser's oversized jaw on the front page and his own behind it. He'd been talking to the cocky's son. When the Captain went to bed the son continued the conversation with me. 'There's nothing wrong with the wide combs, you know. It's progress, just progress. You can shear more, you know, and it's easier on your back. You're not bent over for so long. You blokes are stuck in the dark ages.'

'It's not just about the wide comb. It's more than that, that's what Taffy said.'

'You blokes are always coming up with excuses: it's this, it's that, you can't do this, you can't do that. You want to stay backward; we're just trying to improve the industry, you know.'

'Well, Bernie said if we don't get a pay rise in eighteen months then we gotta shear fifteen to twenty sheep a day more with the wide comb to earn the same as we do now with the narrow one. So what's the point?'

The cocky's son looked surprised. 'Who said that?'

'Bernie said it was in *The Worker*, the union paper. It reckons that unless the courts change the award, the graziers can stop our pay rises, by law.'

'Who's going to do that? The farmers want their sheep shorn.'

'Viking reckons the Kiwis are trying to weaken the industry. First, he says, it's the wide comb. Then they're shearing under the award. He reckons they earn about half in New Zealand what we earn in Australia. They work for six months here, go home, and we give all their tax back. Plus their women do the rousin and cooking sometimes, cutting out other blokes' work. One worker per household, that's the rule. Viking reckons they destroyed their industry, now they're destroying ours.'

The cocky grinned. 'Did you know a lot of shearers are already using the wide combs? Did you know that? And not just Kiwis either – a lot of Aussie shearers are using them too.'

'Viking reckons next thing we'll be working seven days a week. Paying a heap of tax and killing ourselves. He reckons the squatters and cockies and Fraser are carefully orchestrating it. Viking reckons it's a plan, a strategy.'

'You blokes are too negative. Look at all the positives.'

'Viking's not dirty on the Kiwis either, not like these other blokes are. He reckons they're getting used too. Anyway, what are you going to do after this shed?'

'Depends when Dad wants me back for hay carting, if he wants me back. He and Mum are going on a trip they've been planning for a lifetime.' He laughed. 'So I'll watch the farm when they go. That's the least I can do after everything they've done for me. Oh, and next year, a few of us are looking at a volunteer program overseas, working in a poor rural community and helping with some modern farming strategies. After that I wouldn't mind doing a few more sheds. I like it.'

Next day we were back into the Ropelled wethers. They were frantic and nervous when we shore them. They were all on drugs. I wondered what the meat did to us when we ate it.

I started shearing one of them, and when I got to his neck I put my hand on his nose and touched a big ugly sore. Bernie Bourke yelled out, 'Cancer, throw it out.'

'What? Before I've finished it?'

Bernie didn't answer. He was busy coming down the last side of his sheep. Bernie had told me when I used to pick up for him that his back ached so badly coming down the last side he rushed to finish off the sheep because he couldn't straighten up until he had. Some shearers straightened up for a second before finishing, taking the strain off their backs. Bernie didn't.

Draphine, never far away, nodded. 'Throw it out, boy.'

When I positioned the sheep to take the belly wool off, its cancerous nose had already nuzzled into my armpit and around the back of my arm. I pulled the wool I'd shorn off and threw the sheep down the chute. I got paid for it. I used the shorn wool to clean under my armpit and around my arm. Draphine reckoned you probably couldn't get cancer from them but said, 'Them's the rules.'

After work Draphine asked if I could kill a sheep for the cook. The station hand was sick. I said okay and asked would I get five bucks for it, like I had as a roustabout.

'Yeah, yeah,' he said.

I didn't really want to do it. I was exhausted. I went to the yard and there was the cancerous sheep I'd thrown out earlier. I pulled it down, kneeled on its body, and pulled its head backwards around my front leg, exposing its throat.

I remembered the first time I'd had to kill. It was a couple of runt piglets. I didn't have the courage to knock them on the head or shoot them. I tried to save them, telling the manager I thought they were going to come good. He just shook his head and walked away from me. So I drowned them. It was a disaster. They took ages to die.

Smokey had helped me round the sheep up and now sat quietly in the corner of the yard, as if he knew what was about to happen. The sheep knew she was going to die. Her eyes were riddled with terror and her body trembled. I plunged the knife into her throat and cut furiously so I could break her neck simultaneously, making it as painless as possible. The hot blood and frantic kicking of a dying sheep didn't bother me as much as it used to. I gutted her easy enough, except I nicked the bowel cutting open her belly and got a whiff of the putrid smell of fermenting grass. Green, coarse, fresh sheep shit.

I was stuffed from shearing all day and I didn't have the strength to punch the skin off. I got my clenched fist between the body and the hide and pushed and punched one long gap down her back and stopped. Steam was coming off the dead body as the cool air of dusk set in. I left my hand there – it was warm – leant over her and shut my eyes and rested for several minutes. I just wanted to sleep. Her flesh was hot and her skin was tough, hard to rip away from her body. Eventually I got her hide off and lumped her into the meat shed before dark.

Funny, we wouldn't shear the cancerous ones but we'd eat them.

I washed up and went in for tea. I was starving. Haveachat reckoned if you couldn't eat after a hard day's work you wouldn't last long in this game. I should be all right, I thought, I was always hungry.

The next day, after the first run, Gannon looked on the tally board and I had only twenty for the run. He started spruiking. 'Gunna get your hundred today, are you? That's what you bet us last night at the pub.' He knew I couldn't do it, so he was giving it to me. During the run he'd come and count my sheep and yell out to the whole shed how many I'd done. At the end of the run he'd check the board and then he'd get into me.

I didn't get my hundred that day. I was crook, my guts were exploding all morning from too much grog the night before.

On Friday we got into the young ewes and I shore my first hundred in a day. It was October 1977, I was eighteen, and the monkey was off my back. I could now last three, sometimes four, days before I was stuffed for the week. Once I was burned out, I stayed like that until the weekend, when I'd recover. But I was improving. Captain Ahab didn't say anything about my hundred. The other boys congratulated me, and Draphine acted like he'd shorn them himself.

That weekend, Smokey and I went to Sonia's. Ethan was there. They'd been to a concert with a group of others. After he left Sonia and I started talking about our future.

I said it was obvious we were going in different directions. We didn't agree on anything, so we should separate. She said maybe we could get back together when we were older.

I planned on going to Queensland the following year, to consolidate my shearing skills and look for a place I could settle down in, start working up my own run. She had her nursing course, loved the city life, and had plenty of offers to go out. She refused most of them because of me, she said. We agreed to move on at Christmas time.

A few weeks later the shed finished. Viking had rung the shed. We shore about fifteen thousand sheep at Barunah Plains that year. Sure enough, Captain Ahab went for a drink with the owner while the cut-out cheques were being made up. Draphine was sent to Mount Elephant Station. I was sent to Warrigal Creek again. I was glad to see the end of Barunah's squatter and I had some of his money in my pocket. That was the good thing about shearing: if you didn't like a place, you knew you only had to put up with it for a few weeks.

BACK TO LAL LAL

AFTER WARRIGAL CREEK, it was back to another familiar station, Lal Lal, whose shearers' huts of slipped weatherboards and drooped and rusted guttering were in stark contrast to the refurbished family home, with its antique furniture and recently restored stables.

Strands of horsehair pierced my lumpy water-stained mattress and irritated my skin. I preferred separate huts to this dormitory-style rooming. There were no photos or paintings hanging, no bedside ornaments and no sheets. The bed wobbled on the twisted floorboards. The squeaks of the cyclone-wire base quietened with morning. My old green sleeping bag and the remains of my blanket from school were all that came between me and the bitter cold.

'Hands off cocks and onto socks!' *Bang, bang, bang, bang, bang.* 'Hands off cocks and onto socks – it's breakfast time!' The cook going up and down the corridor at six o'clock banging his frypan was a pain in the arse. He'd been watching too many Westerns. But even his noise couldn't stop the weekend's conversation stirring in my head.

Sonia was pregnant. I'd spent every weekend I was at Warrigal

Creek at her place. We celebrated her eighteenth and my nineteenth birthday together, and we hadn't acted like we intended going our separate ways. I didn't know what the gameplan was, I was in unknown territory. And now this. Why now? I wasn't ready for something like this. Fuck, fuck, fuck. Sonia wanted the baby. She said she wouldn't have got pregnant, accident or not, if she didn't love me. She said she was going to have the baby and I didn't have to marry her. Everyone had expected we'd get married and the McHughs had hoped we wouldn't.

At the swarm I drew pen number one. This was my last shed for the season and my last as a learner. I'd been getting my hundred a day since Barunah Plains.

Viking, elbows on his knees, looking down at the floor, said, 'It's time you did the rep's job, boy. Get yourself some experience.'

I nodded okay.

Haveachat agreed. 'It's a good shed for practising in too, and this fella's a good squatter, as far as squatters go. Not like some of them other ratbags.'

Barnesy, the cocky's son from Talbot, was in two. He was still working hard, hadn't made it yet, and he was a year older. He'd shear his forty-six a run. Viking, travelling to the shed from home, was in three. He would get his fifty a run as usual. Haveachat was in four. He'd shear forty-three, forty-four a run and he was travelling from home as well.

Bernie Bourke was in five. He was getting closer to Viking and would get his forty-nine or fifty. He was also close to home, but he was one of those blokes who never left a shed after it started. Bloodshot drew six and he was in a mood. He had black rings under his sick eyes. He'd turned up last night pissed. His marriage was in trouble, his drinking was getting out of hand again, and his car was stuffed. Robert, the squatter's son, was back again wool rolling, and Draphine was overseeing.

The sheep were hard to pull down in the pens. Wrestling them onto their backs took a lot of energy because of their weight. They arched their backs and kicked while I was dragging them onto the board. By the time I got to shear one, I was stuffed. My back ached, especially when the sheep stiffened their bodies. They were the strongest, muscliest sheep I'd ever shorn – straight and good shearing, but hard on the body.

I worried all week about what was going to happen. Dad said I'd disgraced an innocent girl. He said I had to be married within the month. He got out a pen and paper and planned the wedding. I'd had my fun, he said, now I had to pay. My mum cried when she realised she was going to be a grandmother. Ethan sensed something was up between us and asked if anything had happened. So we told him. Ethan thought it would be a special baby. At work I didn't talk much, except to Bernie Bourke. I told him I was stuffed. He said I was burned out and had done well for my first season. He told me not to worry about being tired, it was normal.

Barnesy would come back from home and give a running commentary on the woman he was seeing on the side: the flirting, the rendezvous. Bernie Bourke never said much but he loved to listen with a smile to everyone. Bloodshot never took any notice. Haveachat talked a lot about his granddaughter. I think he saw more of her than he did his daughter; he'd had a blue with the son-in-law. I didn't want to be a son-in-law yet.

Lal Lal wasn't far from Werribee and I drove to Sonia's for the come-for-tea-and-make-it-official. I walked in through the front door. I'd been there many times before, but not under these circumstances. The place seemed more White Kinged than usual. White walls, sparkling floors and a sink like a mirror. I nodded to Sonia's mum, looked the bloke who bought my horse in the eye and said, 'Hello, Mr McHugh.'

His lips tightened, a grimace in place of a smile. His forehead shrank like a concertina and his beady eyes narrowed. He stood squirming in silence, shuffling change faster and faster in his pocket. If he hated me fucking his daughter I wondered how he'd feel now. He said, 'Don't worry, son, I'm not going to punch you in the head.' Mrs McHugh said it could have happened to them too. Mrs McHugh was an efficient mother and polite towards me. Sonia's parents had regularly told her she could do a lot better than me. I sort of agreed with them. They also knew they'd lose her if they pushed too hard and so they dropped off. Now it was different.

We sat down to eat straight away. She'd cooked a roast with crispy baked potatoes and gravy and there was white cauliflower sauce in a little container on the table. I loved cauliflower sauce on my vegetables, and afterwards Mr McHugh flipped the lid on a stubby for me. Mrs McHugh wasn't happy about that.

The following Friday night I avoided Sonia's and drove straight to the centre of the universe, my old local pub. My mates were there. They were mostly doing apprenticeships in roof tiling, fitting and turning, or motor mechanics, and some were in construction work. We drank at the top end of the bar, near the pool tables. We usually talked work and footy – who was tough and who wasn't, whose reputation was in and whose was out. We all talked about women, but never girlfriends.

My eldest brother was in another part of the bar with an older crowd. He'd done form six and was the designated smart one. That was like winning the lottery. Even though I reckoned I was smarter than him, our lives as children had centred on his study. Teachers also had their own designated smart students. It didn't seem to matter that some of the anointed smart students were dumb; as long as they conformed, worked hard, were obedient and neat, and the teacher liked them, they were eventually confirmed as the brighter ones. At least that's how I figured it. And I wasn't any of those things.

My other brothers and I were expected to get trades that provided a reliable income to raise a family. Shearing wasn't considered that sort of job. It was more a single bloke's job.

The old man was drinking down the other end of the bar with a group known as the experts. It included Sonia's father. I wondered what verdict they'd come up with on me getting Sonia pregnant.

I finished up down their end of the bar later in the evening. One of the experts, who'd had a few by then, turned to Mr McHugh and said, 'You realise this boy's fucking your daughter?' The men waited for a response.

McHugh put a tight smile on his face and took a drink. He was not respected by the other blokes as much as he would have liked. And the loud, overconfident bully who'd taken my horse was gone. I felt for him. He didn't like that kind of talk and I hated it.

It was already hot at seven-thirty on Monday morning when the bell went for the first run. Most Mondays I was seedy, but today I was dead sober. The sheep were shearing better in the warmer weather; I was shearing and thinking about Sonia and the baby but I was mostly replaying her mother's earlier words in my head. She thought I wasn't ready to settle down yet and we were too young. She didn't say it to me, but to Sonia.

My handpiece was overheating and burning my hand. Draphine had given me about four different types of handpiece to try this run. None of them were any good. Now he yelled, 'I'm making a ripper handpiece for you, boy – all new parts. You'll shear two hundred with this little beauty.'

He should have been a car salesman, he was that full of bullshit.

The food at smoko was just passable. The cook reckoned he'd been working around Broken Hill – another dishwasher parading as a cook. He copped a few serious bombs from the men, but he only got worse. We would have been better off saying nothing or sacking him. In the end he threatened to poison us and piss in the stew. He was mad. The other cooks the team had sacked over the years all came from Broken Hill too. This bloke kept his job because we couldn't get a replacement in the busy part of the season.

We were sitting down at smoko, resting, when Draphine said, 'You wanta start out of Quilpie in Queensland next year? You can book a pen early if you like. They're looking for shearers now.'

My stomach churned. I thought how I was going to be tied down, trapped for the rest of my life. 'How do I get there?' I asked.

'Bernie Bourke'll tell you. He got a hundred in the cricket match up there, didn't you, Bernie?'

Bernie smiled. Not comfortable talking about himself, he just said, 'Turn left at Cunnamulla.'

'What's this cricket match, Bernie?'

'There's two ten-stand sheds near each other, and the shearing teams have an annual cricket match for a trophy.'

I wanted to get in the car and go straightaway.

That afternoon my handpiece burnt into my hand again. My mind wasn't on the job and I just kept shearing. Next day I had twenty or more blisters over my right palm.

Draphine said, 'You're supposed to stop when it gets that bad.' He looked at me for a moment.

I bandaged my hand heavily and kept shearing. To shelter my hand, I learnt to push the clippers with the knuckle of my index finger behind the tension nut. It was good enough. The sheep were clean, with straight necks.

After work, Smokey sat next to me and licked my blistered hands. I was about to push him away but Robert reckoned dog's saliva had healing properties in it, so I let him lick them.

That night we were having showers and Barnesy was joking about a woman he was keen on. Haveachat said he'd done his balls on her and should wake up to himself. I'd confided in Haveachat earlier that I'd got my girlfriend pregnant and he told the boys I was in trouble.

Barnesy said, 'The only reason I married me missus was she wouldn't have sex with me till I got married. If they ain't like that, they'll probably fuck anybody and they're not worth having.'

I wished I'd never told Haveachat, he couldn't keep his gob shut.

Viking turned to me and asked, 'You gunna cart her around the sheds or what?'

Haveachat panicked, shook his head. 'Don't do that, boy, it's no life for a woman out here. Women in sheds cause problems, you know. Someone'll show her some attention, or she'll get bored and go looking for it, you know what I mean? Next thing, you got troubles. No, stay away from that one, boy.'

I didn't know where to look, so I just stared out the louvre windows at the steam from the showers disappearing into the daylight. I felt guilty just talking about it. That's why I'd only told Haveachat in the first place. I tried being funny and said to Barnesy, 'You won't be able to keep it up to your girlfriend and your missus for long.' I don't know why I said it. It came out all wrong. The showers were a small area and just got smaller. The concrete floor was worn and the stones in the concrete were smooth and protruding.

Barnesy turned on me. 'Give me your mum or your sister or this girl and I'll show you what a man is, boy.'

I was trapped. That was like sticking a knife into my guts.

Barnesy hadn't finished with me yet.

'Come and see me before you go home and I'll piss on you so at least you'll smell like a man when you're fucken her.'

Everyone laughed. I stood there mute, barefoot, naked and dry, waiting for the next available shower. Their bodies were shining from lathered soap under the hot water, the steam rising around them, and they laughed with Barnesy. I felt like I'd drifted into the wrong play area. I never liked Barnesy much after that.

Draphine came out to where the clothesline was at the back of the huts during hut inspection and said, 'What are you doing, boy? Spill your beer all over the mattress, huh?'

I hung my head. 'Yeah, do I have to pay for it?'

'What's a matter with you? Don't worry, I've heard, I've heard. Keep your dick in your pants next time. Come on, come and get your drinks – the cocky's shouting.'

I kept my head down and didn't say anything. Draphine went back where the swarm was. From the centre of the men I could hear Mr Fisken before I saw him. He seemed to love being part of the workers. He was mostly talking to Viking. I was always struck by the cockies' voices. They were so different in the way they spoke and the way they lived. He shook all our hands and thanked us for a job well done, and he meant it.

I said goodbye to most of the blokes. I didn't look for Barnesy. Draphine gave me my cheque. I signed off and was in my car with a big bottle as a traveller. I'd averaged a hundred sheep a day at this shed. That was the best I'd done so far, but these were fast-shearing sheep.

The green undulating land, surrounded by English trees, created a peaceful mood. The weather was hot and steamy and I could smell the sweet paspalum grass I loved to chew. I wondered what it would be like to live in a mansion like this as I drove out the gate.

THE CHURCH

JACK, MY OLD schoolmate and best man, flipped the top off the second bottle. 'This one and we'll go.'

He drove. The dull oak doors with their thick cast-iron fittings were open, waiting for us. I followed the timber boards down the narrow aisle. Herds of shuffling feet filled the pews on either side of me. The bleating sounds of the mob floated up into the saw-cut rafters. Afternoon sunlight shone through the lead-framed windows in the spire, exposing particles of impurities. In February 1978 Sonia was eighteen and I was nineteen. I stood at the end of the aisle waiting for the bell to ring and wondering who was going to win the cricket match near Quilpie this year and said, 'I do.'

THE BRICK FACTORY

THE BRICK FACTORY was about half an hour from home. It was surrounded by abandoned paddocks of volcanic rocks and scotch thistles. The entry road had a brick-breaking machine on the left and a man-breaking machine on the right. The smoko, boss's and despatch huts were also on the left.

I fronted on my first day, broke, married, with a pregnant wife and willing to do anything. Everything I dreaded. I'd been out of work since Lal Lal Station. I signed on and was put on the production line. My job was turning the bricks upright for the loading machine and checking for faulty bricks.

The concrete mixers, furnaces, conveyor belt with its screeching bearings, and the rollers screamed simultaneously. The noise stifled conversation. My hands, which had been soft from the lanolin in the wool, were soon covered in blood blisters from getting jammed between bricks, and my fingers looked like the fat had been sucked out of them.

I started counting the bricks, trying to get a certain number turned every five minutes, racing the production line. Sometimes I thought the clock was broken, so I'd start counting how many

I turned up in a minute, how many a second I was averaging, how many a run I'd be getting if I was shearing. I divided my wages into an hourly rate and divided the number of bricks I was turning up in an hour to try to work out how much each brick cost to turn. Still the clock hardly moved.

Getting out of the factory at knock-off was like a day pass from prison. When the boss offered me overtime he acted as if he was doing me a favour. I couldn't have gone home and faced Sonia if I'd said no. She seemed happy; she even encouraged me to go to the pub with her dad on Friday nights. She wasn't showing much, but had quit her job before the wedding. We were living in her parents' granny flat. They were charging us rent and then buying things for the baby with the money. We had a double bed to sleep in, never had that before, and Sonia cooked me a beautiful meal every night, made me sandwiches for lunch, and got up when I was going to work even though I said she didn't have to.

The boss came from a little town in Italy and so did everybody else. When they were short a man I think the boss would sponsor someone from the old country. Most of the men either couldn't or didn't speak English.

The smoko hut was furnished with a small laminated table. The boss would enter ripping a piece of stale bread from a half-loaf he was carrying. 'Why you no educaesh, no school, what the matter wif you, fucken.' Then he'd shake his head and say, 'Stupid. You come from dissa country, you gotta da language, no educaesh, you stupid, my childer be smarter than you. Won'ta work here likea you. Fucken Aussie. Stupid. Why you like this?'

I tried to answer. He butted in every time. He started talking to the other migrant workers in Italian and looking at me, then they would look. I didn't know where to look. Every smoko he had something to say. In the factory he did the same. My old man would flog me if I called someone a wog. He brought home new Australians from the factory for tea. I tried to be polite for a little while.

On windy days I was sent to a second-floor, open-sided platform to pour the colour dyes for the bricks into the mixer. The dye powder stung when it got into my eyes. On one occasion I went home blurry-eyed and filthy after overtime and Sonia, as she would often do for a surprise, had invited a girlfriend and her boyfriend for dinner. Sonia was a great cook and she made the best steak and kidney pie. I was surprised we hadn't seen much of Ethan, or that Sonia hadn't invited him around. She thought he was still hurt that he hadn't been in the wedding party. I mused on that one. I thought, He nearly was.

Smokos, the boss was relentless. 'Aussie women, they fucken sluts.'

I knew straight away that Dad's mate who'd got me the job had told him my girlfriend was pregnant.

'Not the Italiano girl. Why you get married so young?'

I just shrugged and went back to work. Every smoko he had a different strategy. He got to me after a while, then something inside me kicked in and I got a second wind, then I could take anything this wog dished out during the day.

It got harder to get out of bed and face the line of bricks and then come home to the life that Sonia wanted for us. Her parents in the big house, us in the granny flat, my family up the road. Going to the pub with her dad and my dad on Friday nights. I needed a get-out plan.

Counting the bricks didn't last. Nor did working out how much it cost to turn the bricks, nor every other possible scenario. So I started on a plan. The first plan was to get an apprenticeship. I hated to admit it but maybe Dad was right, I should have done an apprenticeship. Maybe it wasn't too late. Maybe I could still get an apprenticeship somewhere in welding or something and head out onto the rigs or a pipeline, but I knew that seventy or eighty dollars a week apprenticeship pay wasn't enough to live on.

Sometimes I'd pretend the factory was a game of survival. If I lasted the day I got the money and beat him.

Then Dad's mate at the factory was selling his truck. It was a good business and the old man suggested I buy it. His mate was concerned about my drinking and being responsible for the truck. I was concerned there were a million truck drivers and I didn't want to be another one, plus I'd still have to see the wog boss every day. It wasn't much of a get-out plan, but it was a plan. Everybody was in my ear about Being Responsible. As far as I could see, that was another way of saying, Be like us, get a dead-end job for the next forty years, whinge, get drunk on Friday nights, get cancer, die.

I still had five months before the baby was born. Maybe I could find a place in Queensland to live, to start our life.

Then the call came. Blackall Station needed a presser and a shearer to start in ten days. I had my get-out. Six weeks after I was married, Jack – my best man – and I headed to Queensland shearing. On the Friday night I'd been turning bricks up and on Monday I was on my way north. It was all a bit quick for Sonia. Mr McHugh said I didn't need his permission.

THE BARCOO PUB

JACK AND I reached Blackall, in central Queensland, around the end of March. The Barcoo Hotel, named after the river that the town was built next to, had rooms for two dollars fifty a night. It seemed a bit expensive, but we thought we'd start work soon so we booked in for a few nights. The old pub had an upstairs verandah, bore water in the showers that smelt like rotten eggs, and a bar full of shed workers and a few third-grade rugby hacks.

Jack had been doing a bit of everything since leaving school. He worked on the family farm for a while, followed by some tractor driving and truck driving. His last job was chook plucking in Corowa. When I rang him to go shearing he snatched it straight away, like I did from the brick factory.

The contractor rang the pub to let us know there were a few delays and Blackall Station had been put back a month. Our money wouldn't last that long. We gave our names to other shearing contractors and picked up a couple of days at a shed out past Isisford.

The novelty of the outback evaporated with the relentless miles of nothingness. The men were sleeping on an enclosed verandah, not in the huts. I walked into what looked like an empty hut. 'Taken.'

Walked into the next hut. 'It's full.'

Finally a bloke pointed to a room and said, 'In there, mate, in there's a bed.' By this late stage in a shed no one was going to bother to get to know us too much, not when the cut-out was only a day or two away.

It was a ten-stand shed and I was replacing a shearer who was drunk and wouldn't leave his hut. Jack was helping the presser. The shearer's gear was still on the stand and he came up later that day and tried to collect it. I knew him. He'd been at Eynesbury Station when our team was next to them at Greystones. He was too far gone on the Bundaberg rum to recognise me.

There was a caravan near the huts and according to the gossip the old girl in the caravan had thrown her old man out and taken on one of the other blokes. I got a glimpse of her – she was barefoot, with long blond hair and she was pretty. Her ex-old man was from South Australia and now he was back in the herd with the rest of us. There had been a big punch-up and then it was over. I guess the winner got the girl. I don't think the overseer wanted any of them at the next shed.

The sheep shore all right. They were big and clean and we were glad of a couple of days' work and a few good feeds. The rousies were loud and started hollering when wool started coming from my stand. Getting closer to the cut-out meant getting closer to going back to town.

The rousie picking up for me was tall and finely built. The skin around his eyes was damaged and if you looked closely his eyes were slightly crooked. He said he loved drugs more than the booze. He was a choofer. There were a few choofers in the team, he said. I didn't know much about it.

'Yeah, been all over the country. Worked for Brophy's tent

boxin. I was his number one for a while. Best I did was fought six blokes in one night. All tough bastards, but I had the reach.' He clenched his fists and threw a punch in the air. In and out, as if he still had his speed. 'They couldn't get at me.'

'Wool away,' a shearer yelled down the other end of the board.

The rousie ran down and pulled the fleece away from the stand, rolled it and threw it on the table in one motion. 'Anyways,' he said, 'where was I? Oh yeah. They all thought I'd be easy cos I'm skinny. The last bastard got at me, ya know, got through me defences, a nuggetty bastard – broke through and got me. I was stuffed by then, I just couldn't hold on no more. Liked the choof-choof too much. Fucked me in the end ya know. Been on the prawn trawlers and the cray boats. Worked over Broome and down in WA. Come from Gippsland originally, don't tell many that. They hate Victorians up here.'

He was about twenty-eight years old; he had glimpses of youthfulness left and was sharp – better a friend than a foe. He asked me to go to South Australia for a few days with him, he needed a driver, but I didn't need to get into drugs.

The Barcoo Hotel got most of my cut-out cheque. I rang Sonia and said I was working and things were going okay. I told her I had a shed up around Jericho next and there was more work in the pipeline. She missed me, she said, and was lonely. I said for her to come up and we could live here. She said she wasn't coming and to stop asking her. It wasn't fair to put pressure on her when she was pregnant.

'You do know I'm four months pregnant, don't you?'

That ended that. She said she was bored, that was the worst of it.

When I was out shearing Jack picked up some wool pressing. We were earning enough money to keep us in the town but not enough to get out. When we weren't shearing, Jack and I were sleeping in the car with Smokey. At night we would go to the Greek café. One good feed a day could sustain us and we always had a steak and saved the bones for Smokey.

Sleeping in the car wasn't that bad. The only thing was that the vinyl bench seats in the HG were sticky on my skin when it was hot. Otherwise it was as good as a bed. Jack had the back seat because he was bigger and I could sleep without hitting the steering wheel. At night we lay on our backs, put our heads out of the car with the doors open and looked up at the stars. The night sky out here was a mass of stars compared to the light-polluted sky in the city. Jack and I would talk about everything; the stars could do that to you. They were peaceful moments.

Jack was the youngest of three boys and wasn't going to inherit any of the family's properties. He wanted his own trucks and bush block. We both wanted a farm of our own, maybe sharecropping or contract harvesting to supplement the income. I could shear to supplement mine. That was the plan, anyway. Jack wished he was in love, I could tell. He asked what it was like with Sonia and he always talked about the same girl he went out with at school. None of his other girlfriends after her lasted very long, a week or two at the most. He didn't know why. He reckoned most girls were snobby bitches, especially if they were pretty. 'They all want the city blokes, or ones what look like em,' he said. I thought about Sonia and maybe living up here. There were a lot of sheep and the land was cheap.

Jack and I never worried about anything with each other, and we both liked doing the same things. Jack would do anything. He had no fear and he was a big strong bloke. The only thing we didn't like doing was sharing our smokes with each other, except on nights like this.

The talk stopped and the night went silent when Jack started sobbing. Quietly at first. He tried stopping himself but he couldn't. He just kept sobbing until he went to sleep.

BLACKALL STATION

THE MEN WHO fronted at Blackall Station, it appeared, had been together for a while; only Jack and I were new. The swarm was held in the shed. We'd be there for a couple of weeks, if there were no delays.

A big bad bald bloke drew pen number one. He used to sit in the Barcoo drinking and studying the form guide, never spoke to an outsider. He would look right through me. He'd shear for an hour and then sit on a drum and have two or three smokes before starting again. He didn't care about tallies. He was the rep and he didn't seem to like me much. Didn't bother talking to me, anyway. I drew pen number two. I thought I'd just nod at him and see how that went.

An old bloke called Barry drew three; he worked behind the bar occasionally at the Barcoo. He looked like a little old bookkeeper. He was a great barman, but when he started shearing he swore all day and threatened to kill the sheep. I couldn't believe it, he just never stopped swearing to himself. In the fourth pen was a redhead from Tambo. He came up at smoko and said he knew me from the Barcoo pub. Apparently we'd called him a scab. He said he'd told us to fuck off back to where we came from but he could see we were drunk and didn't worry about it. He turned out to be a great bloke. He said we should go to Rocky when the work finished up around here. A good place for a holiday, he reckoned.

In five was a quiet, barefoot shearer. You saw them sometimes, not very often. His feet were always covered in green shit. He might have been a Kiwi once, he wasn't saying much. In six was the redhead's younger brother. He had the same red hair but was twice his brother's size. He didn't say much either, but when I was chasing old Barry in three he would come along every run and throw a sheep down my chute to keep me in front of him. Barry learnt to shear during the '56 strike. The strike didn't mean anything to him at the time. He was one of the novice boys the squatters recruited as a strike breaker. They were given a crash course in shearing before they came and put into a learner's team. That's how they recruited scabs. He said when he started he only shore about ten or twelve sheep the first day. He said the union recruited a lot of us onto their side. We didn't realise we were coming up into a war zone.

After lunch I went to the tally book to see how I was going, and how the rest of the team were shearing. The bald bloke in one had shorn forty sheep and cruised. I had twenty-eight. Barry had thirty-one. Redhead had fifty-five and didn't have a sweat up. The barefoot bloke had forty-eight and the bloke in six had sixty-five. I dropped the book. I thought I was at least shearing equal to him, but he was more than two-for-oneing me. I said how the fuck did you do that? He laughed, everybody laughed. He was a gun, this bloke. I'd never seen anyone shear so fast. I heard later he had a wide comb handpiece he used to bring out after the run started. I didn't believe it.

That afternoon the bald bloke was sitting on his drum watching me shear. He said to me, 'You'd make a shearer if you'd settle down a bit. I thought you were a bit of a scatterbrain, but you got a bit of potential. Take it easy, concentrate a bit and you'll make it.' He wasn't so scary when he actually spoke to me. He finished his smoke. Mostly it just burned slowly, he didn't puff much. He lit his next smoke up and said, 'What are ya doin up here, boy? Run away, have ya? Run away from ya little wife and all?'

I didn't say anything, just buried my head a bit more into the sheep.

'Go home, son. Settle down. Ya been pissed in that Barcoo a few times. Getting ya girlfriend pregnant's all ya talk about.'

I said I'd had a look at a few houses to rent in Blackall, was thinking of settling down here. The landlords thought I was too big a risk, they didn't like renting to drifters. I told them I was staying but no one believed me. The bald bloke said there was plenty of work in the area once you got in, but there was no life here once the kids got older. All the kids went to Rocky or Brisbane to live. There weren't many teenagers in towns like this. His kids were gone and I think his wife was too. All he could do was shear and it was too late for him to change.

I rang Sonia. I told her the contractor had offered me regular work towards the end of June and he had a good run up here. The sheep were a bit tough but he had plenty of work. I told her to come up and we could live here. We could buy somewhere – the land was cheap, the houses were cheap. Maybe we could make a go of it here.

She said I was pissed. There was no way she was having her baby up there, she said, she wanted to be near her mum. I couldn't understand that. We started fighting on the phone; she reckoned I only rang when I was drunk. She hung up on me.

BARCALDINE

THE SHED FINISHED and the rumour was there was work in Longreach. Gannon, the would-be wool classer, was in town and we'd been drinking together. We were both going to the Grazcos office to find out about work. He put on a lot of aftershave to hide the smell of alcohol coming out of his pores and he wouldn't walk with me up the street. He didn't want to be seen with me by the bosses. 'You been saying that since we were both rousin,' I said, 'and I'm shearing now and you're still rousin. You idiot.'

He snickered as if he was superior to me. 'I've been classing. *Class*-ing wool, you know. And running the sheds, doing the books.' He stopped. 'I'm a classer. I'll have me own run soon.' His index finger was up now and he was shaking back his hair. 'You'll never get a pen with me.'

I yelled in his face. 'Dickhead.'

The Grazcos man told me to go and have a look up at Longreach. 'You'll have a better chance of getting work if you're actually there. There's a wool roller from Melbourne up here looking for work too, think his name's Gannon, he might like to go with you.'

That afternoon Gannon, Jack and I headed to Longreach. We didn't get far, only a few k's, before a stone from a truck smashed our windscreen. We set out again later with a brand-new laminated windscreen, this time heading for Barcaldine, the halfway point.

Right on dusk, as the cattle moved in to eat the fresh grass near the table drains, I drove straight into a herd of Hereford cows. One rolled onto the bonnet, fracturing the new windscreen with her horns. The radiator was smashed in and the clutch broken. Miraculously the engine still worked. I had some epoxy ribbon and we patched the radiator as best we could and jumpstarted the car.

We limped half drunk into Barcaldine and pulled up at the hotel in the middle of the street. Everything was shut except the pub. As I walked in, a shaven-headed, angry-looking bloke in shorts and singlet turned from the bar and stared at me. It was a pick-a-fight look: one bloke looks, and if you look back with the same aggression it's a fight. I turned away, looked down. It wasn't that I was weak, or scared, I just didn't want to fight. He was older and I wasn't in the mood.

But it didn't work. He walked towards me, shoved me around to face him and said, 'Outside.'

I went outside, looked for Gannon and Jack. I thought I was going to have to go for it. We were opposite the Tree of Knowledge, the Labor Party's birthplace during the 1891 shearers' strike. The bloke put his stubby of beer down ready to fight, then the lights of a divvy-van came on – a copper was just a few metres away. He drove up behind us and got out and stood behind his off-duty, half-pissed partner. 'Go for it,' he said, giving his mate the go-ahead to flog me.

Jack turned up from behind the shadows of the divvy-van and the numbers were even. The on-duty copper told Jack to leave but he said no. Next thing I knew I was walking backwards and the coppers were coming towards me.

Gannon shot through, he didn't like violence. Jack stayed with the car and Smokey. I was forced into the divvy-van and taken to the police station. The off-duty copper took over. I was okay until he started listing the charges, then I could feel my rage surge up. I couldn't control myself. I upended the desk he was writing on and he jumped me. I threw him off, picked up his typewriter and threw it at him. He started screaming for help. I picked up another typewriter and threw it at him. His eyes were darting around the small room – he could only run backwards for a few steps. He was a miserable, pathetic-looking cunt now.

His mate returned from outside but I had one target in mind. I jumped the off-duty copper, he fell backwards as I landed on him. I didn't care what the other cop did to me as long as I could hurt the fucken pig in front of me. I tried to pull him under me, he was screaming and kicking, his punches were panicked and powerless. I tried to headbutt his teeth out but I couldn't reach, my head was at his chin. I tried one last crack at getting my fingers into his face to gouge an eye out.

I woke the next morning in a padded cell with a hangover and the off-duty cop remorsefully offering me bacon and eggs for breakfast. I was starving but I wasn't going to eat his shit. The sergeant turned up and the cop was sent away. 'Three months, you little cunt,' he said to me, 'that's what you'll get, and you're not getting out till the circuit judge arrives. I'm sick of you drifters fucking up this town and interfering with my Sunday mornings. Pack of useless cunts.'

I was sober now and I told him what happened. The sergeant was wild. He believed my version of events. The off-duty cop had obviously done this sort of thing before. The sergeant fined me for drunk and disorderly, resisting arrest, and assault, said I could get out if I paid the fines and didn't come back into town. I wanted to fight the charges but I didn't want to spend two weeks in the slammer waiting for the judge to arrive. I told Jack to ring home and see if anyone would send some money up. He told me Sonia would only send money if I used it to come home with.

Jack went and found Gannon. They pitched in and I got out. I couldn't afford to fix the car. A new windscreen and the fines and I was done in again. I was sick of being broke, always looking for a job, following a lead, getting fucked over by contractors and sleeping in the car. I had a wife and a baby coming. She wanted to live in the city and I wanted the bush.

Gannon thought it was hilarious that I'd ended up in the slammer for the night. Overnight he'd fallen in love. She was seven months pregnant. He didn't get it. Jack had slept in the car with Smokey. He'd worked out if he turned the ignition on in second gear the car would jumpstart itself, and we became skilled at picking the gearshifts without using the clutch.

We headed back to Blackall and the Barcoo Hotel, where the owners disappointedly gave us a room for the night.

AUGATHELLA

A SHED NEAR Augathella came up with about eight or nine days' work for both of us. A bed and regular food. The corrugated-iron huts had hand-pump showers, kero fridges, carbide lights (there was no electricity), and a copper to wash our clothes.

The overseer asked if I could kill a sheep for the cook, a broken-down shearer with a bad back. The station hands were contract musterers and travelling a long way every day to get out here. He said these sheep were the oldest wethers in Australia – nine or ten years old, due to be shipped overseas after shearing. He reckoned you could boil a leg all day and it'd still be tough as boot leather.

The swarm was in Patrick's room, another Barcoo patron. He came into the pub mainly on weekends, the sort of bloke who'd sit on a beer for ages. But you didn't talk to him in the pub: he was unofficially blacklisted. Don't know why he came in. I was first into the swarm and before I'd said anything to him, he said, 'I didn't shear in '56.' The word in the pub was he did. 'And neither did my old man.' That was the other thing they used to say – his old man was a scab as well.

'Fair enough,' I said, and left it at that.

Barefoot from Blackall Station drew pen number one. He was only getting thirty-seven, thirty-eight a run in these tough old wethers. They were skinny, hollow-gutted sheep. I drew pen number two. I was getting twenty-six a run. In three was a middle-aged, part-time union organiser. He was slogging out thirty-three, thirty-four a run. He said the organiser for that area travelled eight hundred to fifteen hundred kilometres every time he got in the car. At the swarm he called for a show of tickets. Everyone had tickets.

Patrick drew the fourth pen. He was only getting about twenty-one a run. He had no style, a puny body with a big head, a pathetic moustache; his back was stuffed and he had no family, so he didn't need to shear as many as a married bloke. Jack was doing the pressing. The old wool roller, by his own admission an ex-alcoholic, was travelling with the overseer-cum-wool classer. When I saw the wool roller in the showers he had a big scar around his kidney region.

The rousie was a local boy who didn't like school. This was a slow team and a good shed for a roustabout to learn in. The wool roller told the rousie what to do. The young fella reckoned it was a piece a cake. He was a keen worker but unfortunately the fleeces went all over the place. He got plenty of bombs, more from the old wool roller than the wool classer. By the end of the day the wool roller had turned vicious, told the boy he was only a leftover drip out of his old man's cock and was just as useless. I knew how the boy felt. The classer stepped in and told the wool roller to ease up a bit.

The second night, I killed a second sheep for the cook. I decided to do it before tea and before I had a shower – I knew I'd be exhausted afterwards and wouldn't have the energy or desire. The sheep was tied up to a pole in the middle of the paddock. A buckled plywood board lay on the dusty ground next to it, obviously put there for me to kill the sheep on. The cook had given me a sharp knife and a leg iron, the latter designed to put between the sheep's back legs so I could hang the carcass in the meat house when I'd finished.

The sheep was a big stroppy bastard with a big red bulge on its arse. It looked a bit like a baboon's arse. I was tired from shearing and my arms felt heavy; I grabbed its nose, bent it into itself and the sheep went down. I put one knee into its guts, pulled its neck around my leg and cut its throat and broke its neck. The blood ran off the board and onto the dirt and then came the flies. The carcass kept slipping off the board onto the dirt, and the blood didn't help. Every time I tried to punch the wool off, the carcass slid onto the dirt.

Jack came over to see how I was going. He'd already had his shower and didn't want to get dirty but he footed the carcass for me, stopping it from slipping away. When I'd finished I picked it up and lumped it over to the meathouse. I kept saying to myself, Never again, never again. I'm not doing this again. It's too hard. I'm too tired, too sore.

I mustered all the strength I had left to lift the carcass up and hang it in the meat shed. I couldn't reach the hook. My muscles were like jelly, they just wouldn't work. That's when the cook came in.

He said, 'Well done, son, you got us out of a tough spot.'

He picked the carcass and me up off the ground and we hung it together. I started wiping it down, getting the dirt and burrs off the flesh. It had burrs all over its rump and hind legs and now the ribs had a bit of concrete rash. The cook said not to worry, he'd fix it all up and I could go and have my shower. He said there was a plate of food in the oven for me.

I walked back across the flat. The sun was setting and the sky was flaming red. The men were inside and I was far enough away from the huts to feel the sheer enormity of the country. Bush life seemed relentless but the outback was magnificent to look at. And it produced such strong feelings. This was the sort of moment I wanted to share with Sonia, I thought. If she could experience some of the same feelings I had in the bush she'd be happy to leave her family and suburban life.

Under the shower I had to give several pumps to the lever to get the hot water flowing, then I closed my eyes. It was beautiful to feel the water run over my body. I was being brought back to life. I was back in the sea at Newcastle beach on Dad's shoulders; dolphining through the waves at Apollo Bay with Sonia, making love in the shallows. I loved the water. I loved it running over my face. The dried blood covering my arms started to loosen up. The sweat, sticky lanolin, sheep snot and sheep shit came off with soap. The rashes and scratches stung but it was an enjoyable pain. I was clean, hungry, rooted, and ready for bed.

I went back to that same spot every night to see the sunset and feel the outback. Patrick came over one night and we got talking. He was telling me the difference between a tortoise and a turtle. He had beehives that he'd built all around Blackall. He wasn't a big drinker and he didn't have a family. To my surprise I discovered he was a conservationist. He said the rotten-egg smell in the bore water was from oil deposits. Every drought, he reckoned, the oil companies came up here to the dried swamps and drilled and plugged them. Most of the locals knew outback Queensland was full of oil. I began to think I shouldn't have listened to what the others said about him.

Jack was the last worker to finish in the shed at the cut-out. I gave him a hand pressing all the belly wools and locks. He was smiling as he worked, that meant he was stuffed. And he was the strongest bloke I knew. We packed up our gear, collected our cheques and set off.

We headed back to the Barcoo pub. We were five hours away, driving with no clutch, a smashed-in windscreen held together by tape, a smashed-up front guard and bull bar, and an epoxy-puttied radiator. I loved my car. We drove all the way to Blackall in silence.

LONGREACH

BACK AT THE BARCOO I had a couple of messages from home. Sonia was arriving in Longreach by plane on Wednesday.

Early on Wednesday morning I got a day's work, so Jack drove to the airport and picked her up. I was jealous. When we met that night I felt nervous. She'd had her hair cut short, which made her look about fifteen, and she had a belly like a poddy calf. The first thing she wanted to talk about was me coming home. She said no one knew why I was up here.

I said there could be some work in Longreach for me. I had nothing till July down home and I wasn't going back to a factory or her folks' flat.

She said I looked bad – dirty and scruffy. Then she asked me to stop swearing so much, and did I have to have another drink. She reckoned every time I rang her I was drunk. I'd gone downhill, she said.

I wanted to look at some houses here, but Sonia refused. She'd come to take me home.

The next day the three of us went to Longreach. She started working on Jack. Women and mates are never a good mix. He lapped up the attention from her and I got dirty on both of them. It was 30 degrees up there in autumn so we went to the local pool but it was shut. Too cold, they said. We had lunch on the banks of the Thomson River and a swim afterwards.

Jack and I were out of money. There was no work in Longreach – the Grazcos shearing contractor at Blackall had told us a lie to get rid of us. Sonia had the only money and she'd only spend it on petrol to go home. Jack was now agreeing with her and that shit me. He'd backdoor me too, I thought.

We headed home. We dropped Jack off at Daysdale, a little town out of Corowa in New South Wales. The clutch cost two dollars to repair when we got back to Melbourne. It had only been missing a wire. The honeymoon was over.

THE MEATWORKS

AT FOUR-THIRTY in the morning it was pitch-black and cold. There were no lights in the carpark. I could see a dim outline of cars and the glow of a smoke when someone took a desperate suck. A mate from Werribee was working here, reckoned if I wanted to get a start this was the best time to arrive.

A few people were heading to the meatworks from the carpark, so I followed them. They stood hunched over, standing alone; no one was mixing. The moon was still up as daylight began breaking. The figures and buildings came into focus. Bluey jackets and beanies, faded green parkas with fur collars, dirty lumber jackets, overstretched elastic-sided workboots, dirty runners. Old good shoes, usually brown, patterned, outdated, covered in paint. Unless they were smoking, everybody had their hands in their pockets.

The chalky red bricks of the factory made it look old and tired and worn out. Steam was coming out of some of the chimneys. Washed concrete surrounded the place, with a big double gate at the entrance that only regular workers had access to. I stood with a growing number of other men in a gravel area: a large cattleyard. A small office on stilts with an elevated walkway and railing was situated outside the meatworks fence.

By six o'clock the place was packed with blokes old and young. There were all types: Italians, Greeks, Aussies, Serbs, Slavs, Philippines, Lebos, Maltese. The big boss emerged from the office with his clipboard and the murmur and restlessness went up a couple of notches. As workers called in sick for the chain, casuals were selected. The boss scanned the mob. 'I'll have you and you and you.' He pointed to men he recognised. One bloke pointed back to himself, said, 'Me, me.'

'Na, not you, him, him.' Pointing to the bloke next to him.

Some of the men had the look of real desperation in their eyes, others were already broken. A big drunken redhead stood on a drum, started screaming out to the selected men as they walked past him. 'Any you cunts haven't got tickets, I'll find out.' He waved his own ticket in the air.

'Need a meatworker's ticket, you can't start without a meatworker's ticket. None of these other fucken tickets, a meatworkers' union ticket.'

I didn't have a ticket. I had my shearer's ticket, but not a meatworker's. The redhead looked like he'd kill anyone who got on before him without a ticket. Probably black-banned by the meatworks. He wasn't getting a start.

The big boss came back out of his office – a few more vacancies had emerged. He started scanning the mob again. More than half the men got picked up that day. At eight o'clock he came out once more and said to the rest of us, 'That's it for today. Sorry, boys.'

A bloke yelled out, 'The Waterside, see ya there.' It was an early opener.

Some of the blokes nodded. They all knew each other. I didn't go. I didn't know any of them and I didn't want to start drinking in the morning. It was a marker you were an alcoholic. I headed off in my own direction, going from factory to factory, looking for a start.

That night I went to where I knew my mate Johnny drank.

'How'd ya go?' he said. 'Didn't see ya today.'

'I was there. Didn't get on, didn't get picked.'

'You useless little fucker, gotta get seen, eyeball the big cunt, eyeball him, take him on, take the bigger fucker on.'

Johnny was half cut. Eyeball him, he reckoned.

'But it was dark half the time, how can ya eyeball the big boss in the dark?'

'Ya gotta get in there. No fucken excuses, boy, get in there.'

Next morning I didn't bother getting there at four-thirty, five-thirty was early enough. A few men were standing around the yard, so I joined them. This time I got up the front. Not right up the front, otherwise the boss would look over the top of you from his stock-and-station agent's pulpit.

The first round of absentees came in and he started scanning. I eyeballed him. He saw me, paused, and then passed me over. What now? Too young? Maybe. No experience? He went inside, and when he came out he started scanning again. At the same time, Johnny walked past. He looked over, waved to me, eyeballed the boss and said, 'G'day, Dennis.' I waved back. Five minutes later I was picked. Redhead was there screaming and yelling. If I had to buy a ticket I'd be out of pocket after only a day's work. Through the gate and into the change room.

Johnny said, 'Good ta see ya. Good job this, if ya wanna stick at it.'

The foreman gave me a white vinyl apron, gumboots and a sharp knife. I was put on the sheep chain, cutting necks out of the carcasses as they went past. Johnny was on the chain at the other end of the room. You had to be quick or you missed them. It was a low-tally day and I got through to smoko.

I washed up and sat down. I didn't have any food for smoko; a few blokes in the locker rooms were passing around big bottles. They looked at me and pointed with the neck of the bottle. I shook my head. They weren't going to argue, no one wanted to give away their grog. A big wog came up, broke some bread, and with a knife sharper than the one I'd been using on the chain, cut some cabana for me. 'Eat fucken,' he said, and shoved the food into my hands. I said thanks and appreciated his kindness.

Then the Mauritian offered me some red peppers to go with it. I said I was right. Everyone laughed and said, 'Go on, Aussie boy, eat it, have a go.' The big wog said, 'Fucken hot, too hot for you, boy,' then started abusing the men in Italian, Croatian, Serbian, everything. They all threw their hands around and screamed at each other in a lively mood.

Back on the chain, the sheep were still warm when they got to me. A bloke three or four stations along was cutting their heads off. Then someone was cutting open their bodies, including their necks. From another station you'd hear the guts fall to the floor every ten seconds or so. I was cutting out a neck every eight to ten seconds. That might sound like a long time, but I felt under the pump just knowing the conveyor was determining the speed, not my ability. By the end of the day, my left hand was lacerated from missing the necks, slipping, and my general incompetence at knifework.

The shift finished about one p.m. Home time. I said to Johnny I only had a shearer's ticket, did that matter? He reckoned that was all right. If I became a regular I'd have to get a ticket.

'The main thing is, you're a unionist. Comin to the Tarmac for a drink?'

'Na, gotta keep lookin for work, you know how it is.'

'Don't worry, I got my old girl up the duff. Still drink the same, good job here, ya know. It'll all work out, don't worry. The wogs reckon you're all right. If you want a job, keep comin back and linin up. They reckon you're strong like a fucken bull.'

SKIN SHEDS

ON MY WAY home I drove around the western suburbs looking for more work, regular work. I called into the skin sheds to see if they were short a man. The foreman said to be on site before seven o'clock the next day. That meant a guaranteed day's work, not like at the meatworks.

'On the beef hides today, son,' he said in the morning. 'Go out the back, turn left and see this bloke with a cowboy hat on. He's a white blackfella. Won't say much. He's ya boss for the day.'

I found him and a couple of blokes squatting down having a cup of tea before they started work. I said g'day and nodded. They nodded back.

'What d'ya want me to do?'

The boss kept his head down and mumbled, 'Watch for a bit, then join in.'

The first truck arrived from the abattoir loaded with beef hides. Our job was to salt the hides and stack them for drying. The salt, a large granulated type, was sitting in mounds under a big open-sided shed. We would lay out the hide and with short-handled, square-mouth shovels throw salt over it and rub it in.

Then we'd stack them.

My left hand was cut to shreds from the previous day's work. The salt progressively ground into the cuts so that by mid-morning I could hardly hold the shovel. The initial sting was slowly replaced by a deep ache, then a throb. At lunchtime the boss gave me a clean rag and said, 'Wash it and wrap it.'

The lunch break didn't ease the pain. I was glad to get back to work; I wanted to get out of the place as quick as possible. I learned to use my knee for leverage to take the strain off my hand. At two-thirty we finished the last of the hides and I picked up my money from the front office. The foreman said, 'Boys reckon you did a good job, keep calling in. The bloke that's away today will be back tomorrow, but you never know who won't turn up.'

I thanked him for the day's work. Thirty-five bucks wasn't much, but I'd only worked until two-thirty. I'd worry about tomorrow tomorrow. It was drink time.

WOOL SCOURING

TWO MONTHS LEFT. I got up early and went to about ten factories: nothing. Things seemed tight today. It was Thursday, the worst day in the week to try to pick up work. No sweeping or cleaning needed doing. No one was short a man in a gang. Mondays and Fridays were the best days. Usually there was a man down somewhere.

I saw a little wool-scouring factory. I thought about not going in because it didn't look promising, then thought, One last place before I call it a day. No one was going to put anyone on after ten in the morning, they wouldn't get their pound of flesh. And if they were a man down the others would already be used to it, so they'd save a day's wages.

The boss said he had a vat that hadn't been cleaned in years. If I wanted a couple of days' work I could clean it. I said okay.

It was a small factory with only a few workers. A young bloke who'd learnt to use the scouring machine was the main worker on the site. He was fascinated that I was a shearer and wanted to know all about it. Over smoko and lunch I told him stories about different sheds.

The vat was a big wooden container that the wool was soaked in. I had to climb in and clean out the rotten wool. The first time I got in I vomited – it stunk so badly. I didn't know wool could go rotten. It was a combination of mould, mulch and chemical residue. I used a scraper and a bucket to get into the corners and under some of the platforms. I dry-retched all day. Covered in putrid shit, I thought, What the fuck am I doing this for? I wanted a regular job. I wished I was shearing. The money and the work were a lot better than this.

I was there four days. The young machine operator put a concrete-style drill straight through his elbow, removing a core of muscle. When he returned from the hospital he was in plaster, and would be off work for at least six weeks. He was beaming, he was so happy. I asked what was happening with his position while he recovered. The boss was wary of me: would I promise not to leave when shearing started again? I said I wouldn't. He looked at me suspiciously and said I was a nomad. Reckoned I'd get bored doing the same thing every day.

He was right. I didn't think I could cope with the smell or the repetition. It seemed that him using me was okay, but not the other way round.

Every day I went out around the industrialised areas of the western suburbs looking for work. Most days I found something. I'd do anything and I got anything – a day in the freezers, driving a truck, digging ditches, pipe laying, roller driving – whatever gave me enough money to get through to the end of the week. On the odd days I didn't get work I went home depressed. We were back living in Sonia's parents' granny flat. I enjoyed seeing Smokey when I came home. Sonia loved him too.

I didn't think past the day I was living. There was no point. I had to wait for tomorrow to come to see what would come with it.

JERILDERIE

MY FIRST SHED back was at Yanco Station in the Jerilderie district. On one side of Jerilderie were the smaller farmers and the irrigation systems. On the other side was the plains country of the outback.

We shook hands and loaded up. That was the swarm. Max, the cocky shearer/contractor, pulled his handpiece out of gear, pushed the sheep's head over so it wouldn't kick, straightened his own back and said, 'It's dermatitis. Don't worry, just get off what wool you can. They're drenched but I promised this fella I'd help him out last week, know what I mean? He didn't tell me they got wet. Thought he woulda shedded em early knowin we were coming. We got six runs of em if you don't mind doin em.'

I nodded but I must have looked a bit down. Travelling nearly three hundred kilometres to be confronted with virtually unshearable sheep. Broke and a baby due in four weeks.

'Why don't we get to smoko and we'll see how we feel, hey, what about that?'

'Yeah, no worries.'

'Now, watch that dermatitis, boy, the real hard bits are like rock. They'll lock up your handpiece and break your wrist. So be careful.'

We got to smoko and Max said, 'If ya don't wanta continue I can understand, cos they're pretty bad. But we got about six runs and we're out of here.'

In a big shed we wouldn't have shorn sheep this wet, and the union rep would have negotiated a better rate for the ones with dermatitis. But I'd done a lot worse lately than shear a few wet sheep. It was early July and the baby was due in August. Money was tight, but I'd do anything rather than go back to factory work.

That night I followed Max to his house on a little property. A bedroom at the back of the house became my room. He had six kids and a great wife who put on a huge feed. Max had the sort of life I wanted. He said there was a lot of shearing in the district. He'd shifted his house onto the property, it was cheap to do it like that.

I spent the next four weeks with Max cocky shearing. Every night we had a few big bottles to drink on the way home and a beautiful hot meal waiting for us once we got there. My favourite was rissoles and mashed potatoes with gravy, and ice cream and trifle. Smokey wasn't allowed in the house so he slept underneath it, below my bedroom. I rang Sonia every second night. She said everything was fine. The doctor thought she was about three weeks away. She said she was looking through the papers and there were some good jobs around at the moment. One of her dad's mates said he might be able to get me on in the refineries.

Max and I finished a shed at eleven o'clock and started the next at one o'clock. There were no breaks except for the weather. It was great. Cocky shearing was a lot more flexible than working for the big contractors.

We drove up onto a familiar property. I'd filled in for Jack's brother here a couple of years earlier. This time I shore twenty-eight the first run, compared to eleven two years ago. The sheep were good crossbred wethers, big, strong and straight. Max was holding thirty-eight to forty a run.

About eleven o'clock that night Sonia's mother rang. Sonia had gone to hospital. If I wanted to see the birth I'd better come. I drove through the night, stopping for short sleeps along the way.

Sonia was in heavy labour and pushing when I stepped into the ward. She had her hand out, I grabbed it and she squeezed tightly. When the contraction subsided I tried some oxygen, but the nurse said it was for the mother. I felt dizzy and had to sit down. Sonia looked exhausted and couldn't say much. She smiled and I kissed her.

I felt like an intruder in the labour ward with the doctors and nurses coming and going. I couldn't breathe properly with all the disinfectant and ammonia smells and I didn't know what to say when people spoke to me. I needed to smell some sheep shit to feel comfortable. The air conditioning was making me sweat.

The nurse called for the doctor over the phone. That's how I knew the baby was coming. By the time the doctor arrived, all that was left for him to do was sign the papers. I watched as the head then one shoulder came out, then the other shoulder as the nurse manipulated the baby. Then, like a poddy calf being born, a beautiful pink baby girl slipped out.

Sonia insisted I hold her but I was too scared I'd drop her. Eventually I did take her, and left the room walking on air. I thought my life would never be the same. It wasn't.

IVANHOE

LONNIE WAS ONE week old when I left again. I didn't want to leave. Everyone was there looking at the baby. Mr McHugh had put the barbecue on and family and friends were spontaneously coming over. I was so proud of Lonnie.

It was a long slow drive to the shed. I felt like turning back several times. That Sunday night I went to bed in a bare hut without electricity, phones or running water on the outskirts of Ivanhoe in central New South Wales, about thirty k's past Booligal Station. At least I had Smokey. I always had Smokey.

The owner was a young farmer who was trying to make a go of it away from his father's property. The other shearer wouldn't talk to me. The sheep were small hoggets caked in red dust. Once I had a sheep on the long blow, I had to change the cutter, otherwise I had to screw the tension nut down too hard and burned my comb. I shore twenty-eight the first run and used forty cutters and ten combs. I'd have no tools left at this rate. I wanted more money than we were getting here but our tucker was thrown in so I accepted that. The farmer's wife cooked for us and we ate in the family home. He'd bought a dustbowl and he and his young wife looked frayed.

I battled my brain to stay there. Every run I wanted to snatch it and go home. I'd never been homesick like this before. The cocky wanted me to get more wool off the sheep and I wanted him to stop grinding my tools so severely.

Other shearers came to fill the spare pens. They'd put the day in then say they had other commitments. An Aboriginal shearer who was a local gun footballer stayed for a few days. He was tall and had an agile, nimble body. Most shearers' bodies became rigid and the older they got, the more crippled they became. Football and shearing didn't mix.

Spectacular sunrises broke the isolation of those nights in the blacked-out hut. It was almost springtime. The sun was mild when it first came up and it put a soft orange tinge on the bush. You could hear the birds, the rustle of bushes, but mostly you could feel the stillness, the silence. This could have been all there was in the world fifty thousand years ago. Then I went to the shed.

The cocky used Smokey in the shed and offered to buy him. He was worth a man's wages to a cocky. He could get away back and bring the sheep in through a gate since he was a pup. I wouldn't sell him for any amount of money. The cocky did say he was frisky, reckoned he had a go at him, but he liked that spirit in a dog.

The last run on the Friday night of the second week, he told me there was only a day's work for two men left on the Monday. With the other shearer going into town for the weekend, I'd be left on my own here. Did I want to finish up at the end of the run? I said yes and was on my way home by six o'clock that evening.

BOLAC PLAINS STATION

LONNIE, NEARLY ONE month old, slept most of the night. I loved it most when we all slept together. I drove to Bolac Plains on Monday morning and went straight to breakfast. I had my dungarees on and I could organise my hut after work. That way I could stay in bed longer with Sonia and Lonnie.

Haveachat walked into the mess when I was having breakfast. When he saw me he smiled, turned straight back to the flywire door that was still flapping, and yelled out, 'Ay Viking, the boy's here. He's back.' Then he started laughing. 'Where you been, boy? Thought we lost ya.'

Viking walked in right when I had a gob full of sausage, toast and spaghetti. 'He's a mean-looking hogget, isn't he boys? The way he's gouging inta that tucker. How are ya, boy?' he asked me. 'We lose a lotta boys, ya know. See em for a season or two and that's it, don't always see em again.'

I was still trying to eat the food I had in my mouth. I nodded to everyone. I was pleased to see them. Glad to be back in good country, closer to home and with my old team. Life was shaping in my favour. I reckoned I'd get around a hundred and thirty a day in these sheep. These blokes knew me as their rousie and they'd been part of my transformation. At the last shed I'd been homesick, hated the cocky, and the sheep were crap. In the space of a couple of days everything had turned around.

Bolac Plains Station was a green, picturesque property, the exact opposite of the outback. Draphine was the boss, Greeny was the presser, the rousie was a kid from Creswick. Viking was carting the kid around, he'd got into a bit of trouble with the police. Now he was spending his week picking up for us. Good kid with a pretend chip on his shoulder.

Draphine saw me walking across the yard, stopped, stared, stooped, squeezed his beady little eyes and said, 'How are ya, boy?'

'Good, Draph, how's the ute? Still lookin spick and span, ay? And how ya been?'

'All right, all right, boy, go on, get going then. Pick ya pens. Wanna be outa here in thirteen days.' Out of the side of his mouth he said, 'And no fucken wet sheep neither.'

He always had to be a nark. He liked it like that.

We drew for pens at the swarm. Charles drew the first pen and the union rep's job. He was in his mid-fifties, a hard bastard and an ex-drunk with more wrinkles in his face than a Riverina merino. He'd get forty a run. I was in two, I hoped to get thirty-five a run. I was getting faster. One thing about shearing up around the Riverina, I appreciated the sheep down the Western District of Victoria more.

Haveachat was in three and he'd get his forty-five a run. Viking was in four, on 49-plus. He was getting older and his eyes were puffy from drinking but he hadn't slowed down. In five was Bloodshot. He smiled and nodded said, 'How are you, Dennis?' I couldn't believe it. He spoke to me.

I nodded. 'Good, thanks.' He seemed to be back on track. Last time I saw him, at Lal Lal, he looked like he was almost gone. And the rumours about his marriage weren't good.

In six was Gerry from Skipton who'd been the team's learner three seasons before me. He had the best hut. He had heaters, air conditioners, a portable fridge, telly and radio. He liked the comforts of home. He wasn't a fast shearer and was a bit disappointed in himself. Reckoned I'd go past him by next season. He was getting thirty-six, thirty-seven a run. His blows didn't flow when he shore. You needed rhythm in your shearing, like Viking had.

The boys were proud of Gerry's big cock and so was he. The ongoing discussion was about his girlfriend. He had himself convinced she was seeing someone else behind his back. I was a bit confused. If his cock was a chick magnet why was she seeing someone else? Haveachat knew her, reckoned she was beautiful, smart and really loved him, wanted to marry him. No one could convince Gerry, so he dumped her.

The wool here was soft and the sheep smallish – a bit cranky, though. I had the first one out in three minutes and ten seconds, just under the forty-a-run speed. Viking yelled out, 'Look out, Dennis's on the loose.' A few roughies and a bomb from Draphine slowed me up.

Conversation among the blokes stopped. It didn't matter what happened in life, work took over. Maybe that was a good thing.

Draphine came up to me. I thought, Here we go, he's going to bomb me. He said, 'Ya dog's loose, boy. Rounded up all the sheep we let go, brought em back to the yard. I'll use him a bit if ya like, take a bit of the sting outa him. He needs the guts worked out of him, otherwise he'll be trouble.'

'Yeah, thanks Draph.'

The next day Charles, shearing in one, pulled up. Knelt down on one knee and had his other leg up, leaning his forearms on it. Said, 'Now listen, boy, just on that dog of yours. There've been a coupla complaints about it barkin and all at night. It's my duty as rep to tell ya that dogs have to be a certain distance from the huts. Don't worry, there's a nark in every team. But ya have ta follow the rules, boy. And your dog's tried to bite a couple of station hands as well. No one's complained about that yet, so watch him, ay.'

'Yeah, yeah, I will. Thanks Charlie. I'll take care of him.'

Something was up with Smokey. I didn't know what it was. He'd had a go at the cocky at Ivanhoe too.

At smoko Haveachat asked on behalf of the boys what happened with my girlfriend.

'I got married and she had a little girl.'

Gerry said, 'So you're a mongrel little daddy. A fricken little daddy. I'd shit meself and I'm nearly twenty-five. How old are ya now?'

'I'll be twenty soon.' I didn't say much. I didn't want another attack like Barnesy had given me at Lal Lal last year.

'What are ya gunna do now?' Gerry asked

'I was thinking of finding a place where there's a lot of shearing and settling down there. Even somewhere like Skipton would be all right. How much shearin is there around Skipton?'

'Heaps, but I come from Skipton and I can't break in. Can't get any sheds meself, that's why I'm out here. It's all sewn up, you know.'

Sonia and I had been thinking of getting a van and travelling around Australia shearing. Gerry said his sister had a caravan for sale. I went out and had a look at it and bought it. The next week I brought Sonia and Lonnie out and we had a week in the van on the property. Sonia and Lonnie never left the caravan, it was so cold. Lonnie was good for most of it but started to cry with a bit of colic. The boys said they never even got to see what she looked like. I was too scared I was going to cop ridicule from them so we kept to ourselves, but I didn't like the feeling of having my family in a caravan at a shearing shed. At the end of the week I took them home and went back on my own. It was a good experiment but I wouldn't do it again.

The shed took sixteen working days to complete. We had a few wet days, which put us a bit behind. We shore about thirteen and a half thousand sheep at Bolac Plains. The team averaged about a thousand a day, I averaged thirty-four a run.

Sonia and I were in love with Lonnie. Leaving them and a warm bed on a Sunday night for a bed in a bare hut was a bit of a comedown. But I was only two or three hours away from home, which wasn't too bad. I was really happy, happier than I ever thought I could be. I was a shearer. I could get a hundred and forty sheep a day and I was only in my second season. I had my own family. And I could see it now – a bush town and a bush block to raise our kids. I'd be a local shearer and then get my own contractor base and we would have a great life. I thought, I'm close, real close.

BARUNAH PLAINS AGAIN

BARUNAH PLAINS WAS a good money shed. All the team were there – Viking, Haveachat, Captain Ahab. Draphine was overseeing and Gannon was wool rolling. He still wasn't a classer. Even old Russell the owner wasn't the ogre I thought he was. He still walked up and down with his riding whip and his riding boots. It must have taken him half an hour to get dressed just to impress us.

Draphine reckoned I was rough with the sheep. He told me to slow down and shear them properly instead of worrying about how much money I was making. I was shearing about thirty-two a run in the wethers and about thirty-six in the ewes. My mind wasn't on money, though, it was on Lonnie and Sonia.

I left for the shed as late as I could on a Monday morning, went home Wednesday nights, and was first out the gate Fridays. I couldn't stay away from my family. Sonia would wait up for me on Wednesdays and we'd put little Lonnie in the bed between us and go to sleep. It was fantastic. I didn't want to go to work, I just wanted us to be together. But at four-thirty I'd get up, Sonia would make me breakfast and a cup of tea, and I'd head off.

Close to the shed, I'd be driving into the rising sun. I'd want to shut my eyes for a couple of seconds and break the sleepiness. My eyelids were like lead weights. Once, I woke up because of the gravel noise from my tyres: I was heading straight for a gum tree. I wound down the window, turned up the radio and had another smoke. I'd get to the shed about six-thirty and have another breakfast.

Some nights I'd be in my hut and say to myself, I could be home under two hours if I left now, and so at nine or ten o'clock on a Tuesday or Thursday night I'd leave for home. I didn't want to be in the sheds.

When a shearing contractor in Werribee offered me a pen at his depot shed, I told Grazcos I wasn't going on with them after this one and the boss came out from Melbourne and spoke to me. He pointed out that Grazcos had given me a learner's pen after only one season, and given me all the off-season work as a rousie. Now, when other shearers were set in their runs in the busy part of the season and it was hard to get shearers, they wanted some loyalty from me in return. I agreed, and rejected the contractor's offer, partly because I didn't want to live in Werribee.

Draphine laughed. 'You're not going anywhere, boy.'

But I wasn't a boy any more.

TITANGA STATION

SONIA WAS LOOKING forward to getting away from the family. She said my mother claimed her mother was getting all the time with the baby. Sonia told her that her mum worked all day and didn't get home till six in the evening.

Schultz was cooking at Titanga Station and he looked fantastic. I'd last seen him at Gunbar, in the horrors. He told me his drinking had got worse after Gunbar. He went out to the meat house at another shed, picked up a bottle and sculled it – it was sheep dip. Nearly killed him. He hadn't had a drink since. He'd bought a flat in Williamstown and only went cooking in sheds in the second half of the year now. Never did the hot runs any more. Now that he didn't drink, he didn't need as much money as he had in the past. He travelled a bit in summer, went on the dole, or got another job for a while.

Titanga was an eight-stand shed on a property out of Lismore, off the Hamilton Highway. Springtime in the Western District of Victoria was full of rainbows, undulating plains and plantations. The well-grassed paddocks and rich soil allowed for a high number of sheep to the acre. The bluestone shed was heritage-listed, built by convict labour. The huts weren't. They were made of corrugated iron and furnished with a bed and a side table.

Apart from that, the squatter was a fair man. He always tried to keep the shed full and the sheep dry. He stayed out of the way of the shearers and respected our space. I liked cockies like that. They had their lives and we had ours.

The swarm was late starting. Men were slow to get out of bed and others were late turning up on the property. Draphine was a bit jumpy. He grabbed me, said, 'Get em going, boy. We wanna be outa here in fifteen days. Get em movin, will ya. And give us ya dog. He can help down the shed for a while this morning.'

In pen one was Charles's son. Twenty-four, a bit lazy. Had hair down to his back – spent a lot of time looking after it. He'd get thirty a run in these sheep. Bernie Bourke was in two, he looked good. He'd shear his forty-seven. It was good to see Bernie again. I reckoned he would catch Viking this season. I drew three. I was aiming at thirty-five a run. Good money. I was saving now as well. In the fourth pen was Eddy, who took the rep's job. All he talked about was the Kiwis and the wide combs. He'd shear thirty-seven a run, but he'd rather a fight than work any day.

The shed was built with four stands on one side facing four stands on the other. The bales for locks and belly wool were sunk into the floor in the middle of the board. On the other side of the board to me, in five, was Charles. He'd hold his forty a run in these sheep, he was on fire at the moment. In six was Haveachat. He looked good and he seemed happy, though he wasn't quite the same without his comrade Viking, who'd gone to a shed near Mount Elephant. In seven was Gerry from Skipton. He would hold his thirty-five a run. I reckoned I could get him at this shed. In eight was Brian, a left-handed learner from Rushworth. He'd been the rousie last year. He was very particular and methodical.

He was getting his twenty-two to twenty-three a run. He was good, he had sheep shit on the brain. I knew how he felt.

The shed went smoothly for a while. I was getting my thirty-five a run. I started planning during smoko how I could get faster. I thought, One complete blow around the crutch, rather than doing it in two halves. Turn the sheep around ready for the long blow while shearing the neck and taking off the top notch. Keep yourself in perpetual motion – like Viking does, always moving around the sheep. Keep the sheep calm and well positioned.

If I did all these things, I thought, I should be able to catch Gerry. I didn't.

Lunchtime was a long walk to the mess from the shed; most of the guys jumped on the back of a ute. I reloaded my handpiece and walked, trying to stretch my aching legs. Lunch was a banquet with Schultz – he even had trifle and ice cream for sweets. I ate the roast with the crispy baked potatoes and headed straight back to the shed for a lie down. My stomach was bloated. I wrapped my towel up and stuck it under my head. I was out to it, until the noise of the men back in the shed preparing for the next run woke me up.

While Haveachat was looking through the tally book he said, 'How'd ya go, boy? He got ya for a couple, ay.'

Gerry laughed. 'He's right up me arse.'

Bernie Bourke said, 'Ya shearing more than I did in my second season.'

Haveachat smiled. 'Yeah, ya come on well, boy. You better watch out, Gerry, he'll get you soon enough.'

'He's nearly got me now.'

The boys joked around but Gerry was confident he could beat me. He played it down because he was in front. I'd challenged him, now I had to stick with it for the rest of the shed or they'd say I had no heart. Gerry outshore me that shed, but chasing him helped keep my tallies up so I got a good cut-out cheque.

Our little war was a good diversion from the other subtle competition going on in the shed. Haveachat had Bernie Bourke in his sights. Bernie Bourke was gettable in good sheep and good conditions. He was untouchable in tough conditions and wrinkly sheep.

At night Gerry's room was the drinking hut. He had a fridge and a heater – cold beer and a warm room. The evenings were mild early then turned cold quickly. The sunsets were usually wild, with ever-changing variations in the clouds. Eddy, as union rep, got around like an ambassador, checking on everybody. He came and sat on the steps out the front of my hut for a chat and said in a quiet, calming voice, 'Ya dog's causing some problems.'

'What's wrong now? Draph's had im workin, reckons he's doin a good job. He reckons Smokey's got a big future.'

'Some of the men have complained about him.'

'Who?'

'Doesn't matter, the point is he's bitten a couple a people. Including one of the kids helping out.'

'Well, they shouldn't tease him and stir him up. It's not his fault.'

'Draphine reckons there's something wrong with him. Something you can't fix.'

'It's just a phase he's going through, he'll get over it.'

Draphine came along. I thought, Here we go, this is a set-up.

'Draph,' Eddy called out. 'What was that thing you said was wrong with the pup?'

'Distemper,' Draphine yelled back. 'I reckon he's got distemper. You might have to put him down, boy. You had him at Greystones, didn't ya?'

'Yeah.'

'Did you get his shots?'

'What shots?'

'Greystones's got distemper in the ground, boy. Ya can't get rid of it once it's in the ground. Now your pup's got it, nuthin you can do. Sorry, boy. I'll put him down for ya if ya like.'

Eddy and Draph nodded and walked off to the mess together. I grabbed Smokey and rubbed his ears, he loved that. I scratched his body hard. He looked up at me with his beautiful black eyes. Smokey could stare you right in the eye. Then he started licking my knee.

No one was putting my dog down. He was the best friend I'd ever had. I thought, He'll come good, be all right. I wasn't putting him down, that was for sure.

That night I went into town to ring Sonia. I missed her and Lonnie and this shed was too far for a midweek trip. I rang on the public phone outside the post office in Cressy. Lonnie had started crying a lot, screaming sometimes. The doctors were sure it was just colic. Sonia, being a new mum, was still getting on top of things. The spring wind blew the rain into the open booth in gusts. I wanted to talk about Smokey but Lonnie was screaming again and Sonia had to go.

We were at Titanga fourteen working days and the team shore around fifteen and a half thousand sheep. We had a few wet days and short Fridays but I got my thirty-five a run, a hundred and forty a day. Schultz was cheap as well as a good cook, but tax was five hundred dollars. I hated tax. That left me with thirteen hundred dollars for the shed. On my own I could live a long time on the cheap with that money, but it wouldn't go so far now I was married.

Eddy called a swarm. He said there was a stop-work meeting at the Mechanics Hall in Inverleigh next week about our claim for a pay rise and our ongoing battle over the Kiwis and their wide combs. Everyone was expected to be there, a show of solidarity. Fraser wanted to break our solidarity. I didn't want to have a break from shearing. I wanted to keep making money.

Draphine came up on the last day and said, 'If there's no strike, go to Devon Park out of Dunkeld next week, boy, and this one's royalty.'

THE STRIKE

DUE TO SHEARERS being spread all over the state, the union held meetings in various districts throughout Victoria. The votes for and against from each meeting were sent to the head office and compiled for a statewide result. Three hundred and twenty-seven men met in Inverleigh to discuss the dispute. The union had applied to the arbitration commission for increased allowances. Only about half a shearer's wages came from shearing, the rest was made up of allowances for things like travelling and tools.

Viking, Haveachat, Captain Ahab, Gerry and his brother-in-law were there. Haveachat was talking about our last real pay rise. The story went that in 1974, when we'd been trying to go from $32 per hundred sheep to $45, Justice Mary Gaudron took the court out to a shed so they could witness the men shearing. We won the fight and things changed. Haveachat reckoned Gaudron was the shearer's hero.

This dispute, over incremental rises in our allowances, had started in New South Wales, but it was more than a wage dispute. It was about showing Fraser and the graziers that we had balls. We were under pressure from the invading Kiwis and we wanted their tax loophole closed, to make it fairer on everyone.

In Inverleigh we voted to go on strike indefinitely, and the votes coming in from around the state echoed our decision. We wanted to put as much pressure on as possible. But the Inverleigh vote was not unanimous and the dissention among the men left us feeling a little vulnerable, so we agreed to meet again in two weeks.

I liked the idea of going on strike. I didn't like the idea of blowing a season of savings. Feeding a family, trying to get ahead of the bills – it was hard. The way we voted was to split the room: non-strikers on one side and strikers on the other. It was confronting. Nobody wanted to be identified as being on the graziers' side.

At the second meeting a fortnight later, the contractors made their presence felt by sitting alongside their men. Cranky Eddy put up a motion to ban the contractors from being at the meeting, citing conflict of interest. The union said that since the contractors were also shearers and had tickets, they were entitled to be there and vote. The union officials at this meeting wore suits. Mum always said never trust a bloke in a suit, you never knew whose side they were on or when they'd pull the pin.

This time the Inverleigh men voted to go back to work. The vote was 326 for, one against. The stronger members weren't at this meeting, they'd gone down to bolster the Casterton/Hamilton meeting. And instead of dividing the room, there'd been a show of hands. This was far less confronting, a strategy to defeat the strike and get us back to work.

Despite the one-sided vote at Inverleigh, the statewide decision came down to a few votes and we were only narrowly defeated. Inverleigh had fallen to the right and we went back to work. The organisers said it was in our best interests to go back while negotiations went on, but we thought otherwise. With pressure from wives to return to work, mortgages, and Christmas just around the corner, the blokes buckled.

The conversation outside after the meeting turned to the Labor Party and its chances of getting into office. If we had Labor in power we wouldn't have to be fighting all the time. Viking claimed Bill Hayden wasn't good enough to get the Labor Party elected. He said we needed someone like Hawke as prime minister. Haveachat didn't agree, he was for Bill Hayden. He reckoned Hayden's last budget as treasurer was so good, that was the reason the Liberals blocked Supply. The Liberals knew they'd be in opposition for ever. He said Hayden could do the job if he won the election.

I headed home and packed my gear. Sonia was happy I was back at work. Grazcos rang and said Devon Park on Monday. I was glad to be working too but I had a bad feeling about the strike. I didn't think we were as strong as we sounded. We had some strong voices in the union but we were soft underneath. It was hard to be militant when you had no money.

DEVON PARK STATION

DEVON PARK STATION was the last shed for 1978. I arrived too late for tea and too early for bed. The kitchen light was on, so I went looking for Graham to see if I could get a bone for Smokey. Graham seemed pleased to see me, not so pleased to see my dog.

He'd got there a bit after three. 'I always come early, you never know how bad a condition the mess and stove are in at some of these places.' Squatters, Graham reckoned, hated spending a cent on shearers' huts. The wealthier the grazier, the stingier they were. 'Because I come early and all, I've seen them clearing out the huts the day before shearing starts. They'll put anything in them – grain, chemicals, spray guns, even seen a heap of tractor parts in a hut once. They just give them a quick sweep-out the night before. Mice and rat shit everywhere, sheep dip and grease stains on the floor. Then we got to fucken sleep in em.'

Devon Park was about ten kilometres out of Dunkeld in the Western District. Beautiful lush country, and when the wind blew, the grass rippled like a sea of green waves. The driveways were lined with poplars and there was a sprinkling of native trees across the paddocks. The weatherboard shearing huts faced the Grampians, giving a spectacular view in the evenings.

The owners belonged to the blue-blood squattocracy and lived on an estate a few kilometres away, out of site of the men's quarters.

The next morning at the swarm, Harold nominated unopposed for union rep. I didn't think I'd see him again after he collapsed at Ulonga, but he'd recovered and had been shearing for a couple of months during the busy part of the season. The boys didn't say much at the swarm. Everybody wanted to make some money and get home for Christmas. Despite the uncertainty around our work, the first thing Harold said to me as we left the swarm was that there was to be no dogs in the huts. He looked at me. 'You know the rules, follow em.'

He didn't have to be such an arse. But it seemed the men's tolerance for Smokey was gone. He wasn't a pup any more.

On the way out Lewis, who I'd last seen at Gunbar Station, pointed his finger at me and said, 'If your dog barks fucken once I'm shootin it. You've been warned.' With that he turned and walked up to the shed.

I was too scared to argue with him. I knew he'd do it. Lewis hadn't mellowed at all since Gunbar. He wasn't a big bloke but his reputation was. He was one of the strongest men in the sheds and he could snap at anytime. And he was worse on the drink.

Smokey sneaking onto my bed at night was the last thing I'd remember before falling asleep. And I always knew when he got off – that was time to get up. He was my alarm before the alarm. He was part of my family.

Draphine still took Smokey out to work in the yards. If he barked around the huts during the day the cook went ballistic. Graham was a good bloke but he didn't have much tolerance. Things seemed good though until Draphine came in during a run and pulled me up. He put his hand on my shoulder as I was going into the pen for another sheep.

'What's wrong, Draph?'

'Smokey's bitten a couple of the contract musterers and a visitor.'

'Well, they shouldn't stir him up and that. It's not his fault.'

'You'll have to shoot him.'

'I'm not shooting Smokey.'

Draphine started on me. 'Well, you know I reckon he's got distemper. That's why he bites. The brown stain on his teeth, it's distemper. The squatter reckons the same. The dog's survived somehow but he turns on people, goes a bit mad, and you can't pick it. If your dog's got distemper there's nothing you can do.' Draph shook his head. 'I'll put him down. Sorry, son. Really am. Good dog and all, been a good companion for ya.'

'No one's putting my dog down. He'll come good, Draph. He'll be all right. I'm not puttin him down.'

I put Smokey in the car where he was safe and went back to work, apologising, saying that it wouldn't happen again. They left me alone but it was an uneasy truce. One more problem and he was gone. Or I was.

At the end of the third run, late in the first week, the team had settled and there was a fierce battle between Bernie Bourke and Viking to ring the shed. Harold was in one and shearing about twenty-five a run. Morgan in two was holding thirty-five. Havea-chat in three and the Captain in four were holding forty-five a run. In five was Lewis, he was holding forty-eight. Bernie Bourke in six was holding fifty-one, fifty-two, Viking in seven was holding the same and I was getting about thirty a run.

I was Viking's penmate. I pulled an old cracker ewe out before the bell rang for smoko. My back was killing me and my comb and cutter were blunt. I screwed the tension nut down to push one more sheep out before smoko. I rushed the first blow and cut her from brisket to crutch. I didn't even realise I'd got the end tooth of the comb under her skin.

Viking glanced across a couple of times. 'Sew it up, boy. Shut the cocky up.'

It wasn't a deep cut but it looked worse than it was. The squatter came along and started helping. He was wearing his moleskins and a flash shirt. He smelt of aftershave. I smelt of lanolin and sheep shit. My flannel was dirty and my dungarees were drenched in wool grease. I hadn't noticed how much I smelt until he came near me. I started stitching the old ewe but I was running out of cotton.

Viking yelled at me, 'Your stitches are too close.'

By that time I'd put about thirty stitches into the belly; now I was covered in blood to go with the sheep shit and lanoline. To break the tension, the squatter yelled out to Viking that there were only seven stitches in a wheat bag. The team laughed and the squatter laughed, but his lips remained tight and his face was strained. I had to stay behind during smoko and finish.

I wasn't happy. I only sewed the cut to shut the squatter up. He might have laughed but he wasn't happy either. And the team had been laughing at him trying to fit in with us, using one of our sayings with his plum-in-the-mouth voice. He was trying to put me down with a joke because he wasn't allowed to bomb me. He had to go through the overseer if he wanted to complain. Even though it was his shed, his sheep, his farm and his money, it was my pen. My stand. My job. And the squatter hated that. He would have liked to shoot my dog as well, so we weren't friends.

The squatter was mainly talking to the old ewe, pacifying her. I didn't know what to say to him. I couldn't even look at him. I wanted to say something that sounded smart. I guess I wanted to impress him, or for him to like me, so to break the tension I laughed and said, 'It's only an old cracker ewe anyway.'

He didn't laugh at that. He mumbled something under his breath.

I was sweating, exhausted, and my back ached. I was shaking

from holding down the fretting sheep. I realised the squatter wasn't really helping me. He was protecting his sheep, his property. The sheep meant more to him than I did. Then his smell, his clothes, his resentful look, the way he ignored me, made my skin crawl. I wanted to smash his tanned face with my handpiece. The way he held the sheep made the sheep fight more. He was useless, a private-college boy. I figured he'd never even worked on his own property before. I wanted him away from me. I wished I was on strike right now.

I eventually sewed the old ewe up and shore out the last run in silence. The weekend was one day away.

Draphine rang the bell for the start of the last run on Friday, then he and Harold came over to my stand. Harold said a decision had been made about Smokey. 'He's gotta go.'

'But he's been sleeping in my hut at night and in the car during the day. I've done everything you asked.'

Harold stared at me. 'Turn it up. He barks all day, never fucken stops. The cook's threatened to snatch it. Ya pup's drivin him crazy. You were told. And you know the rule, no dogs in the huts. You either shoot him or pack your swag. We don't want to see you go, we know you need the money this close to Christmas, especially coming off a strike, but we've had enough.'

Draphine started after Harold finished. 'If Lewis doesn't shoot him someone else will.' He put his hand on my shoulder and turned me into him and said softly, 'I'll shoot him for you. It's better that way.'

'No.' I couldn't stand the thought of anyone else shooting my dog.

After work Smokey looked up at me. He knew he was in trouble. His tail was down, his ears back. He'd gone too far this time. I'd told Draphine I'd keep him tied up, out of sight from the huts. I couldn't afford to miss this work, not with my commitments.

Draphine relented. 'Keep him right away from the shed and the men and don't bring him back, understand?'

I'd survived and Smokey had just survived. But I couldn't bring him back to these sheds. I went into town and rang Sonia. I needed to hear her voice and tell her what was going on. She immediately started talking about Lonnie. The doctors said she had colic from gulping her milk and not being burped properly. Sonia thought the doctors were treating her as if she didn't know what to do with her baby. Lonnie was screaming like she'd been stabbed and Sonia couldn't pacify her any more. She had to hang up the phone before I got a chance to talk.

I'd tied Smokey to a big gum tree and used a hubcap as a water bowl. After ringing Sonia I sat with my back to the tree for a while. Smokey crawled onto my lap and laid his head down, looking up at me sheepishly. He gave a whimper and settled in and we sat there and watched the moon.

Viking and Bernie Bourke went blow for blow for the whole shed and in the end there was one sheep in it. Viking held off Bernie but his time as the gun was coming to an end, someone would beat him soon. I was glad Viking won. I didn't want to see him beaten, even though I liked Bernie Bourke.

The team shore about thirteen thousand sheep over twelve days at Devon Park. At the cut-out Draphine told me to report to the Bourke office in New South Wales. 'And it's fucken hot up there, boy,' he said.

It was Christmas. I'd earned good money this season. I'd bought a caravan instead of a house. A house was a noose around your neck that the boss could hang you with.

BOURKE

ROWS OF SQUARE fibrocement houses with industrial air conditioners lined the red-gravelled backstreets. Tucked behind a tyre factory and edged on the Darling River was the caravan park. It was four days after Christmas and we'd driven for three days in 45-degree heat with a crying baby and no air conditioning. We were pulling a 27-foot van behind my HG161 with a reconditioned radiator.

This was one of the biggest shearing districts in Australia and there was so much work my shed was starting on the second of January. The morning after we arrived, Lonnie's knees were pulled up tight into her belly. Her stomach was hard. Her body was red from the heat and screaming. Her lips were tight, bloodless with pain. Periodically there was a cycle when no sound came for a couple of seconds. Smokey had crawled into the annex next to her bed, his ears flopped forward and his eyes drooping. He sat looking up at the bed while Sonia fanned Lonnie and replaced the face washers on her belly and legs.

She said, 'Maybe it's just the heat.'

'Or the car trip is still unsettling her.'

'No, she loves the car. She slept half the way here. Do you want to take her for another drive, do you think that would help?'

'Na, it'd be 60 degrees in the car now. I'll go and get her script.' I'd dropped off a script from our doctor at the chemist. He said he needed a couple of hours to fill it.

When I got back there he still hadn't filled it. He couldn't read the writing. I had to go back to the caravan, get the doctor's details and surgery address from Sonia, and take them back to the chemist. He said he'd ring the doctor and find out what the script was for.

I went back again late in the day – he hadn't been able to contact the doctor. Fuck. How hard could it be to fill a script? The chemist in Werribee did it every week and all of a sudden it was a major issue. The chemist said to call in the morning and he'd have it ready for me.

Back at the van we got the pusher out and went for a walk. It was a little cooler in the evening, not much. Lonnie had moments of quiet and settled a little. When we got back we put her to bed and she slept. The problem wasn't solved: in the middle of the night she started crying again. Sonia insisted on nursing her. I passed her dummies, bottles, face washers. Someone in another van yelled, 'Fuck off,' but the rest of the park, which was full of meatworkers, shearers and contract railwaymen, were patient. Fatigue seemed to beat the pain in the end.

The next morning I went straight to the chemist. It was shut until ten-thirty. Two hours to kill. We took Lonnie for another walk. She was a bit better in the pusher, but it wasn't long before the crying started again.

When the chemist saw me at ten-thirty he ducked behind a partition. I told the attendant I was there to collect a script. The chemist came out trying to read a bottle of pills, glanced up, eyes darting, and said, 'Give me twenty minutes, will you? Thanks.'

I had no confidence in him but I was desperate to stop Lonnie's crying. I waited outside. I looked through the window and the chemist came out from behind the petition and gave me a nod. It was ready. I went in, collected it and paid. Walking out I said how pleased I was to finally have the medication. I said, 'The baby's been crying for a couple of days now.'

'Baby? It's for a baby? I thought it was for you.' He charged around the counter and snatched the prescription off me. 'Come back this afternoon.' And with that he disappeared behind the partition again.

Lonnie improved during the day and we went for a swim. The other shearers were getting dropped off at a bridge about six kilometres away and floating down the Darling River in tractor inner-tubes to the caravan park. Sonia and I took it in turns to look after Lonnie and have a go on the tubes. By late afternoon Lonnie had started crying again and I went back to the chemist.

In the caravan with the medicine at last, Sonia opened the bottle. By this time Lonnie's screaming was as intense as it had been the other night. Knees up, lips bloodless, body red, stomach hard. Her crying was quivering. She was a few days short of five months old. Sonia poured some medicine onto a teaspoon and stopped. Something was wrong. 'What?'

'It's not her usual medicine.'

Lonnie was lying in front of us buckling in pain. It was dusk, but still 43 degrees. We decided to give her half the dosage. We lifted her head and poured the medicine in. Put her down.

She stopped crying. Then started shaking, quivering. Her eyes were turning in. Sonia grabbed her and squeezed her. They weren't big fits, small really. They went on for twenty minutes, her arms wavering in and out, and her little body vibrating.

WARATAH STATION

WE HEADED OVER to the shed about eight-thirty in the morning. The heat from the red sand seeped through my boots, burning my feet. I put my towel over my head to stop the weight of the sun. Roos and emus were scattered through the distant paddocks. A young contract musterer on a motorbike was barely visible in the dust; he had a hankie tied around his mouth and was slowly bringing in another mob. The tin shearing shed was like an oven.

In the first pen was Alex, a South Australian in his mid-thirties. He had some type of zoo or farm with exotic animals. The drought must have hit him hard. In the second pen was Fitzroy Bobby, named after the Melbourne suburb where he grew up. He was twenty-two and had been shearing about the same time as me – learnt to shear around Longreach. He'd had a job in a factory and shot through.

I was in three. In four was Danny Khan from Byrock. He was a good bloke, a descendant of Afghan camel drivers. He also had the mail run in the area. In five was Larry from Nyngan. He was old, had been knocked around by the grog and the sheds. In six was Nigel from Bomaderry, on the coast, looking more like a surfie than a shearer.

The expert/overseer was also the wool classer. Paddy from Hughenden was the cook. His brother-in-law, a wool roller, was travelling with him. They had owned a restaurant. Think they drank it.

The bell rang and we were into it. The sheep were black, covered in burrs as hard as tintacks. The first blow down the belly, the burrs tore into my hand. Every place I opened up a sheep – the belly, the first leg, the neck – the burrs tore the flesh off my hands and arms. Then the lanolin got into the open wounds and stung like fuck.

After lunch it was 47 degrees, and that was the town temperature. In the corrugated-iron shed, surrounded by hot sheep, we reckoned it was at least 60 degrees. The first few runs I shore the whole two hours. During the third run, Larry stared at me and shook his head. 'Ya got all year to go, boy, don't haveta burn yaself out in this heat. Keep the noise down in the break – give us a fucken break too, ay.'

I wanted to keep busy. My mind wanted to sleep, my hands and arms were stinging, and my muscles had no energy. I'd drunk two waterbags by lunchtime and it was washing me out. I'd added some Staminade, trying to put some salt back into my body.

When the day finally ended we hit the showers. The water, even in the cold taps, was boiling. The cocky hadn't bothered to dig the pipes into the ground. The showers were in a small tin hut that had cooked in the sun – it was so hot you couldn't touch the tin – and with the boiling water running it was worse than a sauna.

I'd been dreaming about a shower all day. There was a slight draught through the louvre windows. My naked body drenched in sweat, I moved backward and forward, trying to pick up the weak air movement. Finally I splashed the boiling water onto myself and soaped up out of the shower, then briefly endured the pain of the hot water on my body to get the soap off.

It was too hot to eat, yet I knew I had to. I managed some mashed potatoes and cold meat. I hadn't thought I could drink hot beer, but I did. It was that hot I had to sip it. Our beds were spread out on the claypan to avoid the sweltering huts. The best time was about three in the morning, when the temperature dropped under 40 degrees for an hour or two. It was beautiful.

Late in the week, after smoko, the overseer gave me a message to call home. I could ring at the cocky's house. The owner was a German builder who'd married a local girl and taken over the farm. From the hallway of his house I rang the manager of the caravan park. He said Lonnie was in hospital and Sonia wanted me to come home.

I packed the car and headed to Bourke. Waratah Station was on the Barwon River, about thirty k's out of Brewarrina and a hundred and twenty k's out of Bourke, near the Queensland border. Sonia met me in the hospital foyer. She locked her arms around me and squeezed. Her hair was unkempt; her clothes were wrinkled and dirty. That wasn't her. When I broke free she started talking fast, but wasn't making much sense. Lonnie had been an outpatient all week and the doctors had done a series of tests. The fits had continued. Some days she had up to twenty clusters of fits. You couldn't hear her when she was fitting. In fact that was the sign: when she went quiet. The doctor called her type of fits salaam spasms.

The hospital had arranged for further tests to be conducted at the children's hospital in Melbourne. They wanted to test for hypsarrhythmia epilepsy; the prognosis for that type of epilepsy wasn't encouraging.

Lonnie was giggling and playing with me in the hospital. She was fat and bubbly. After I'd strapped her into the baby capsule in the car, she went into more fits. She had her eyes half shut and her body vibrated. Her head rose and fell while her arms went in and out, like a windup doll. The fits seemed to last a few minutes and then she fell asleep.

I drove all night and the next day, and dropped them off at the granny flat. Then Smokey and I drove back to Bourke. I had to get back to work.

I was late to the shed after the weekend and the overseer was furious. The penner-upper was abusing me because he'd lent me his car battery to get to town after Sonia rang, and then I'd driven to Melbourne with it and he thought I wouldn't be back. No one cared that I'd just driven four days straight. The cocky wanted his sheep shorn, the contractor wanted his shed finished, and the other shearers wanted out.

The temperature had reached 49 degrees in the town. There was a storm brewing, as was usual after a big hot spell. The owner and the young musterer panicked and rushed the sheep into the shed. They were scared of being caught with wet sheep. The mob came into the shed panting and sweating dangerously.

Sheep are tough. Sometimes they had fence wire tangled through their bodies; they lived with broken legs, surviving in seemingly empty paddocks by digging up the clover burr in the ground. Crows gouged their eyes out, maggots nearly ate them alive, foxes stole their lambs, and wild pigs were known to eat lambs straight out of the vaginas of distressed ewes. Yet they survived, even thrived. But a sheep will drop dead of a heart attack quicker than any other animal if it's pushed to run too fast in the heat.

These sheep were starting to drop dead in their pens, and the heat coming off them was worse than shearing wet sheep. Larry called for a swarm. We told the overseer that if a sheep died while we were shearing it we wanted double for it. It's twice as hard to shear a dead sheep as a live one. The wool becomes clammy and sticky. The contractor agreed. Fitzroy Bobby thought getting the wool off might help cool them down and save some lives. It didn't.

When they slumped or stopped kicking I knew they were dead. Sometimes, shearing down the last side of a sheep, its head would flop. Or I'd take their belly wool off and the burr in their neck would hit the back of my arm and I'd know it was dead. I kept forgetting, and pushed the head out of the way.

The shed was in a panic. People were running around everywhere. Going in to pick a sheep, Danny yelled, 'Look for a sheep with a tongue that's not blue.'

The carnage went on all afternoon. Some died in the pens, some while we were shearing them, others when we threw them down the chute. The cocky and the station hand were at the bottom of the chutes, pulling the dead ones out of the way. They were blocking the chutes up and more sheep were panicking and suffocating. It was a massacre.

We worked through the run without stopping on the hour for a smoke and got as many shorn as possible. Larry said, 'They bomb us for cuttin a few, look at em now. Stupid bastards. What a waste.'

In the end, the owner lost about fifty sheep. I'd never seen anything like it.

We were near the end of the second week of the shed when the two old wool rollers began hitting the grog pretty hard. They didn't fall asleep like the rest of the team, they just kept drinking. I found myself drinking more and more with them. One had been educated and when he was pissed he talked about his businesses. The other talked about the family he'd left behind in Orange. He'd been a builder. We kept drinking until it was dark and we were sleepy. I was talking as much as I was drinking. I couldn't shut up. I was talking about anything except Lonnie.

I went to town on Friday with the overseer to ring Sonia. She said the hospital was still doing tests. Lonnie was having brain scans and they were trying different medications to stop the fitting.

I said, 'But what did they say? When will she be right? When can she come home?'

Sonia didn't have any answers. The doctors, she said, never told her anything much. But it didn't look good. At the moment Lonnie was fitting up to fifteen times a day. The more Sonia talked, the vaguer she seemed. I asked her when she was coming back. She said once they got the medication right. I said I'd ring tomorrow. Her voice was fading and we were being drowned out by the noise in the pub. When the yelling stopped the call had flatlined; I hadn't heard her say goodbye and I didn't get to say 'I love you.'

The shed finished midweek but there was no cut-out. We stayed in the huts and travelled to the back station, thirty minutes further inland. Including the days I'd missed taking Sonia and Lonnie home, I averaged eighty-five sheep a day. I was just getting my hundred in a full day's work. The team shore 6200 sheep in the ten days. Not what you'd call a fast team. Nigel the surfer rang the shed.

THE BACK STATION

WE HAD A FEW new shearers for the back station, a shearing shed on a neighbouring property owned by the same man. Larry and Nigel left for other sheds and Radleigh, a gun shearer, and Connell, a show shearer, turned up.

These sheep had tight fleeces and we had to push hard to get the wool off them. Radleigh could shear. He was cruising because of the heat, but ten minutes out from the bell he whipped off five or six sheep, which kept his tallies respectable. It was a more open shed. The stands were on the back wall next to the counting-out pens, so we had the chutes behind us with air coming in and big windows above the chutes that we propped open with a stick. There wasn't much breeze but it was better than the claustrophobic feeling in the last shed.

That was until a dust storm swirled around on the board in the 49-degree heat, getting into our teeth, eyes, under our armpits. The station owner and his hands shut all the doors and windows and put bags over the counting-out chutes, but the dust penetrated every crack and opening in the shed. We looked at each other from time to time – if one stopped we could all stop, but nobody did.

I kept saying to myself, Just do one more, concentrate, concentrate on the end tooth of your comb. I kept going but my resolve was gone. I kept going because I didn't know how to stop. I didn't know how to not do something. I didn't know when giving up was good for me. What was I doing here, why was I doing this? Snatch it, pull the pin.

There was no escape from the heat, the work and the pain.

That night, we were sitting on our beds out on the claypan. The stars were out and Smokey was curled up next to my feet. Connell, one of the new shearers, said, 'There's trouble brewin, I'm telling ya. I heard that we're headin for a blue. Ecob's been talkin. In the next coupla weeks it's gunna happen. There's a big meeting at Dubbo comin up.'

'Who's Ecob?' I asked.

Someone said, 'Ernie Ecob, he's the AWU's leading organiser in these parts. He's the one doing all the fighting for the union in New South Wales against the wide combs and the Kiwi tax loopholes.'

The show shearer told us that Ecob would have his hands full with the National Farmers' Federation. They were out to get us and the meatworkers.

I lay down to sleep. At night the pain of the work seemed bearable and the nights seemed to last forever. I'd rung Sonia on the weekend. She said the doctors had confirmed Lonnie had hypsarrhythmia epilepsy and had suggested we put her in a home. They said she might never walk or talk.

Smokey crawled on his belly, a few inches at a time, along my bed until his head was over my arm and he went to sleep. That was his favourite position.

The heat-breaking rains came a few days later. There were about three hundred sheep left, so the owner declared the shed. We made it through the black soil to the huts, had a shower, packed and headed into town. The relief from the heat was fantastic. We drove out racing the rain and the boggy soil. The overseer said he'd meet us in the Brewarrina pub and give us our cheques.

BREWARRINA

I WAS STARTING to feel better. I'd had a couple of bottles on the way in and the grog was kicking in. Sonia and Lonnie were due back soon. My hands had swollen up and had a red glow. The tops of all my fingers were scaly. It had taken a while for them to harden to the burry sheep but I was starting to acclimatise.

In the pub, smoke and the smell of stale beer hit me. It was dark – no lights on, no carpet on the floor. The concrete was wet with spilt grog. The stools had no upholstery left. A couple of wrecked couches were out the back. People were drinking out of wine bottles leaning up against the wall. The bricked wall behind the bar had wooden shelves stacked with smokes. Havelock, Log Cabin, tailormades. Some windows had sheet metal in them. The only picture was a signed photo of Lionel Rose.

I fronted the bar to order a beer, looked around for the overseer. A couple of older women came up and said g'day. A couple of young men with billiard cues dressed in rugby tops stood behind them. Men were singing, arguing, and a fight seemed to be breaking out in the billiard room. Then the pub noise dropped. I could feel my heartbeat quicken.

'What you fucken doin in here, ya white cunt? Ay?'

'Yeah, fuck off outa here.'

I backed out onto the footpath and a bloke said, 'Wrong bar, mate, round the other side's the bar you're lookin for.'

I opened the half-timber, half-smoked-glass door to the bar on the other side of the pub. The carpet had a red print of a waratah flower on it. My reflection in the mahogany bar made the place feel small. I asked for a beer. The shelves were full of exotic drinks: Galliano bottles, a variety of whiskies and different rums. Behind the glass shelves was a mirrored wall. I looked up and saw the overseer come in.

'Found it all right I see, son.'

The other men from the shed began dribbling in. We started a school between us, and other shearers from the area joined. Down the other end of the bar the rain had brought a few local cockies and their station hands. We came face to face at the bar while ordering a beer. It was always a nod or a g'day, but not much conversation until they got pissed.

Then it started.

'You blokes going on strike? That's the rumour.'

The show shearer yelled back, 'Dunno, meetin's on Saturday, find out then.'

'Well, whaddya ya reckon and all? Whaddya think?'

The show shearer walked to the bar, leaned over, lowered his voice and said, 'Never know what the men'll do. Won't think for emselves or nuthin, that's for sure. They're like sheep. They'll do whatever they're told. They'll whinge and whine and carry on and all, but in the end they'll come outa that meeting wantin to go to war. We'll go out for two weeks, lose maybe seven, eight hundred bucks, right when we need it, then get three or four cents more a sheep and go back to work. We'll never make that money up. It's gone. Fucken gone. We're fair-dinkum stupid sometimes like that. Fair-dinkum fucken stupid.'

'It's good to hear you talking like that,' the cocky said. 'You blokes have to be careful, I'm telling you. This McLachlan and his new National Farmers' Federation is out to get you blokes. I'm not for him myself. He's too ruthless. Everybody needs rules, you know. He wants to destroy the rules, have no award at all. That's not good. No good pushing the shearer out of the industry.'

Another drinker joined us and said, 'The boongs are into it out there, killing themselves.'

'They could've nailed my arse before, but they didn't.'

'What are you, a boong lover? Not saying all boongs are bad. Some are all right. Not many, though. The government's the biggest problem. They get the dole and black money. I wish I was black, I wouldn't have to shear them mongrel wethers.'

Fitzroy Bobby said, 'Like your kids to be black?'

'Fucken smartarse.'

The show shearer, trying to be funny, said, 'They're smarter'n us, they're not out there shearing them mongrel burr-infected bastards in 50-degree heat. We're the stupid bastards, doin that.'

I was out of there. Fitzroy Bobby wanted a lift back to Bourke, so we left together. I collected my cheque and the overseer said, 'If you're not on strike, report on Monday to Charlton Station.' It was about thirty k's out of Brewarrina on the Tarcoon road.

Radleigh, the other new shearer, wanted a lift too – he had a woman in Brewarrina West, which the locals called Dodge City. We drove out there. It was an eerie feeling driving through a completely black township, separated from the rest of Brewarrina. Mums and kids stared at us as we passed through their part of town. Some houses were partly torn down, unpainted, the front doors and windows smashed. Overgrown grass, used fridges and car bombs cluttered the front yards; there were diffs and wheel rims on the nature strip, and two or three mongrel dogs to each house. The atmosphere was electric. I dropped Radleigh off and said g'day to his woman, a gorgeous-looking half-Chinese, half-Aboriginal woman.

On the following Saturday, Ernie Ecob opened the union meeting in Dubbo. He welcomed everybody and laid out our case. He said we had a fight on our hands. If ever we needed to be strong it was now.

'*Now,*' he emphasised. Then he introduced Charlie Oliver, the best union official I ever heard. He spoke with sincerity and respect for us. He outlined the nuts and bolts of the claim. Then another union organiser got up; he was the designated stirrer in the meeting, a real Bozo the Clown. He bent over like a footy coach and tried to inject some anger and aggression into the men. *Blaa blaa blaa,* that's all I heard. Charlie Oliver had convinced me of the need to go on strike, the need for solidarity in these uncertain times. That's how I felt after the last union meeting at Inverleigh. We needed more solidarity, I could see we weren't strong enough. I felt Fraser was going to do everything he could while he was in power to destroy us.

A resolution to put a case for a wage rise to the arbitration commission was passed by the meeting. If we didn't get the right response we would commence industrial action the following week. Ecob and Oliver wanted to attack, take the fight to the graziers and the Liberals. Meet them head on. We had to meet here next Saturday. I was in.

Shearers all over the northwest of New South Wales had come to the meeting, and a lot of blokes from all around Australia were shearing in the area. A few young overseers still had tickets from their wool-rolling days and they'd come to listen and spy. They reported back to the Grazcos men and the Grazcos men reported straight to the Graziers Association. They were real scabby little pricks.

CHARLTON STATION

SONIA AND LONNIE had returned to Bourke by bus and I wanted to have another night with them, so I didn't leave for Charlton Station until Monday morning. Sonia had been taking Lonnie to the Bourke hospital because the fits, which had been under control for a few days, resurfaced. The doctor said he could manage her from Bourke. We'd started a range of different medications and dosages and we thought it wouldn't take much to get her back on track again.

Lonnie seemed healthy to me. She still laughed and giggled, she liked being pushed in her pram, and she loved Smokey licking her. The only difference was the fits, and afterwards she'd fall into a deep sleep.

Pretty much the same team from the last shed was at Charlton Station. The wool rollers both looked crook from the grog. I didn't know how long they would last. Paddy the cook sang at night and played his guitar. His wife was camping with him. It was a six-stand shed. The team were Danny the Afghan, a new bloke called David – a clean-cut type – me, Radleigh the gun, Connell the show shearer, and Fitzroy Bobby. By the look of David he was a cocky's son who'd missed the lottery, born fourth or fifth in line for the farm. So he had to work like the rest of us.

The sheep were South Australian merinos, big and straight, the same breed as at Gunbar. The intense heat had gone and the temperature fluctuated in the high thirties. The water we showered in was muddy. The huts were falling down, the beds were wrecked, and the thunderboxes were full and stank.

The presser, from Gundagai, was the first bloke I ever saw drink pineapple juice after work. He said he'd drunk a farm, a café and a family away. On Wednesday he told me he was going into town to ring his AA sponsor. I thought this AA must have been some sort of secret society. Radleigh reckoned they were pretty tight with one another.

The next day at smoko a small plane landed on the claypan in front of our huts. It was amazing. A couple of blokes thought it might have been the sheriff coming to get them. It was a film crew. They were working on a TV miniseries called *The Thorn Birds* and the team were collecting photos and footage to remake the shearing shed back in America. They were astonished at the roo dogs climbing on the back of the sheep. The film crew took photos of the tree-trunk posts, the flywheels that drove our down tube, the pens, the chutes, the wool tables and wool bales. Then they had lunch with us before they flew off again.

Friday afternoon, the leftovers of a cyclone heading down from Queensland were threatening to break the calm. All through the last run we monitored the blackening sky, waiting for a sign to run for it. No one wanted to be trapped at the shed over the weekend. The winds hit first, the shed buckled, the sheep grew ominously quiet and it went dark, like during an eclipse of the moon. We downed tools and ran to our huts, the rain hitting hard and fast. Most of the blokes gave up quickly. They knew the roads.

Fitzroy Bobby and I had planned to head off together. As we

ran across the claypan, he yelled that we didn't have time for a shower or to get any clothes. If we couldn't get out past the claypan now we were stuffed. Within moments the water was pooling around the huts. We jumped into the car and headed off.

I looked into the rear-vision mirror and saw Smokey running after me, flat out through the water. I told Bobby I had to stop and get my dog, but he said we'd be bogged for sure. I was torn between driving off on Smokey and getting back to Lonnie and Sonia. I floored it and didn't look back. Once we were out of sight, I thought he'd stop chasing.

At the gate of the property, there was a choice of routes to Bourke. The longer way, to the left, was over red soil. The road to the right was over black soil, and shorter. Red soil was safer in the wet, but we decided to take the shorter route. We figured the rain hadn't soaked in too deeply and we'd get through. We didn't.

Every kilometre we went we got slower, until we had a rock on the accelerator, the car in first gear, and Bobby and I were on either side stopping it from sliding into the table drains. Rain was still falling. Wearing only thongs when I left the shed, I pushed in bare feet. I yelled out to Bobby that the car was boiling.

'Don't worry, it's only a sign the engine's hot. It needs to be hot to run well.'

I kept waiting to get onto solid ground but it didn't happen. When the rain stopped the car was down to the axles. Eventually, after several hours, we were bogged. The sky was a wild blue and grey and I couldn't tell the time, couldn't see the sun. We guessed it was about six o'clock at night. Which way to go? Back to the shed or try to walk into town? We headed back. After an hour the light was fading fast and we walked into a property where we knew some of Bobby's mates were shearing. Maybe we could get put up for the night. But the huts were empty. The blokes had got out before the rain.

Back on the track, we talked as we walked. I told Bobby all about Lonnie. I hadn't spoken about her to anyone. Bobby had grown up in the city and he talked about the different factories he'd worked in before shooting through to the bush. He thought if we started running we might get back to the station before the dark set in. I ran for a while, but I'm not a runner. I was barefoot and my back ached from slopping through the mud. Bobby became a dot on the horizon as night set in. Then it was dark. Pitch-black and scary. I heard something rattling but couldn't see anything. I heard Bobby calling. We kept yelling until we came into contact. He'd stopped running when it got dark and waited for me. It was too dangerous to be alone in the bush at night.

We couldn't see more than three feet in front of us. We walked like we were blindfolded, never straying too far from accidentally brushing one another. A bird or something rustled the trees and both of us jumped and screamed, then quickly composed ourselves, pretending we hadn't just done what we did. When a dog barked we shat ourselves, and next thing it jumped on me and I screamed. It was Smokey. He had run all the way. He was frantic, wagging his tail and jumping all over me.

We continued walking for hours, and on a hunch walked up a driveway and there was the sign, CHARLTON STATION. Now we were only a few k's from the huts. There had been a huge, rogue wild boar in the area. We didn't want to get cut down by the razor-sharp tusks it was rumoured to have, and I didn't want Smokey to get hurt or killed. I picked him up and carried him. If a boar could eat a lamb while it was being born, and eat distressed ewes, it wouldn't hold back if it could get at us.

'Snake, snake, d'ya see that? Swimming through the water. Fucken hell.'

I said, 'Where, where, Bobby? Where? Don't fuck around, will ya, not with fucken snakes and all. I'm too tired.'

The lights from the huts were in sight. The huts were on a low-lying claypan, and after the torrential downpour it had become a shallow inland lake. All the snakeholes were full of water. This was the last part of our journey, getting back across a snake-infested watercourse. We were exhausted, hungry, thirsty, and desperate to get back. Without speaking a word or looking at each other, we fumbled around in the dark and found each other's hand and walked across the lake hand in hand to safety. We never mentioned afterwards that we'd done that.

After seven and a half hours of pushing the car and walking through mud, I ached all over. We took a few cold chops from the fridge, and even though I was hungry I filled up quickly.

I lay on my bed covered in mud. I was too wrecked to have a shower or take my clothes off. I thought when the mud dried I'd just shake it or peel it off my mattress and blankets. My body was like a machine slowly shutting down; each muscle let go and relaxed one by one, moving up my body, until I slumped and my eye muscles collapsed. The last thing I remember was feeling relief and thinking, We made it.

I surfaced at about eight o'clock. I didn't know how to get a message to Sonia. I was bent over and crippled when I walked. My feet were damaged for weeks. My body felt like it had broken bones all through it.

We were on strike now. The message had come through from the manager to the overseer. We couldn't get to the meeting because of the rain. The manager sent a station hand over in a four-wheel drive and piled us in the back and drove us to Bourke.

'What about my car, Bobby? I can't leave it in the middle of the road. Someone'll flog it.'

'If we couldn't move it, no one else is gunna. Don't worry, we'll come back in a coupla days to get it.'

When I got home the van was shut up. The park manager told me Lonnie was back in hospital. I headed around there on foot and Sonia and I walked home together.

I got the car okay. It was caked in dry mud. With a few tugs from a towrope it came free. Toughest car in Australia, my old Kingswood, couldn't kill it. We were on strike for two weeks. The union said we could pick up casual work as long as we didn't shear. Bobby and I went hunting for jobs. A day's work would give us some breathing space, something to do, and keep us off the grog.

I did a day at the meatworks salting hides, another day throwing sheep and cattle guts down a chute. I tried the dole office but they knew we were shearers. I even got the odd day's work on the council. One day we went out past Louth and dug a trench. It was getting hot again, 45 degrees. The truck driver took us there, showed us what to do, then sat in his truck. Bobby and I did a day's work in two hours. The boss offered us full-time work.

We shook our heads.

Lonnie was put into hospital yet again, and her medication altered once more. The fits came two or three times a day now and she had between ten and twenty spasms a fit. A visiting paediatrician from Sydney's Prince of Wales Hospital gave us some suggestions but they didn't stop the fitting.

We won the dispute: a few cents a sheep. Ernie Ecob was trying to build a more militant team of workers for the impending fight with the Fraser government and the National Farmers' Federation.

Back at Charlton Station we immediately went out on strike again. It wasn't just that the shower heads were blocked with silt from the dam and the water was murky, that the bedframes were stretched, or that the thunderboxes were full and the dunny seats wooden. (Wooden seats had been banned years ago because they apparently carried bacteria that plastic didn't.) The sheep had scabby mouth. Scabby mouth disease, which causes ulcers in the gums, results from sheep digging burrs out of the ground, usually in a drought. But in this case it was because there wasn't enough to eat due to overstocking. We tried to get the Brewarrina police out to deem the property a health hazard, since scabby mouth was contagious, but they said there was no way they could come out.

I rang the local union with no effect, so I decided to ring Charlie Oliver. I explained we couldn't get a union official on site. Next day, Ernie Ecob turned up, driving all the way from Coonamble. He said the owner of Charlton, who lived around Parkes somewhere, was well known to the union and he blackbanned the shed straight away. I was sent to Butterbone Park Stud.

BUTTERBONE PARK STUD

I HEADED BACK to the van first. I reached the caravan park and saw Sonia's parents' car reversed into the opening of the annexe on our van. At first I thought they'd come to visit. As I got closer I could see Sonia packing. Her father was checking the water and oil in the car. The McHughs had made a decision to drive up unannounced and get Sonia and Lonnie. The paediatrician in Bourke had assured us that Lonnie would be looked after just as well here as in a hospital in Melbourne or Sydney, but that didn't matter to the McHughs. Sonia acted powerless but it seemed to me she wanted to go.

I slept in the empty caravan and headed out the next morning to Butterbone, which is near Warren. I was there about four days. It was a hostile team. I'd seen the young overseer at the union rally: one of the squealing rats. He was always spruiking that the industry needed modernising – wide combs, working on Saturdays, more flexibility – reckoned the Kiwis were good for us, created competition. Australians were union-mad, he said, lazy bastards. The Kiwis created options for struggling farmers.

I'd lost interest. The overseer's old man was a coalminer from

Muswellbrook. I wondered what he thought of his son's political position.

The cook came down and started shearing after smoko to help with the cut-out. Ecob turned up and I snatched it. I left there thinking, We don't have a chance.

Back in Bourke, the contractor said, 'No work.'

The park manager said, 'That's crap. They can't get shearers. You've been black-banned for snatchin it, that's all. They'll get over it. They always do.'

I rang home to talk to Sonia. Lonnie was back in hospital.

'Do they know what causes it?'

'They said this type of epilepsy is normally associated with a severe head injury.'

'What about the heat, coming from Melbourne to Bourke?'

'No, they said she'd have had to have her head rammed into a furnace.'

'What about the medication? Did they test the contents of that bottle?'

She said no, but the doctors had assured her the medication couldn't have caused this. She said the social workers wanted to know where I was and she didn't know what to tell them. Then the social workers suggested a home for Lonnie.

'She'll be better soon. She's going to come good after a while.' I started thinking of how she'd giggled and held onto the coffee table at the hospital in Bourke, trying to walk round it. She was so proud of herself.

I asked Sonia when they were coming back. She said she didn't know. She wanted me to come home.

The phone was beeping and I'd run out of change. I didn't think of her parents' granny flat as my home.

I went to the Royal Hotel and got into a school with Wally, the show shearer, Radleigh and Fitzroy Bobby. Sculled the first couple to get the kick. The show shearer was telling us about the family he'd walked out on.

'Did her a favour, ya know? Yeah, I was no good for her. On the piss half the time, never home, going from one shed to the next. Broke one week, rich the one after. I shot through. Let the kids have a life with someone else. No good confusing em. Fucken painful, though, seeing em once a week an that. Dropping them off on a Sunday night and driving home alone. I couldn't hack it. I nearly necked meself.'

It was mid-afternoon. I thought I'd go back to the van for a while. The heat hit me when I left the pub. I didn't think I'd drunk that much. I crashed for a couple of hours and woke up thirsty, real thirsty. Dry, wanting a drink.

I bought some stubbies and sat drinking in the park with another school. Fell asleep again and woke on the grass in the dark this time. I stumbled around, tried to climb a barbed-wire fence. Nothing seemed normal. I heard skin rip, didn't feel anything. Flat on my back – got up, walked down the street to the club. A bloke yelled out, 'Fuck off out of here.'

Two blokes come from nowhere, grab me, and I can't defend myself, can't move my arms. I slur out, 'Get fucked.' I'm thrown onto the footpath. I get halfway up and girls' legs in stockings walk by – miniskirts, giggling, boobs and perfume. I think about their soft skin and soft lips. I want a fuck. Girls walk around me. I try and say g'day. The boys following them walk over me, not around me. I stand up; the two security guards standing at the gate tell me again to move. Up the steps there're lights flashing and a big window. Inside is dancing and music. I head off away from the party. Don't know where I'm going. Am I back home? Was that my missus I saw? Is she in there? That dirty rotten slut. The coppers turn up. A voice booms out, 'Hold it there.'

There's a scuffle. I can't fight, I can't move my arms. My head hits the ground. My shoulders are being twisted off. Smokey goes ballistic and the cop pulls his gun. I yell no and tell Smokey to sit. Smokey sits. I'm thrown, not out, but in the slammer. I land on musty grey blankets and the lights are out. There are a dozen others in the cells. All black. I go into a rage. Screaming, banging the lock up and down on the steel bars. The boys tell me to quieten down. One says he wants some peace and quiet and if I don't shut up he'll shut me up.

I stop. Sit on the blankets. I start to calm down. My rage is replaced by fatigue. I don't move. I don't want to move. For the first time in a long time I'm still, not racing somewhere. My head has stopped. I feel strange, peaceful. Not happy, not sad. Nothing.

Lonnie. Lonnie's in hospital fitting. I'm in here drunk. I can't find my life. I've always got plans. I've looked for my place, thinking something will hit me and I'll say, This is it. Or, That's it. But it hasn't happened. I work my arse off and don't end up with any money. I seem to spend my life running from one place to the next, always on the go. I look for a place that feels right but nothing ever fits.

I can't find a future. Lonnie has no future. Who will look after her? What will happen to her when we're gone?

I want to feel something – love, maybe. I don't know what I'm missing. I just know I'm missing something. I want to be held. I want to be touched, cared for. I want to be happy. I want to be happy more than anything. I don't know how to be happy any more. I used to be happy.

I try and hold it back. I feel ashamed and cry myself to sleep.

A young Aboriginal woke me. 'You all right, fella. We be havin breakfast soon. Bacon and eggs on a Sunday. You had some pretty wild dreams, ay, last night. You be all right now, ay, feelin better.'

I looked at him; I looked at all of them. Their doors weren't locked.

'We just cuttin out a few fines, that's all. It's not hard. We gettin our three meals a day. It's okay, we from the community. We gunna be debt-free in a coupla weeks, ay.'

I was exhausted, but strangely okay.

A big cop said, 'Go home, son. We got enough problems up here without putting up with little cunts like you. And that's some loyal dog you got there. He wouldn't leave and we couldn't get near him. Ya lucky we didn't shoot him, he's mad.'

I felt dead. Smokey and I walked down the street, following sounds of music into a church. Aboriginal children from the community were singing 'The Little Drummer Boy'. *Pa rum pum pum pum, rum pum pum pum.* There was a statue of Jesus on the cross, and above it God looking down from heaven. Below it the prayer of confession. *Bless me Father for I have sinned* . . . What had I done wrong?

Did I die and go to hell? I'd always imagined that when I died I'd remember the lead-up to and the moment of death. A car accident, for example, where I should have slowed down, or cancer, and the regrets I had as I approached death. Remembering the people I left behind and the people who loved me. I never thought that when I died I wouldn't remember dying. I just assumed that, because living people had memories of the dead, dead people had memories of the living. What if in hell you didn't know that you'd died? What if going to hell was as simple as changing a lens, or slipping through a door?

WONGA STATION

THE NEXT DAY, the park manager helped me find my car. I'd smashed it, but not that bad; he said he could help me fix it. I had no job, no money, and was still black-banned. I had no way of getting home even if I wanted to. I didn't seem to care any more. I couldn't feel anything and my mind seemed in neutral. I had no answers.

The park manager gave me a contractor's name, said he was looking for some shearers. I rang him and he picked me up in his one-tonne ute on Sunday afternoon. We headed out the other side of Wanaaring to Wonga Station, three hundred kilometres out of Bourke.

I sat in the back on the tray, opposite his dogs, my swag and my toolbox and Smokey tucked in between my legs. I stared into the rising dust we left in our path. This was sandy country. We were as remote as I'd ever been before, with thick, stunted scrub all around us.

The property was owned by cockies from West Wyalong. They were great people, completely down to earth. It was a four-stand shed. The other men were decent enough blokes. A couple had travelled up from West Wyalong, and myself and another bloke from Bourke made up the team.

The sheep shore well. The spinifex grass kept their belly wool and leg wool stunted so they shore fast. The swarm was quick and the owners used Smokey all week in the yards. They put a muzzle on him, they told me. Otherwise he was too dangerous. Said he was a great dog but I'd better watch him.

On the weekend I went to town. My car had been fixed. I paid up all my debts with a sub from the contractor and drove back out to the shed on Sunday. The shed lasted nine days. I averaged thirty-eight a run, which gave me a hundred and fifty a day. But the tally didn't mean anything to me any more. I was thinking of money to get back to Sonia and Lonnie. The contractor fudged the tax for me and the tucker was only seven bucks a day. I left with about four hundred in my kick, after I'd paid everybody in town.

I wondered whether this was part of growing up, surviving failure and being beaten. Learning to accept less in your life. I didn't know what growing up meant, really. I'd always wanted control, to be the master of my life, and I wasn't.

SMOKEY

LONNIE'S SUNKEN EYES looked up when I opened the door. Her chin was red from dribble. She'd been a fat baby in Bourke, now she was skinny. I picked her up and her head flopped back, her flaccid legs dangled like a rag doll. The Lonnie who had walked giggling around the Bourke hospital coffee table was gone. I was shocked at her deterioration. Sonia was pleased to see me. She said the fits were continuing and the medication mucked up Lonnie's sleep patterns.

I spent a couple of days looking for work. I knew I couldn't take Smokey with me to the sheds any more and I couldn't leave him at home when I was job hunting and risk him biting Lonnie. I didn't think he would, but I couldn't risk it.

Mr McHugh offered to take him down the swamp and shoot him with his rifle, but I didn't want anybody else shooting Smokey. Sonia suggested the pound but I couldn't do that. I rubbed Smokey's ears, he loved that. Smokey was small, fast and energetic; his eyes were wired. People envied me for having such a loyal dog. No one could win him over. They could pat him but he didn't take to anyone except me.

I put a rope through his collar and tied a knot. He looked up at me; he knew his fate. His tail was down, his ears back. He crawled and whimpered along the road to the swamp.

Once I'd found a good place to bury him, I dug a hole. I knew I wouldn't be able to dig it afterwards. The ground was cold and slimy. I would have preferred a grave where the earth was warm. Smokey whined and gave little yelps as I dug. He kept crawling around in circles. I felt sick. I undid his collar and put the gun to his head.

He sat there and looked into my eyes. His two front paws were lifting alternately, pleading with me. The old rifle was a single-shot, bolt-action .22. The timber butt was faded. It had only been used for killing sick and injured animals. Smokey heaved and cowered back. I pulled the eye of the barrel about a centimetre back off his skull. If the barrel's too close to the body the bullet's impact is weakened. 'Don't jerk the trigger,' I told myself aloud. 'Don't jerk the trigger.' I had to get it right. I pointed the barrel down, about an inch above his eyes in the middle of his head.

It was silent in the swamp, beyond daylight but not yet dark. Smokey and I looked into each other's eyes. Where other people saw wild eyes and a wild dog, I saw sad, soft eyes. I thought back to when I first saw him in the litter with his mum; to him licking my blistered hands at Lal Lal Station; sleeping in the back of the car on long trips; finding me in the bush at Brewarrina; waiting for me when I got out of the slammer in Bourke. But mostly I thought of him curling up near me when he wanted a cuddle.

I pulled the trigger. The shot broke the evening silence. Smokey convulsed on the ground yelping, saliva running from his mouth. The bullet hadn't killed him. I panicked. I didn't want him to die. I was confused. Fumbling with another bullet, I reloaded, put the rifle to the back of his head and pulled the trigger once more. A trickle of blood came out the side of his mouth and with a few small sighs Smokey died. My knees buckled from under me and I sank into the mud, leaned over and burst into tears. I hated myself. I kept crying until my ribs hurt, until I couldn't cry any more.

When the night air set in I got up. Smokey was already getting stiff. I pushed him into the grave, buried him and said goodbye.

THE BEER CAN FACTORY

I WAS RANKED as a second-class process worker on rotating shiftwork. The factory clerk, a balding, neat little guy, only said what he had to. I reported in, filled out my details: tax forms, driver's licence, next of kin, medical insurance, things like that. Then I was sent to the travelling nurse for a medical. She made me cough and gave me a pass. Next was the store. The storeman, an old fitter, took my card and issued me with two pairs of green overalls, two pairs of earplugs, one pair of gloves and protective glasses. He explained that I had to bring back my issued clothing and equipment when they wore out or got damaged, otherwise he couldn't replace them.

The foreman met me at the clock-on machine. My card had been made up and put in the rack. I was number 124. I had to clock on before my shift started and clock off when I finished, leaving my card in its proper place. No one was allowed to clock on or off for anybody else, that was automatic dismissal for both parties. The foreman asked was I crystal clear on that point. I nodded. He took me over to my machine.

My job was to feed flat pieces of tin into a machine that turned them into beer cans. I had to make sure the tin sheets were square when I put them in and that I didn't overload the machine. Then I had to go down the other end of the machine and make up cardboard boxes. Any problems, I had a red emergency button. The foreman finished off by saying, 'Put ya hand up if ya wanna go to the dunny an someone'll come an take over. If anythin goes wrong with the machine the fitter'll come over. It's a good job here – reliable, you know. You're only a young bloke still. Got a chance to consolidate yourself here, know what I mean? The note says you were shearing. That's hard on ya back, isn't it? Country life's good, my uncle's got a few sheep, but there's not much work, is there? We used to go up for the shearing and help the shearers. Did you know a Johnny Gamble?'

I shook my head and mouthed, 'No.'

'Yeah, I wanted a few acres meself. No money in it. Well, ya haven't done much with your life yet, you're only twenty. See how ya go here. Too old for an apprenticeship, but if ya stick at it I might be able ta offer ya a traineeship.'

I could do it now. I started work at seven on morning shifts and two-thirty on afternoons. The pay was that bad I had to get overtime to make ends meet. But it was close to home in the industrialised area of Laverton. The boss was okay. He said I was a good worker and offered me a harder machine if I wanted to learn it. He knew I needed money. Said he was married himself, and the best-looking girl on the production line was sort of his girlfriend as well.

I was home every evening now for Sonia and Lonnie. I spent most of the day at work dreaming. Lonnie never looked at us any more and that was hard. The hospital gave us plaster splints for her legs and we practised walking with her. She would just flip-flop. We used to make it a game and pretend she was doing the walking, trying to make her laugh, but it wasn't much fun. She dribbled all the time; we were always wiping her mouth, trying to dry out the sores on her chin.

The noise of the machine became a rhythm. I tried to imagine it was playing songs. At the end of my first shift the sheets had cut my hands to bits, so I relented and started using the gloves. But I couldn't come at the protective glasses.

On a production line the machine is the boss. I spent my day with something that didn't wait for me. If I hit the stop button a red signal went off and the fitter would come over and want to know why I'd stopped it. He didn't mind as long as there was nothing wrong, as long as he didn't have to fix anything.

One Scottish bloke with thick glasses and a scraggy face wouldn't let the fitter oil his machine. He had his own oilcan and rags, reckoned the fitter didn't give a fuck about his machine so he wouldn't let him touch it. The fitter said it was his job and he'd call the union and shut the place down if the Scot touched the machine again. Every morning they'd have the same blue. One of them was always cornering someone to lend support.

I hated my machine. At the end of the day I was bored. At the beginning of the day I was bored. Smoko, lunchtime – bored. I went home bored. At home I pretended Lonnie was going to get better, but I had a sinking feeling in my guts about her and I didn't think I could survive the factory for much longer.

After a few months I got a phone call from Grazcos. Greystones was starting and I had the offer of a pen. I took it without telling Sonia. Two weeks' shearing was better than a month's pay in the factory and I thought I'd see what happened after that, anything would be better than this job. Sonia wasn't happy, but neither was I. I could be a better provider and buy a home if I could just get a break. Something I could get my teeth into, but she was going for all the safe options. Just like her parents.

I gave a few days' notice and quit the factory. The pay-master said sign here and here and walked away. The machinists had the same earmuffs on, the same protective glasses, the same overalls, and the same expressionless look on their faces. Nobody looked up, nobody waved or said goodbye. They lived for the smoko card game and the monthly social nights put on by the union reps. And there was the foreman giving the same drill to the bloke who was taking over my machine. When the foreman put his hand up, showing the new bloke what to do when he wanted to go to the toilet, I left.

GREYSTONES AGAIN

DRAPHINE SMILED, SAID, 'Getay, boy.' He seemed different, softer, and he wasn't yelling. He asked about using Smokey up the shed.

I shook my head. 'He's gone now, Draph.'

'Sorry, boy, really am. I know ya loved that dog, son.'

All the regulars were there. It was great to see the blokes again but I had a bad feeling that this was it for me. I'd promised Sonia I wouldn't go away again, and here I was, away again. I said I'd take whatever I could get close to home. This shed was close to home, but the next shed wouldn't be.

I had breakfast at home and was late to the swarm. I drew the first pen and took the rep's job. Viking drew two and we were penmates again. Big Laurie from Hamilton was in three. Monahan from Albury was in four, Haveachat in five, Barnesy in six. Bernie Bourke was in seven and Morgan was in eight.

Viking said he hadn't been doing much except annoying his wife and going to the pub early. Haveachat had been sitting home playing with his grandson and getting fat so he'd have something to work off in the season.

We headed to the shed loaded up with our waterbags, toolboxes, rags and towels. I had on two jumpers and a beanie. It was a freezing foggy morning with low-lying clouds in the valley. The smell in the shed was high – sheep shit everywhere. This much shit meant the mob had probably been in the shed all weekend, in case of rain. They'd be hollow-gutted for sure – the belly wool would be harder to get off, but at least they'd be a bit lighter to drag out.

The run started and sure enough the sheeps' guts were sunken. Along the long blow they dipped in a bit but they weren't that wild. I always reckoned sheep were best shedded for a day before shearing. If they came in straight off the paddock they were wild, full in the guts, and they shat everywhere when you were shearing.

The first full run I almost kept up with Viking. I thought, I'm getting there. The last time I'd been here, it had been my first shed and I shore thirteen for the run. This time I had thirty-eight. The main thing wasn't the tally, but the pecking order. I was starting to beat Laurie, not all the time, but one or two runs a day I'd get him by one sheep. He didn't like it.

Halfway through the shed a regular job came up with the Water Board, delivering water to farmers. It came with a house and it was outdoors. Sonia and her mother thought it would be perfect for me. Sonia applied for it before she told me about it. I knew what the market gardeners were like, and despite a bad interview I got it.

The boys, especially Haveachat, said I was doing the right thing for the kid. Draphine reckoned I should hold on, Greystones was shearing the lambs the following week and I'd probably get my first two hundred in them. I rang the Water Board to ask if I could start the following week. They said no.

On the Friday night I packed up my tools. Draphine told me

how many sheep to shear the last run and he made my cheque up early. I said goodbye to the blokes and left.

Driving out of the station, I felt tired. I'd been waking up every night from the same nightmare. I was being lowered into an old brick bottomless well. I had thick ship's rope around my waist, I couldn't see who was lowering me, nor could I see the bottom. The descent was steady and smooth. The funny thing about the dream was I wasn't fighting back. I was calm, I was just descending. But I'd wake up fighting for breath, as if my chest had been squashed.

THE WATER BOARD

MY FIRST DAY on the new job I went in to give Lonnie a kiss goodbye. Her blankets were off and she was having another fit. Her hands and arms were moving in and out in slow motion, as though she was going to pray, and her little body shuddered.

At the work depot I was given gloves, a shovel, a file for my shovel, and put into the back of a ute with blokes on a work-for-the-dole scheme. We were sent out to shovel mud out of two hundred kilometres of channel. So much for the advertised position. Even with a house and low rent, the pay was crap. I told Sonia I'd stay for one year and not a second more. After a couple of weeks, the job came down to who got to drive the ute.

A few months later, coming home dejected, I tried to talk to Sonia about how unhappy I was. Before I'd finished she said, 'You promised, you promised.' She squinted her eyes and tightened her lips and let out one more emphatic 'You *promised*.'

And that was it.

At the start of summer the job changed. I had to release the water to the farmers and check the waterwheels. One lunchtime early in the season, I was walking down the street when a market gardener wound down the window of his Mercedes and yelled, 'Where's my water, you arsehole?' He shook his fist out the window and looked around to see if anyone was watching.

It was a long summer.

My old onion paddock was still there, with a new house beside it. The first generation of market gardeners lived in trains, the next in weatherboards, and this generation lived in mansions. I stopped and looked at the paddock where I'd picked all those onions. I saw the mansion of that miserable market gardener I'd worked for. I'd thought I would have done more with my life by now.

THE DEPOT SHED

SONIA LIKED THE security of the Water Board job. No one could understand me leaving a government job that came with a house to move into a rented farmhouse with a sick child and a pregnant wife and go back shearing. But I was dying in the Water Board job. I found it excruciating to go to work and the money was crap. When I was shearing I was the boss and I could earn good money. It wasn't the fantastic job I'd thought it was going to be, but I had pride in myself when I shore. When I looked out the chute and saw the sheep shorn it made me feel good. When the fleece rolled off the sheep and I had my rhythm I felt good, I was my own man and I was part of something. Shearers cared about what they did. Shearers had a say in their work. I liked that.

So when Powell, the local shearing contractor – the same one who'd offered me a job when I was at Barunah – rang with eight or nine months of solid shearing I took it. I didn't want to live in Werribee, that was a compromise, but it didn't stop me looking for a place in the bush to live in later on. The weekend prior to my starting, in August 1980, we moved into a farmhouse near my old onion paddock. The little house we rented had been used for storing cardboard boxes and needed cleaning; a few rats persisted even after the clean-up. When Sonia brought the new baby home from hospital, we made a rat-proof bassinet cover for the crib and Jade slept in our room. I didn't want a rat climbing into her crib in the middle of the night and gnawing her face.

Lonnie was now staying awake for up to thirty-six hours at a time. The medication was making her sleep patterns erratic. She'd started walking, in a fashion, but she still predominantly rolled and was still chewing anything she could put her mouth around. There was no room to roll in this house and there were outside dangers, with a water channel flowing next to it, a main road and tractors going by.

I pulled up at the depot shearing shed on the first morning stuffed. It was one thing to go to a bludger's job at the Water Board after Lonnie had been awake all night, but doing a day's shearing on no sleep was another. Trucks were unloading sheep out the back and the diesel engine that ran the shearing gear was warming up. Farmers brought their sheep to this shed, we didn't go to them.

I walked in. Men were already on the board loading up their handpieces and adjusting their combs and cutters. I'd slept in. The overseer was grinding a few tools and the wool classer was organising the wool room. Men looked and said hello. We got straight into it and the pace was on. I took it easy for the first run. I knew I'd be exhausted later in the week. The sheep were good-shearing crossbreeds. I got kicked out of place a bit by them but I was glad to be back. No lunch was supplied. Sonia had made me a salad but I was used to a roast for lunch and I was starving.

In pen one was Tony Smith, a barrel-chested bloke who'd won the Golden Shears a few years earlier and was crowned Australian Champion Shearer. He'd shorn forty-seven in his first run, despite dodgy hips. Jimmy Mott was in two. He was also a show shearer and had an Australia-wide reputation. He was regarded as one of the fastest shearers in the country but he couldn't keep up his speed for two hours, both his knees were gone. He used to squeeze the sheep like a concertina, making it smaller to shear. In the last ten minutes of the run he shore nine sheep. Just over a minute a sheep. I couldn't believe it.

Chamberlain was in three. One of his hips needed replacing but he was holding on because he still had one kid at school and he wouldn't be able to shear once he had the operation. He shore thirty-seven, not bad for one hip. Jimmy Pine was in four, a nimble bloke in his prime. He got forty-four. He'd bought a house off Powelly the contractor and now he was trying to pay for it. I was in five. I didn't draw for my stand, I was given it. Everybody had their own stands. I got thirty-five but knew I could get forty a run in these when I was fit. That was my plan: to shear forty a run every run until I got a house. In six was Chopper. He hated shearing. He got twenty-eight. In seven was Tommy Hickey. Tommy had never married – racehorses and the racetrack were his life. He got twenty-three. Brendan Smith was in eight. His dad was Tony Smith. Brendan wasn't as fast as his dad but he was as clean. He shore thirty-two.

So here I was, working for a small private contractor, sugarbagging it, suburban shearing. I was in enemy territory. My old team might have thought I'd switched. The blokes in this shed were solid. Most shearers after a few years try and get out of travelling away all the time.

During smoko Tony Smith gave a union report on developments with the National Farmers' Federation. The secretary of the Victorian Riverina branch of the AWU believed the NFF was building a fighting fund to defeat the shearers over the looming wide-comb dispute, and apparently it had more than a hundred thousand dollars already put away. A former official from the clerks' union had joined the NFF and was orchestrating the attack.

Smithy went on to say that the union thought Western Australia was lost. 'It's almost a complete scab state.'

Afterwards one of the shearers asked me if I'd seen any Grazcos men use wide combs.

'No way, the blokes I worked with were staunch.'

'Well, Grazcos is the graziers' company.'

'I don't care what they are, the men I worked with were always solid.'

I never thought anybody would've thought the men I learned with were less than 100 per cent solid unionists. We went back to work. It hadn't taken long and I was back into all the politics.

Powelly walked into the shed. Chopper, shearing next to me, leant over as if whispering and said aloud that the contractor was that tight he made his missus darn his old undies.

Powelly came up to me and watched my style. He was hunched and old but had a sharp eye. He told me there was plenty of work at the moment. When we finished here we had a few months down at the Board of Works farm.

'So do a good job,' he said. 'Listen to old Herb the overseer and don't go bringing those troublemaking New South Wales ways down here. We're all good unionists – just be sensible, understand me?'

Piney in four told me Powelly had been a shearer and a labourer during the Depression, so he knew what he was talking about. I nodded, but I didn't agree. As well as being a shearing contractor, he was also a property developer, plus he had farms all over Australia, so Piney reckoned.

We finished at five o'clock every day instead of the regulation five-thirty. The third week in, I was coming home late from the Thursday-night barrel at the footy club and I hit some water lying on the road. The HG went into 360-degree spins and I wrapped the old car around a pole. She was a write-off. I dislocated my shoulder and had several hairline fractures in my ribs, near my spine. I went to work but I could only shear about sixty a day. It was better than no money at all: so much for my forty a run, every run.

In November we took Lonnie back to the children's hospital for a check-up. She was two years and three months old. They evaluated her as functioning at the level of ten or eleven months, and in some respects seven. Lonnie still didn't acknowledge us. I'd gotten used to her not responding. Jade was totally different. She was sharp and took in everything. She wanted to be where the action was. Lonnie seemed oblivious to having a sister.

Towards the end of the year I went to the bank and asked about a loan for a house. They said I'd need four or five thousand dollars' deposit, so I arranged to sub a minimum wage off Powelly every week and leave the rest of my earnings with him until the end of the season.

After the depot shed we went down to the Board of Works farm and shore there for a few months. In late March I got a cheque from Powelly for over four thousand dollars and went and put it in the bank. This was the richest I'd ever been. I applied for the loan: rejected. I hadn't had the money in the bank long enough. They suggested the money wasn't mine and they didn't think shearing was a very stable job.

Around the same time, Lonnie was going through periods where we couldn't touch her or pick her up. She would whine and squeal for hours on end. I had to lock her in her room sometimes to get away from her. My nerves felt raw. I couldn't stand it. Sonia's mum would always offer to take her. She'd come and clean the house and do the washing. Lonnie was hospitalised several times to give us a break, and to try different drug therapies. Her little body was gaunt. She was always sick with throat infections and ear infections. Her body made jerky actions. Nothing flowed. The helmet, and the splints we put on her legs for therapy, made her look worse.

Near the end of the off-season, Lonnie's fits were going for ten days at a time, then she'd stop for two days, then she'd have another eight of fitting and three off, until they seemed to stop. Sonia started taking her off the medication – she was crazy on it – and her improvement was encouraging rather than dramatic. She acknowledged us a bit more, and responded to noises around her a little better.

In the off-season I bumped slates onto roofs and Sonia finished her nurse's aide course. I didn't touch one cent in the bank. The following August, the shearing season got off to a good start and I put another thousand dollars in the bank and bought a car on hire-purchase. It cost four thousand dollars and it seemed too expensive, but we'd never had a good car and things were looking up so we bought it. I went back to the bank again and they had some other excuse why I couldn't get a loan. They didn't really believe the money was mine. I spoke to Powelly and he told me about a bank that was looking for business and recommended me to them.

But Powelly wanted me to buy one of his houses. The old Housing Commission house I'd looked at cost $27 000 and his house was around $42 000. We went for the Commission house. He wasn't happy with me. Reckoned cheap house, small growth. The more expensive the house, the bigger the growth. But I didn't want to be dependent on him for work like Piney was. We moved in and it was great to be out of the farmhouse and in our own place. It had a big garage and backed onto the Werribee River. I thought we had the best view at half the price. Mrs McHugh cried when she saw the house and offered Sonia money to get a better one.

Then we went on strike. The union secretary called a statewide strike opposing the proposed wide-comb trials. On the second of December 1981 the arbitration commissioner, despite union objections, approved the trials. There were reports of scab teams being raided by carloads of shearers, and a few blues were starting to occur.

Between August and December I'd paid all the bank and legal costs for the house. We'd bought our furniture from the Care and Concern shop and Sonia made lampshades for the lights. At Christmas time Powelly came up to me and said that was all the work he had. The other men did painting jobs or went trapping or had time off. My mortgage and car repayments didn't change. I didn't want to leave the family and I didn't want a crappy, low-paying factory job.

BILLYBINGBONE STATION

BILLYBINGBONE STATION WAS about 250 kilometres on the Dubbo side of Bourke and a twelve-hour drive from home. It was close to Charlton Station. The drought had hit Bourke as well. This country was dry enough in a normal season but now it was bare-dusted paddocks.

The shearing shed and huts were the only buildings on the place. I grabbed a hut away from the kitchen. The shed had sheep in it but there was no cook, no men, no rousies, no life anywhere. I couldn't find the generator. Then I heard a noise. I panicked. In the dark corner of a hut I'd only glanced into, a person was stirring. The room ponged. He was drunk and had shat in his pants. I put my swag in a hut, shut the door, went to bed and waited for nightfall. It was this, the factory, or labouring somewhere.

The next morning the team turned up at six. The cook cleaned up and put on a simple breakfast for us. The contractor was a good bloke. The temperature was in the low forties, not too bad for this time of year, and I was a more seasoned shearer than last time I came up this way.

The sheep were hard to shear. Pushing the comb through the

wool was like pushing through steel wool. My wrists were aching. I tried not to hold onto the handpiece too tightly because I didn't want to end up with tendonitis in my wrist again. I was averaging about thirty-five to thirty-seven sheep a run, and at the end of the shed I'd saved more than a month's house payments. I'd adapted to the heat much easier this time.

I drove home for the weekend and got there in the early hours of morning. Sonia had waited up but I was drunk and tired when I arrived.

Lonnie's initial improvement after going off the medication had plateaued. We gave up on getting any real help from the hospital. She still wore her helmet but it didn't stop her crashing, or tripping over her own feet, it just lessened the damage. She still chewed anything that could be chewed, as though her tongue was her only form of stimulation. Jade was crawling early, walking and feeding herself at eight months. Despite Jade's best efforts, Lonnie ignored her.

I told Sonia that my next shed was close to the town of Nyngan, which had a caravan park near the river. She decided to come up for a few weeks, get out of the house for a while. We packed the car and headed off with Lonnie and Jade in the back. After about eight hours of Lonnie screaming I had an overpowering urge to drive into a tree.

The caravan park was a dustbowl. The river was further from the park than I remembered, the shed a little further out than I'd said. Sonia walked the kids every day but there wasn't a lot to see. They mostly played games indoors, in the air conditioning. Sonia saw the park manager standing at the toilet block at the same time every morning, perving on her through a gap in the curtains. Her knickers and nighties were stolen off the line.

I only made it back to the caravan every second night. I was paying for the cook and the tucker at the shed, paying house payments and bills at home, and paying park fees. On the Friday night I came home and Sonia was packed and ready to go. I drove all night, slept for a while, drove back.

After the second shed, the work thinned out and drinking filled the gaps until the late-payment notices came. The contractor said the drought had knocked the numbers around. I headed back home. The car got repossessed and I bought a bomb to get around in but we kept the house.

THE ROAD-MAKING GANG

THROUGHOUT 1982 THE wide-comb trial continued, the drought persisted. I got a job paying six dollars fifty an hour and Lonnie stopped crying. She'd stopped making any noise at all. She flattened out, back into her own world. I had lost my confidence. I could feel it – nervous when I didn't need to be, always trying to prove myself. I didn't really know what to do next. I was married, had two kids, a mortgage in the suburbs, and I wasn't earning enough money to pay all the bills.

I got a job on a road-making gang in a construction company. Every week they'd sack the worst worker – the slowest or the least skilled in the gang. I thought I'd be better off on the dole, except that Saturdays were paid at overtime rates. I had to work all the available overtime and every Saturday to make ends meet. If I was sick and had a day off I wasn't allowed to work the Saturday, and my pay wouldn't last the week.

An Italian concreter and I started work on the same day. His job was the stormwater pits and mine was rolling the road, compacting the crushed rock after it was laid. Up and down, backward and forward, a thousand times a day. I'd roll the road in and then roll the road out, creating the camber. When I wasn't on the road gang I was building all the walking tracks around Brimbank Park, or laying sewer pipes in estates in St Albans. I had to watch for cave-ins doing that work. We weren't even allowed to smoke roll-your-owns on the job, the boss said it took too much time.

There were no strikes here. Nobody complained, or spoke out against the company. Any talk of dissatisfaction, you were suddenly out of a job. If you were merely difficult they'd send you miles away from your home. Either way they got rid of you. I waited for my tap on the shoulder. I'd rather die than go home and tell Sonia I'd lost my job. I had to keep it. I'd taken it thinking I'd learn how to drive a machine, get another career, maybe learn a backhoe and work for myself. The boss knew I'd do whatever he said, go wherever I was told, put up with any conditions. After having the car repossessed, I didn't trust my own decisions. At home Sonia continued to assume more authority. After buying a car without telling me, she invited some friends around for tea and delivered the news in front of them. Ethan, one of the guests, thought she was brilliant. It seemed that as my confidence diminished, hers blossomed.

I started looking elsewhere for better-paying work. Driving around to worksites was expensive. I could only put five bucks' petrol in my car at a time. I dreamed of the day I could drive into a petrol station and fill up without worrying about the cost. I lived on a quarter of a tank. I rolled thin roll-your-owns and kept the butts. Then when my money ran out, usually on Thursdays, I'd smoke the butts. Some Sunday mornings I got a job cleaning out the vats in a milk factory – that was drinking money. The smell of sour milk after a night on the grog made me spew. Sonia was always at me to quit drinking but I was hardly drinking. She whinged about the money I was earning, and I was working six or seven days a week.

I hated her lists. I don't know why she had to keep putting 'cut the grass' on them every week. As if I didn't know. She whinged and complained she had no help and then redid everything I did, from hanging out the washing to making the beds. The more she redid things, the less I tried. The house was White Kinged and the sink was always like a mirror. I fantasised about wheeling in barrowloads of dirt and putting it all through the house.

Over winter we'd started an exercise program for Lonnie and I had to be home in the evenings to do it with her. There was no guarantee this would help but we had nothing to lose.

I had a couple of offers for pens shearing locally. I took one and snatched the road gang. I knew I had the spring, and maybe summer, shearing before I had to worry about looking for another job. I couldn't take being poor. The worst was being parked outside the milk bar ripping up the floor of my car for dropped change, or putting my hand down the backs of seats to find a couple of cents. I hated that. Friday night's treat was a fried dim sim each to go with the chips and potato cakes. I hated that too.

THE WIDE-COMB DECISION

I WAS SHEARING with a small contractor on the outskirts of Melbourne. It was a lot of travelling but I was home every night. One day, after about six weeks, I shore my first two hundred. It didn't mean as much as shearing my first hundred had, but I could feel my confidence returning. I felt better shearing than I did doing anything else. At work I was my own man, at home I was Sonia's gofer.

It was a four-stand shed. I was travelling with Johnny Eddy. The third shearer was old Gordon. He was drunk on the stand. The fourth was a Kiwi, Clutterbuck. Johnny punched out his hundred a day. Gordon was about the same. He did his in three runs because he was blind drunk by three o'clock. The Kiwi seemed like a broken gun. He was shearing about forty-five and cruising. I was getting over forty a run in the bigger sheep.

Clutterbuck didn't seem to care about the whole wide-comb thing. He talked about it as if it wasn't his problem. Johnny Eddy told me the Kiwi's three kids had burned to death in a car explosion at a shopping centre. Story was he stayed home for two weeks then came back to work. He didn't know what else to do.

I went back to the depot shed for Powell and shore another

two hundred sheep in a day. One run I got sixty. They were small, easy-shearing older lambs. At home Sonia and I communicated through the list of jobs she'd leave for me on the fridge. Evenings we did the exercises with Lonnie but nothing was happening. On weekends I took the kids swimming.

Houses were going up everywhere in Werribee and now they were putting in traffic lights. Soon there'd be no sheep left in the area. I thought of moving to the bush again.

In December 1982, Commissioner McKenzie came down in favour of the use of wide combs. The union appealed, and the combs couldn't come into use until that was heard, but it didn't look good.

The word was, Fraser was going to call an election, and if Hawke replaced Hayden we might win it. With a Labor government in power we could shut the Kiwi tax loophole, get things back on track. It was rumoured the National Farmers' Federation was already planning a push for a lower rate of pay per sheep, because of the predicted increase in tallies with the wide comb.

The other thing we heard was that Grazcos were organising scab teams in the event of a strike. I didn't believe it. No way would Viking and Haveachat and the boys scab, they were solid.

One old-timer said to me, 'Get out, son, it's fucked. And it's only going to get worse.'

Get out into what, though?

That Friday, Sonia was offered a last-minute night shift. It was close to Christmas so she took it on the proviso I didn't drink. Even though it was the end of my working week, I promised I wouldn't drink.

After I'd put Lonnie to bed I stalked around the house. I went out to my stash. I thought, She owns everything else but she doesn't own me. I opened the first bottle and took a swig. I felt it go down and hit the spot. I sat back and thought how we'd win the big fight. Hawke would win the election and we'd beat the Kiwis, we'd move to the country and get our own farm. A horse in the side paddock for the kids, a ute full of shearing equipment. I was the contractor and Sonia did the bookkeeping. When I'd finished the bottle I stashed the empty in the bottom of the rubbish bin and went back inside. I sat down to watch the tellie and thought, Things are good, Lonnie and Jade are asleep and I've got the house to myself, why not have one more and go to bed, no harm done.

So I went back out to my stash, grabbed a bottle and envisaged me giving the victory speech after we'd defeated Fraser and the squatters. Fraser hated us and I hoped he'd be banished for life after he lost. I grabbed two bottles. This was worth celebrating.

The next morning I woke up, jumped out of bed and ran outside. I felt panicked. I was sure I'd heard Lonnie screaming from out on the street last night.

I stood on the footpath frantically looking. I started yelling out her name. I ran down the street for ten metres and then ran the other way. I ran across the road and back. Maybe she was out the back in the sandpit. The river – maybe she'd climbed the fence and was down the river. What if she'd fallen in? Maybe someone had taken her.

I must have had a nightmare. I'd been trying to move my body, to rescue her from the cold, from a wild dog. She was terrified, defenceless. Locked out with only a nappy on. Every muscle fibre in my body had been trying to make me move but I was trapped in a coma. In the dream I was blind, I couldn't think, I couldn't feel, but I could hear her screaming. I could still hear the screaming.

It was a nightmare, that was all. I relaxed, took a deep breath and went inside, repeating to myself, I'll never drink again. Never drink again. I walked into the girls' room. Jade was asleep. Lonnie was gone.

I thought of ringing the police but I couldn't do that. I couldn't bear the thought of them pulling her out of the river, or finding her body dumped somewhere. I would find her. I ran through the house, out the backyard, back into the house, into her room – maybe I'd missed her. I looked behind the curtains, sometimes she played there. She couldn't talk. She lived in her own little world. I went back into my room, back out to the yard. I jumped the fence to the river, then I jumped back. I couldn't even think about finding her in the river; maybe I'd missed her somewhere else in the house. She was playing behind the couch or somewhere. I ran inside.

But she wasn't anywhere. I thought about the police again. Sonia.

In my room I looked for a shirt to wear. I felt naked. I threw the doona back and there she was. Asleep at the end of the bed. When I'd thrown the doona off to get out I'd covered her. I was in a cold sweat. I felt dizzy. I lay next to her and touched her soft white arms. I pushed my nose over her body, smelling her. Breathing in her familiar smells, I felt better. She had beautiful Shirley Temple curls.

Funny though, she was wearing just her nappy, the way she had in my dream, and why was she sleeping at the end of my bed? If she got into our bed she usually climbed in next to me. She wasn't the best walker but she was a great climber.

Sonia came home and went straight to bed. I didn't tell her about the nightmare, I still had a sickening feeling about it. I didn't know what had actually happened. For once I was glad Lonnie couldn't talk.

That evening a new neighbour we hadn't met yet came over from across the road. She introduced herself and then started telling a story. She said, 'About three o'clock this morning I heard someone crying, and I could hear your next-door's pitbull barking and pawing at your fence. I looked out the window and saw your little girl crying under the streetlight.'

I started sinking. Sonia glanced at me; her face was curdling.

The neighbour watched us eyeing each other off and continued. 'I got out of bed, I thought if that dog next door to you got free, you know what he's like, and ran over to her, but your dog wouldn't let me near her at first. Anyhow, I went slowly, grabbed the little girl and picked her up. The dog let me do that. I knocked on the front door and yelled, but it was locked and nobody answered. I went around the back and the door was open. I turned the light on and went through the house, going from room to room looking for someone. I was terrified, I thought for a minute one of you might have been killed and I was going to find a dead body. I got to the last room, your room,' she pointed to me, 'and turned the light on, not expecting to see anybody.

'I got a shock when I saw a man – you, I guess – half naked, flaked out across the bed. I only had my nightie on and I panicked.

'I just threw the baby on the bed and ran out. I thought I'd better come and say something now, considering I'm new in the street, you know, in case someone saw me coming in or leaving your house at three in the morning. I don't want to get off to a bad start in the neighbourhood.'

And with that she left.

Sonia's cheeks had tightened, her eyes and lips were narrowed. She looked at me. She didn't speak. She made a phone call, packed a few things and left.

ROOF SERVICE

SONIA CAME BACK on the proviso I stayed off the grog and didn't go shearing again. Lonnie's exercises were going well and she was improving. We found a kindergarten for her. The doctor had recommended a special kindergarten but she was accepted by the regular one.

I got a casual job cleaning pigeon shit off the Fitzroy Town Hall. It was hot, dirty, itchy work but I was used to that.

On the fifth of March 1983 Bob Hawke was elected prime minister. Eighteen days later Commissioner McKenzie brought down a second decision in favour of wide combs in the shearing industry. It was the off-season but the strike had started. Reports were coming in of big fights between Kiwis and Australians around Moree, Hamilton and Dubbo. The brawl in Moree made the papers, sheds were being torched, and down in Hamilton people were being shot at. Grazcos was accused of running scab teams to break the strike. The union in Victoria was using spotter planes to see who was shearing.

In early May the new Labor government intervened. But not in the way we'd hoped for or talked about for years. They intervened to broker a resolution. They cut us loose. Ernie Ecob went back to the table on health and safety issues. Commissioner McKenzie agreed to an investigation into the health effects on shearers of wide combs. In the meantime the men resumed work; the wide comb was allowed to be used. The NFF's industrial officer, who'd once been an official with the clerks' union, was furiously recruiting inductees to the wide comb during this time. He was reported as saying how he loved screwing workers more than he loved screwing the bosses. Most unionists thought the fight had been lost.

Later that month Sonia had an unplanned baby girl. Lonnie's acceptance at kindergarten was short-lived. Sonia got a phone call to come and collect her. Lonnie apparently walked through games, fell over everything, walked out during reading time. They said she couldn't even hold a pencil or crayon in her hand and she didn't mix or communicate with the other children. She needed one-on-one care and they weren't staffed for that. They asked if she'd been tested for autism.

We thought Lonnie had improved dramatically with the exercises. At the time of her diagnosis, the doctors had said she might never walk or talk and now she could do both. But the teacher said they couldn't understand her when she spoke. They thought it was more like babbling.

Powelly offered me a pen shearing hoggets. The local shearers said that most of the men weren't using a wide comb; they were going to beat it on the ground. Powelly still had a few sheds left but his shearing contracts were winding down. In his real-estate business he was selling farmland as housing estates. Soon the depot shed would have a suburban street through it and brick veneers and backyards on it.

I got on the grog, badly this time, and lost three days from my memory. I woke up the other side of Hay, flat-lining. I'd let Lonnie down not being there for her exercises and further estranged Sonia.

I'd go to work, come home, do the exercises. Sonia would prepare tea, do the dishes, write out her list for me, put it on the fridge and go to bed. I'd sit on the couch after everyone had gone to bed, have a drink, fall asleep, go to bed when the TV woke me. Sometimes I'd try and get close to her. A clenched fist would come back with a 'Fuck off' on the end of it. The next day I'd do it all again.

TUMBARUMBA

IN OCTOBER 1983 I picked up a shed near Tumbarumba in New South Wales. Sonia didn't mind, there was no other work around, and she had her life and I had mine. The contractor had been an employee of Grazcos and had taken all their work after the strike. Grazcos had been black-banned for their strikebreaking activities. I didn't know what had happened to Viking, Haveachat and the blokes. The commissioner's final decision on the health risks associated with the wide comb was due in six months.

The rain was relentless and we sat around playing cricket in between the downpours. Then we started drinking but I couldn't get high. I couldn't get happy. I didn't want to drink any more, I'd had enough, but I couldn't stop. That's when I started on the wine. After two weeks I was in debt to the contractor for a hundred and sixty dollars.

I couldn't go home in debt. We went to town and I ended up in a brawl and went down for a kicking. I was too drunk to defend myself. I woke up black and blue. All I remembered was covering my temples, hoping they wouldn't kill me. I knew something was wrong with me when I felt good about the beating. On the Sunday I got out of the slammer. Then I remembered being at an old school friend's place after I'd got the kicking. It was late. He had no grog. I was standing in the doorway of his laundry, looking for anything to drink. The embarrassment of getting caught stopped me searching further. I left. The rest was blank, but I thought I couldn't be that bad, otherwise I would have gone through his cupboards. The back page of Monday morning's paper had a photo of my house. While I'd been locked up the Werribee River had flooded and my house had been evacuated along with everyone in the street.

We finally got back shearing and I worked my way out of debt. I went home with a few dollars, and then the same team from Tumbarumba went to Titanga, with the addition of Draphine as overseer. We caught up and had a few laughs; he hadn't changed. He said a lot of blokes had switched to the wide combs.

'Not because they want to. It's just they're losing money now if they don't. The fight's over. The wide comb's in, boy.'

We started shearing but it wasn't the same. Bernie Bourke was there. He shore twenty-eight for the run. I said, 'What happened, Bernie? You were shearing forty-five to fifty last time we were here.'

He smiled. 'I burned out. I'm stuffed. Can't stop shaking all the time.' He walked in and got another sheep. He was about thirty-five years old. Draphine reckoned he'd worked too hard in the heat too many times.

On the Wednesday night we went into the Mount Elephant pub and I ran into Haveachat and Viking. They were the contractor's guard men now. Haveachat said they were using the wide combs. He said they went out for ten weeks for nothing. Everybody was using them. He said we had to make a decision: either get out of the industry or change with it. He reckoned he and Viking were too old to get out.

The shed finished after about eight days. I packed my tools, looked around at the bluestone shed, said goodbye to Draphine and Bernie, and drove out the gate. I heard that Draphine died some years later and that Viking eventually retired. Bernie Bourke continued on, walking rather than running in and out of the pens. I think he got his house. I wondered if he ever got to Lords to see a test match. I never heard what happened to the other men or how their lives panned out.